**Suicide Bombers**

*Liberté • Égalité • Fraternité*

RÉPUBLIQUE FRANÇAISE

This book is supported by the French Ministry for Foreign Affairs,
as part of the Burgess programme headed for the French Embassy in
London by the Institut Français du Royaume-Uni

# Suicide Bombers
## Allah's New Martyrs

Farhad Khosrokhavar

Translated by David Macey

Pluto Press

LONDON • ANN ARBOR, MI

First published 2002 as *Les Nouveaux Martyrs d'Allah* by Flammarion.
English-language edition published 2005 by Pluto Press
345 Archway Road, London N6 5AA
and 839 Greene Street, Ann Arbor, MI 48106

www.plutobooks.com

British Library Cataloguing in Publication Data
A catalogue record for this book is available from the British Library

ISBN   0 7453 2284 0 hardback
ISBN   0 7453 2283 2 paperback

Library of Congress Cataloging in Publication Data applied for


10   9   8   7   6   5   4   3   2   1


Designed and produced for Pluto Press by
Chase Publishing Services, Fortescue, Sidmouth, EX10 9QG, England
Typeset from disk by Stanford DTP Services, Northampton, England
Printed and bound in Canada by Transcontinental Printing

# Contents

# A Note on Terminology

The terms 'terrorism' and '*jihadism*', 'terrorist activity' and '*jihadist* activity' are used here as though they were interchangeable. They are used, that is, in the sense in which they are used in the West and in the press, and have no predetermined value. What one side sees as terrorism or *jihadism* can be experienced or perceived by the other side as a war of national liberation or an attempt to fight the global hegemony of the West. It can always be argued that only tiny minorities are involved in so-called terrorist activities and that they are not recognised by the moral majority they claim to represent. Al-Qaeda claims to represent a global Muslim community which is not, in many countries, prepared to follow it, even though bin Laden may be celebrated as a hero. Similarly, Italy's Red Brigades and Germany's Rote Armee Faktion claimed to represent a working class that did not support them, even though a few working-class individuals may have hero-worshipped them. In general, we will describe as 'terrorist' activities that take a totality or group as an ideal reference or principle of legitimacy, even though that group or totality does not actually support its members' actions. In some Muslim societies, bin Laden is glorified as the man who took symbolic revenge on an arrogant America and, more generally, an impertinent West. Such societies may well hero-worship him, but they do not want him as their leader. His role is rather like that played by Che Guevara in Western countries and in Latin America in the 1960s and 1970s.

# Introduction

Throughout the twentieth century, the modern world strove to relegate religion to the realm of the private affairs of the individual. Over the last decades, however, we have seen the return in force of ostentatious forms of religiosity that defy the public space they invest. They reject society, and may even declare war on it.

Far from representing relics of an archaism faced with extinction, these violent religiosities are part of the modern world. The dynamic that produces them is the same dynamic that defines our cultural and political conditions of existence. Often characterised by the preponderant role played by death in their worldviews, they affect almost all religions, even though we will be looking exclusively at Islam here simply because the author of these lines is not competent to speak about other religions.

In the West, the problem of Islam and its activist forms arises for many different reasons. On the one hand, old barriers are breaking down as globalisation makes it difficult for the discrete and watertight civilisations of the past to go on existing. A hundred years ago, the population of the West was overwhelmingly Christian. That is no longer the case. In less than half a century, the upheavals of the modern world and the intermingling of peoples of different origins within it have resulted in the establishment of sizeable Muslim minorities in almost all countries. Muslims are now part of the cultural and religious landscape, be it in France (some four million), England (one and a half million), Germany (over three million), elsewhere in Europe or in the United States (some four million). The globalised world also generates a number of interrelated symbolic and cultural phenomena, thanks to the modern media and new forms of communication, mass population movements from one corner of the globe to another, and the formation of ever more varied diasporas. Events like the war in Bosnia or the struggles in the Palestinian territories are watched in real time by television viewers all over the world and inspire an almost simultaneous feeling of compassion, indignation, solidarity and revulsion. This too is breaking down the barriers between the various parts of the world.

The overwhelming majority of Muslims living in the West adapt to their host countries and are eventually integrated into them. A tiny minority become radicalised for the specific reasons examined in the following analyses. There are various reasons for this. There are, to begin with, problems relating to the independence of former colonies after the Second World War (the Muslim territory of Kashmir, where the Indian-controlled area has given rise to conflict between Pakistan and India), but there are also problems relating to the creation of Israel and the Six Days War, and to the collapse of the Soviet Empire (Bosnia, Chechnya or even Afghanistan). Those Islamic forms of struggle that result in *jihad* or martyrdom relate to the establishment of new nations that find obstacles in their way or, as in the case of Iran, to the formation of nations that find themselves at war with other countries. Despite the differences between the cases of Iran, Palestine, Chechnya, Algeria or Afghanistan, the one thing that they do have in common is that they are inspired by Islamic movements that have a clearly identified goal. The enemy they are fighting is also clearly defined. In Iran, the goal of the war against Iraq was, on the one hand, to preserve national independence and the gains of the Islamic Revolution on the one hand and, on the other, to fight the Iraqi enemy. Anti-Western rhetoric made the anti-imperialist struggle one of the issues at stake in the Islamic Revolution, but that goal was quickly marginalised.

A fundamentally different form of martyrdom came into being as a direct result of the collapse of the bipolar world and the Soviet Empire. This is al-Qaeda's form of martyrdom. Although it does have many things in common with national forms of martyrdom, the subjectivity that inspires its actors and the form taken by its hatred of the world are fundamentally different.

The interpretation offered here is based upon the analysis of texts, my field experience as a sociologist and anthropologist working in the Islamic world and in France, but also upon interviews carried out over a period of 18 months in French prisons with Muslims. Some were jailed for associating with wrongdoers in order to plan acts of terror, whilst others were radical Islamists or accused of belonging to Islamist networks. These interviews reveal the specificity of their commitment and of the way they live their subjectivity.

One myth dies hard. Martyrs are described as 'Allah's madmen'. They are described as being motivated by something approaching dementia, or as being out of step with the Western life way of life. They have personality problems, or quite simply have not succeeded in integrating into our societies. They are, in other words, not modern and are simply incapable of behaving as responsible and autonomous individuals. They have also been marginalised and excluded, and they react to their social and economic exclusion by rebelling against society. This is to some extent true of the young people in the suburbs in French cities, and in poor neighbourhoods in England. A minority of al-Qaeda-style martyrs would recognise themselves in this description. But the vast majority of the network's members cannot be categorised in this way. Their subjectivity is not that of marginalised or wretched individuals who have been excluded or rejected by society. They are often from the middle classes and have no major problems in integrating. In most cases, they are in fact much more integrated than the average citizen. The Islamist activists who become al-Qaeda-style transnational terrorists are much more complex than most people imagine. They are usually described as representatives of something archaic or simply naive creatures who are not strong enough to come to terms with the complexity of contemporary society, and who are being manipulated by a few masterminds. Even if these descriptions are in part accurate, they miss the essential point. On the contrary, such terrorists are, in a way, products of our world. Their ideal is to create a transnational neo-*umma*, but its myths and fantasies are as vague as those of our modernity, at least amongst those who have been brought up in Europe, converts and many second-generation immigrants from North Africa, Pakistan or other Muslim countries. They construct their individuality on the basis of a new relationship with the contemporary world. The logic at work in their groups is to some extent similar to that at work in modern cults.

Whilst we have to note that contemporary Islamic martyrdom can take different forms, we must also avoid two pitfalls. If we regard each case as though it were unique or, on the contrary, identify radicalisation with mere fundamentalism or Islamism, there is a danger that our analysis will be flawed. We will try, insofar as it is possible to do so, to penetrate the subjectivity of these actors and to describe in phenomenological terms their motivations, their intentionality, their mental construction of the world, and their way of inserting themselves into the world whilst protesting against it at the same time. This by no means implies an apologetic conception of their actions or their representation of the world. Understanding is not legitimisation. A sociology or anthropology that makes no attempt to understand and condemns their subjectivity out of hand or gives a traditional or premodern vision will get us nowhere because it makes it impossible to think seriously about the ills of our modern world. The second pitfall is to categorise as 'Islamism' all radical modes of action that claim to be Islamic.

This study, which is based upon my experience of Iran between 1977 and 1991 and my fieldwork in France and some Middle Eastern countries from 1992 onwards, is intended to be a contribution to our understanding of extreme forms of subjectivation. Islam provides the backdrop. References to Islamic theology and anthropology do to some extent give religious radicalisms a form of legitimacy, but we must go beyond that and look at the interaction between religion and modern living conditions, and at the way in which new forms of subjectivation can lead Islam in what are often unsuspected directions.

## TWO FORMS OF MARTYRDOM

In Muslim societies, the martyr is a figure who stands midway between the hero and the saint. Saints certainly exist in popular forms of both Shi'ite and Sunni Islam. And yet there are no saints in Sunni orthodoxy: there can be no intermediaries between Allah and his creatures. Even the Prophet himself is, strictly speaking, no more than a human being. It is local customs, as well as brotherhoods, Zaouias and maraboutism, that surreptitiously introduce the notion of sainthood by referring to *baraka*, or the ability to increase wealth, to prevent or cure illness or, more generally, to make life propitious by granting the wishes of the faithful.

In Shi'ite Islam, the twelve imams can be seen as equivalents to Catholicism's saints.[1] They act as mediators between men and God because they are indirectly descended from the Prophet via his son-in-law and cousin Ali. A martyr is not a saint but, once he has embraced a holy death, he can be compared with the saints and can become their companion in Paradise. There is also something of the hero about the martyr, but his heroism is not of the worldly kind. He commits himself to a noble religious cause governed by the logic of being rewarded in the next world. The Sunni martyr is one who dies 'in the path of God' by taking part in a *jihad*. In Shi'ite Islam, martyrs have something in common with the tragic saints that we find, for similar historical reasons, in southeast Europe.[2] Ever since the period when models of sainthood were established after the Occultation of the twelfth imam in 874, Shi'ite communities have often been persecuted or, which is more important, have perceived themselves as being persecuted by Sunnis. Just as in the Balkans, Shi'ite martyrs are traditionally the object of a cult of suffering.[3] 'Creating martyrs', in the sense of creating more candidates for a holy death, is, on the other hand, an activity that developed in the modern world, despite the classic theories of secularisation which predict that social modernisation would put an end to it.

The appearance of new martyrs is not due to the reproduction of traditional structures with Muslim societies, and still less is it due to the desire of certain communities to oppose modernisation. The new martyrs are indeed, sometimes in excessive or even pathological form, new figures of emancipation from tradition. They espouse forms of legitimacy that claim to follow a tradition but at the same time marginalise it in the real world. We are dealing with the paradox, which has become a classic problem for sociologists of religion, of a new religiosity that breaks with traditional forms of communitarian life and at the same time conceals the break behind a more 'authentic' version of early Islam. Much of the novelty of the so-called 'Islamist' phenomenon lies in its ambivalent use of the register of religious tradition in order to undermine it.

If we define martyrdom as self-sacrifice for a sacred cause, it can be found in most religions and particularly in the Abrahamic religions. In both Christianity and Islam, it is associated with the notion of bearing witness, which is itself tied up with the idea of the struggle against injustice and oppression. Leaving Islam aside, there is a close association between the two in the Sikh religion. The link is established by the idea that injustice results from a refusal to recognise God, or the idea that the oppressor is a heretic. The fight against heresy and infidelity can therefore be seen as forms of martyrdom because fighting those who adulterate religion to the death goes hand in hand with denouncing tyrants and oppressors.

If we look at modes of action, we can identify two types of martyrdom. The first is a defensive martyrdom. Its goal is not to lead a violent struggle against heretics and oppressors, but to bear witness – even at the point of death, to the righteousness of the cause by opposing heretics and oppressors by adopting a non-violent attitude of defiance. The Christian martyrs were classic examples. They rejected violent action, but they also refused to obey the orders of the Roman Governor or Emperor who wanted them to follow the official religion. Christianity is not the only religion to promote defensive martyrdom. Buddhism can also have recourse to it, as we saw when Buddhist monks in Vietnam in the 1960s immolated themselves in protests against the military government.

The second type of martyrdom is offensive in nature. It implies an active, and if need be violent, struggle against those the believer regards as oppressors and heretics. Self-sacrifice implies a desire to annihilate the enemy in the course of a fight neither party can win.

Whilst both types of martyrdom are inspired by the idea of self-sacrifice, each has specific forms of action, which makes them fundamentally different.

### Defensive martyrdom

'Martyr' derives from the Greek word *martur*, which becomes *marturos* and *martures*. Its essential meaning is 'witness'. The expression was used in Greek courts. Until the second century AD, it did not mean dying for a cause. With the appearance of that new meaning, the old sense of 'bearing witness' in a court gradually became blurred and gave way to the new meaning. This does not mean that the wish to die as a martyr did not exist amongst Christians until the second century. There are many examples, including Ignatius of Antioch at the beginning of the second century. Having fallen in love with death, he looked forward with joy to the tortures that awaited him.[4] The 'martyr affect' did exist, even though there was no word to capture its semantic specificity.

Christian martyrdom came into being in the Roman Empire and was, from the outset, closely linked to that historical and cultural situation.[5] Its appearance provoked stupefaction and incomprehension on the part of the Romans. How, wondered the Stoic Emperor Marcus Aureleus, could a rational being commit 'irrational suicide', especially when he caused the fatal blow to be struck by others?

Pagans saw the voluntary martyrdom sought by Christian as a sign of dementia. They were astonished to see people rushing headlong into death by intentionally provoking the wrath of the Governor or Emperor. They could understand their wish not to make sacrifices to them. But acting ostentatiously and imitating those who had refused to make sacrifices in order to be put to death was simply irrational.[6]

According to Eusebius of Caesarea, who was writing at the time of Diocletian, the first martyr was Procopus, who refused to make a sacrifice to the gods in the presence of the Emperor.[7] He said that he recognised only one God and was ready to sacrifice himself to Him. His head was then cut off. Martyrs were sometimes so rash as to physically prevent governors from making sacrifices. The young

Apphianos was one example. He walked up to Governor Urbanus, who was pouring a libation, took him by the right hand and stopped him from making his sacrifice. He then exhorted him to recognise the error of his ways and to give up making sacrifices to idols. According to Eusebius, the Governor's entourage tore him to pieces like wild animals. In the eyes of the Roman authorities, the profane dimension of martyrdom was bound up with its ostentation, which was intended to spread Christianity through proselytism. The condemnation of groups of martyrs gave their deaths an even greater impact. According to Eusebius, Pamphilus suffered martyrdom in February 310 together with eleven companions. Twelve was a holy number because Christians believed that there had been twelve Apostles. The twelve had spent two years in prison and were put to death together with a number of Egyptian Christians.

The possibility of female martyrdom is a further feature of the Christian religion. Women were in the minority, but they were bold enough to challenge the legitimacy of the pagan gods. Valentine was one example.[8] She was exhorted by a Roman court to save her own life by making a sacrifice to the gods. She refused, and was dragged by force to the altar. Rather than comply, she knocked the brazier over. She was tortured and put to death.

Christian martyrdom was sometimes accompanied by miracles. In one case, when Christians were refused burial – their remains were scattered and left to be devoured by wild animals – it rained and drops fell on the stones of the columns of the temple. The rumour was that the earth wept because it could not bear the sacrilege inflicted on the believers.

Christian martyrdom is, in a word, characterised by a refusal to obey Caesar in matters of religion, and the death meted out by the authorities is the result. And yet, as in all attitudes involving death, there is also the issue of limits. Death is no longer an indirect consequence of transgression, and becomes an end in itself. Martyrdom is transformed into the ambition to die per se. It is an act of witness to not only the rejection of an inauthentic religion, but also to a 'burning desire' (the expression was used by the early Christian martyrs, and was also used by Shi'ite martyrs in twentieth-century Iran),[9] to leave this world, which is a vale of tears. The martyr despises this world and rejects its pretences. The expression 'thirsting for death' (*tes maruriasr epithumia*) was also used by Iranian martyrs (*tesnhe ye shahadat*).

The shift of meaning is, therefore, in some sense implicit in martyrdom itself. What was once the possibility of an unwilling death in the service of a religious ideal was gradually transformed into a death that is desired because it would guarantee the martyr a glorious stay in Paradise. The justification for martyrdom is always the vanity of this world, its inconstancy, despair at living in it and the ambition to leave it to join the blessed in another place: the Paradise in which God's chosen ones dwell. What was originally a Christian challenge to the legitimacy of Roman polytheism or a challenge to a political authority that goes against authentic religion (revolutionary shi'ite martyrdom in Iran) is transformed into a quest for suicide at the hands of an external agent (the Roman authorities for the Christian martyr or the Iraqi army for the Iranian martyr). That agent is demonised, but is in fact colluding with the martyr who is put to death by him.

Martyrdom produces an inversion of affects. Death normally provokes fear and sadness. Yet the texts speak of the radiant joy of martyrs, of their satisfied smiles and even of their laughter at the moment of their execution. On the whole, the literature of martyrology speaks of the equanimity of martyrs and their yearning for death, and of affects characterised by inner happiness, and sometimes even exultation. This type of attitude can also be found in the Iranian, Lebanese or Palestinian martyrs of the twentieth and twenty-first centuries.

The essential point is that, insofar as it expresses a deliberate wish to die, martyrdom is bound up with situations in which the martyr believes he is being persecuted by the forces of Evil. For the early Christians, persecution meant Rome's repression of Christianity –or at least that is how it was experienced by followers of Christianity. In the case of Iran, it meant persecution by the forces of Evil, namely the West as embodied by Saddam Hussein, the Iraqi head of state. Martyrdom can also be characterised by a further 'pathological' feature if the 'burning desire' is focussed on the persecutor. Death has to be administered by the agent of evil, who brings about both his own damnation and the glorification of the martyr, whilst secretly granting him his wish. One example is provided by Ignatius of Antioch who, according to Bowerstock, displayed an excessive willingness to die at the hands of his persecutors. The burning desire can only be fulfilled by another person. If it is not to be identified with suicide, death must be inflicted by the magistrate or the Roman governor. The relationship established by martyrdom is thus triangular, and involves the self who must perish, the third party who must put him to death and the God who must accept the sacrifice.

In the Roman Empire, the burning desire to die as a martyr became so widespread during the third century and at the beginning of the fourth that the theologians had to step in. Whilst the desire to preserve the faith and to fight those who wanted to impose a false religion was considered legitimate, the conscious wish to die and thirsting after a holy death was deemed to be blasphemous. Augustine denounces this type of death and extends the commandment 'Thou shalt not kill' to all human life, including that of the martyr. Henceforth, putting oneself to death was murder, 'for to kill oneself is to kill a human being'.[10]

Following the logic of taking things to the limit, the martyr takes the legitimate defence of the faith to mean self-sacrifice, and then a quest for a death that is quite independent of any circumstances that might make it legitimate. This dialectic is still of contemporary relevance. Tragic circumstances can set the mechanisms of martyrdom in motion. There comes a moment when the fascination with death is often divorced from the religious logic that previously reined in the passion of dying, and it becomes divorced from the religious goal. In such cases, we have a passionate love for death and a desire for self-annihilation, and they replace the desire to ensure the legitimacy of a sacred cause by risking death.

### Offensive martyrdom

The offensive martyr is inspired by a desire to destroy the enemy by resorting to a legitimate violence that is sanctioned by religion. The struggle implies killing the infidel and oppressive adversary. This idea, which is the inspiration behind Muslim martyrdom and that found in other religions, can also inspire nationalism, as with the Tamil Tigers in Sri Lanka, the patriotism of the First World War, or the revolutionary phenomena of 1789.

In the Sikh religion, martyrdom has undeniable similarities with Islamic martyrdom.[11] The martyrdom of the fifth guru, Guru Arjan, led to the militarisation of the Sikh religion in 1606. That of his grandson Guru Tegh Bahadur, who was the ninth Sikh master, led to the creation of the militant Khalsa elite, which was founded in 1699 by Gobind Singh, the tenth and last Guru. The term used to designate Sikh martyrdom is the same as the Arabic expression, which is also used in Persian: *shahid* (plural: *shuhada*). Its two overlapping meanings are also found in Islam.

On the one hand, there is the idea of a sacrifice (*qurban* in Arabic) that brings one closer to God because of the blood that is spilled: the notion of *qurb* (proximity) is implicit in the word *qurban*. In Sikh martyrdom, a second notion – which can also be found in Islam – is central, quite independently of the first: the struggle against oppression, and bearing witness by dying in the struggle against injustice. The two notions reinforce one another. Self-sacrifice for the sake of religion is part of the struggle against irreligious oppressors. The Chahid gives his blood in order to preserve justice (*dharma*) in tragic circumstances and to bear witness to the truth of his religion. The ideal of resistance is extended to mean death in the service of a sacred cause.

# I
# Islam

The expression 'martyrdom' (*shahadat,* from *shahid* or 'martyr') has had a strange destiny in Islam. In the Koran, the word means bearing witness and not dying a holy death. Whenever dying for Allah is mentioned, we encounter expressions such as 'slain in the cause of God' (II: 154), 'fight for the cause of God' (IV: 74) or 'fled their homes in the cause of God and afterwards died or were slain' (XXII: 58). 'The cause of God' (*Sabil ellah*) is the major expression used to designate what will subsequently become known as martyrdom (*shahadat*).[1]

It was, in all probability, after the Muslim conquest of Palestine in the seventh century that the notion of 'witness' (*shahid*) took on the explicit meaning of 'holy death' and the connotations of the Greek notion, meaning both 'witness' and 'martyr'. The expression *shahid* refers to Muslim martyrs who died on the field of battle whilst fighting the infidel, and who were promised great rewards in the life to come. The underlying sense of 'bearing witness' makes the martyr both the protagonist of a holy death and a witness to the truth of his faith.

In Christianity, acceptance of holy death was an act of witness testifying before men to the sincerity of one's faith before God and to the righteousness of the cause. The same twin meanings can be found in Islam. The Muslim *shahid* does, however, differ from the Christian *marturos* in one fundamental respect. In Christianity, death results from the Christian's refusal to obey the will of a powerful figure who wants to impose his religion upon him. The Christian does not seek to inflict death upon the Roman pagan who wishes him to foreswear his faith. He simply denies him the right to force him to go against the precepts of his religion. In the case of Islam, martyrdom is a death resulting from the fight against the enemy of the religion of Allah. It is dying for the cause of God that leads to the believer's death as a martyr: 'Whoever fights for the cause of God, whether he dies or triumphs, on him We shall bestow a rich recompense' (IV: 74).

According to the official Saudi-approved French translation of the Koran this *surah* should read: 'Yes, Allah has bought believers, their persons and their goods in exchange for Paradise. They fight in the way of God; they slay, and are slain. This is the true promise He made them in the Torah, the Gospel and the Koran. Who is more true to his commitments than Allah? Rejoice, then, at the exchange you have made; and that is the greatest success.'[2]

'They will fight for the cause, they will slay and be slain.' This key phrase from the 'Repentance' *surah* is, in theory, the justification for martyrdom in Islam. 'They will slay or be slain' and are promised 'the Garden'. This founding text does not, as has sometimes been said, use the expressions 'martyr' (*shahid*) or 'martyrdom' (*shahadat*), which would later become a key notion in the idea of 'holy death'. The idea of dying a holy death 'in the way of God' is, however, explicitly formulated and will be adopted by the various Islamic traditions.

In Christianity, the physical violence comes from those who hold authority and the Christian does not react with equivalent violence; in Islam, the fight against the enemies of Allah is characterised by legitimate violence, and one can slay or be slain. The enemy is not accorded any privilege and is not allowed to strike with impunity. If God's warrior slays, he will be rewarded by God; if he is slain, he has his place in Paradise. At this level, martyrdom takes on a totally different meaning to the meaning it has in Christianity. The Muslim's use of violence is legitimate and his fate will be decided at the end of the fight 'for the cause of God'. The violence is no longer one-sided; it does not come from the enemy alone, and is accepted by the believer who resorts to it quite legitimately and in accordance with the precepts of his faith.

Martyrdom can therefore be summarised as follows:

- One who fights for the cause of God, has immense merit.
- One who dies in the course of the fight is a martyr and will go to Paradise.
- Martyrdom is the non-intentional result of death on the field of battle (or in similar circumstances) at the hand of an enemy confronted with the express purpose of neutralising or killing him, and without seeking death at his hands.
- The ideal type of martyrdom involves an active commitment on the part of the Muslim. He will be slain or slay, and will use legitimate violence against heretics or unbelievers who pose a threat to the religion of Allah.
- Unlike Christianity, Islam does not renounce the use of physical violence against an enemy. On the contrary, there is an express will to neutralise or kill the enemy in a battle that

can just as easily end with the death of either the 'infidel' or the believer.

## *JIHAD:* HOLY WAR

Muslim martyrdom differs from its Christian equivalent because the violence involved is reciprocal. It is closely linked to the other seminal notion of *jihad* or holy war. The major difference between that notion and the Christian notion of the crusade is that it has a theological basis in Islam, whereas 'crusade' has no theological basis in Christianity, despite all the exactions that were committed by the Christian religion in the name of the crusades and, subsequently, on pretext of converting the Indians of the South American continent and elsewhere to Christianity.

The notion of *jihad* first emerged in Arabia as a result of Islam's ideologicalisation of tribal warfare.[3] Incessant warfare between various tribes was frequent in Arabia, where the heterogeneity between different religious communities (Jewish, Christian and pagan) and divergent interests resulted in constant fighting. Islam gave this type of warfare a unitary meaning by giving it a religious content. Initially, the meaning of *jihad* fluctuated to a greater or lesser extent.[4] It gradually took on the codified meaning of 'for the cause of God' as the universalism gradually established by Islam transcended tribal rivalries and intertribal economic struggles.

In Islam, holy war is closely associated with martyrdom, even though, as has already been mentioned, the latter expression is not used as such in the Koran and is a later addition to Islam's body of doctrine. The classic texts do not provide much information on this subject, as it was of minor importance of outside the domain of jurisprudence (*fiqh*). *Jihad* was associated with the division of the world into two parts: the territory of Islam (*dar al islam*) and the territory of war (*dar al harb*). Shafi Muslims also refer to the third category of 'the territory of the treaty' (*dhar al ahd*), where a peace treaty has been signed with non-Muslims.[5] When non-Muslims signed an armistice with Muslims and paid them tribute (*kharadj*), their territory was that of peace (*dar al sulh*).

A *jihad* can also be declared to defend Islam against the threat of a non-Muslim offensive. In such cases, every Muslim is under an individual obligation (*fard 'ain*) to join it. When a *jihad* is proclaimed to ensure Islam's expansion across the world, it becomes a collective duty (*fard kifaya*) and an obligation for the whole community; a

Muslim can decide not to take part as an individual and still come to the aid of the community by supplying goods and services.

There is, in short, an essential difference between offensive war and a defensive war in the name of *jihad*. That is why, during the expansion of the Caliphate or Sultanate, holy war was not the duty of the individual believer, who could delegate his military obligations to a Muslim army. It is only in the nineteenth century, when Muslim societies came under the domination of European armies, that we see the return of *jihad*, especially during the early period of European domination when the struggle against European colonisation took the form of politico-religious movements.[6] Be it in late nineteenth-century Central Asia or in Iran's struggle against Russia's hegemony over the North West provinces in the early twentieth century, the fight against non-Muslim foreigners has been justified by reference to *jihad*.

Any discussion of *jihad* must make one further distinction which is usually scorned by radical currents but which is strongly emphasised by those new mystical currents that reject radical Islam. New religious reformers in Iran such as Motjahed Shabestari and Abdolkarim Sorush are cases in point. Inspired in this case by the traditon, they make a distinction between a lesser *jihad* (*jihad asghar*) and a greater *jihad* (*jihad akabar*). One is seen as a war against unbelievers, and the other a struggle against the believer's own tendency to transgress the laws of God. References to this form of *jihad* are found mainly amongst Muslim mystics who were striving for an inner purification that would allow them to welcome Allah and who were therefore not afraid of dying for love of him – often at the hands of other Muslims who regarded them as 'godless'.[7]

The mystical form of *jihad* is primarily addressed to the Ego, whose prime duty is to master its own propensity to transgress the laws of God. According to this view, the subject is, like Satan, inclined to rebel against God. The subject's rebellious ego (*nafs e ammareh*) prevents him from welcoming God. The novice (*salek*) must fight against this rebellious *nafs* so as to embrace God and merge into Him. The battle is with the self and not an external enemy. For the radical tendency, the finger is pointed at the external enemy and the struggle against the self is subordinated to that. According to this militant view, the self is motivated by an apathy that encourages it to abandon the struggle and abnegation for the cause of God in order to find its own peace. The believer must both join the struggle against the infidel enemy and overcome his own egotism in preparation for the supreme sacrifice.

We can thus see how the two registers of *jihad* (against the ego and against the enemy) are differently articulated. For Islamic radicalism, the Muslim must fight the heretical enemy and, in order to do so, must be prepared for self-sacrifice. For mystical quietism, the fight against the enemy is no more than one more facet of the non-reality of the outside world (*madjazi*). The believer must devote himself to his inner purification in order to reach higher levels of spirituality by climbing its different stages (*maqamat*). These two versions of *jihad* coexist within Islam and the antagonism between them has often led to internal struggles resulting in the banishment of Sufi mystics, but on the whole Islamic thinkers reject the quietist and mystical vision. Sometimes, a combination of both versions can be found in radical thinkers such as Khomeini, who transformed the mystical tendencies in the martyr's devoted love into martyrdom for the cause of God. Love of God inspires a desire to merge with Him (*fana fil lah*) through martyrdom.

### The Koran and *Jihad*

The Koran is a book with multiple dimensions. In it, we find verses (*surrah*) that praise the mercifulness and goodness of God, *surahs* that give a spiritual version of faith, and others that emphasise the wrath of God and the punishment He reserves for sinners. The same multiple dimensions can be found in the Old Testament.

If we divorce the Koran from the context of the traditions (*sunna*) based upon sayings attributed to the Prophet (*hadith*) or the consensus reached by the *ulamas* on various subjects over the centuries, certain *surahs* may offend modern sensibilities (as does the Old Testament). That is why the radical versions of the religion of Allah that base themselves on the Koran are no more than one of the many tendencies within Islam, and by no means the only tendency or the sole possible interpretation of this religion. They stress certain *surahs* of the Koran at the expense of others. Those who emphasise the *jihadist* dimension of the religion of Allah often refer to verse 29 of the Repentance *surah*: 'Fight against such of those to whom the Scriptures were given as believe in neither God nor the Last day, who do not forbid what God and His apostle have forbidden, and do not embrace the true Faith, until they pay tribute (*jizya*) out of hand and are utterly subdued.'

This *surah* refers to the 'peoples of the book', or in other words Jews, Christian and, according to some, the Zoroastrians, who have, according to certain Islamic traditions, received a sacred book. It recommends war until such time as the people of the book agree to pay tribute. Taken independently from the other, this *surah* can be used to justify waging all-out war on non-Muslims.

Other *surahs* in the Koran add, however, a degree of explanation that attenuates the effects of this verse. Verse 190 of the 'Cow' *surah*, for instance, reads: 'Fight for the sake of God those that fight against you, but do not attack them first. God does not love aggressors.' Only those who fight are to be fought.

*Jihad* is mentioned in verse 39 of the 'Pilgrimage' *surah*: 'Permission to take up arms is hereby given to those who are attacked, because they have been wronged. God has power to grant them victory.' Here, *jihad* is obviously defensive and concerns only those who have been attacked.

Alongside the *surahs* that recommend holy war as a way of protecting or spreading Islam, there are others that emphasise clemency or tolerance. Thus verse 256 of the 'Cow' *surah*: 'There shall be no compulsion in religion. True guidance is now distinct from error.' Similarly, 125 of the 'Bee' *surah* reads: 'Call men to the path of your Lord with wisdom and kindly exhortation. Reason with them in the most courteous manner. Your Lord knows best those who stray from His path and those who are rightly guided.'

Here, an exchange of views and debate are recommended. The condemnation of unbelievers is an attribute of God and not his creatures, who must not pronounce any judgement on those who stray, because He knows them best.

In verse 29 of the 'Cave' *surah*, we read 'Say "This is the truth from your Lord. Let him who will, believe in it, and him who will, deny it".' Once again, religious belief and denial are a matter for the intelligence and perception of the individual. According to this *surah*, compulsion must not be used to convert others to the religion of Allah.

In verse 99 of the 'Jonah' *surah*, it is written: 'Had your Lord pleased, all the people of the earth would have believed in Him, one and all. Would you then force people to have faith?' Here, the omnipotence of the Lord is invoked to justify tolerance in matters of religion. Had it pleased the Lord, all the people of the earth would have embraced Islam. He did not make them do so because He had his own plans, and it is not for his creatures to take the place of Him and His wisdom and make them do so. Compulsion is ruled out on the grounds that God is all-powerful.

Whilst we do find verses in the Koran about *jihad*, we also find others about peace. Verse 61 of 'Spoils' *surah*: 'If they incline to peace, make peace with them, and put your trust in God. It is surely He who hears all and knows all.'

The Koran thus contains *surahs* that are against war and in favour of peace, just as it contains *surahs* in favour of *jihad* and opposed to a peace that is regarded as humiliating for believers. The absence of explicit rules about this is remedied by reference to Tradition (*sunna*) and to the stories attributed to the Prophet by his closest disciples (*hadith*) or reported by other witnesses, and to the consensus (*Ijma*) by the Ulama (*Ijma*) in some Islamic traditions. Interpretations vary according to the socio-historic situation and the call for *jihad* changes in accordance with historical circumstances and the emergence of new groups with varying degrees of militancy.

The essential problem that preoccupies Koranic exegetes is to demonstrate that these different *surahs* are compatible and to arrange them into a hierarchy when they appear to contradict each other. To take a recent example. In his interpretation of the Koranic texts that oscillate between recommending peace and war, or even clemency and harshness, the Shi'ite cleric Motahhari distinguished four types of *surah*:[8]

- those that preach holy war in absolute terms;
- those that make holy war conditional on factors such as the unbelievers' decision to open hostilities or their desire to subdue Muslims;
- those that quite clearly assert that obedience to Islam is not obligatory;
- those in which Islam declares itself in favour of peace.

When, according to Motahhari, a *surah* speaks of holy war in absolute terms and with no restrictive conditions, its meaning must be subordinate to that of *surahs* preaching *jihad* on explicitly defined conditions (such as an attack by unbelievers or the oppression of Muslims). This hierarchy means that the Koranic text must be cited and applied carefully and with reference to other quotations and references.

Many Ulamas are agreed as to the defensive nature of *jihad*. The problem is that the restrictive conditions (such as an attack by unbelievers or the oppression of Muslims) can be interpreted from different perspectives. The radical currents that have always punctuated the history of Islam interpret repression in its broadest sense. In the contemporary period, the presence of Infidels in the Holy Land in Jerusalem or in Saudi Arabia is regarded by certain Sunni groups as aggression. Similarly, Western cultural aggression (*tahadjom farhangi*) is regarded as a casus belli by Shi'ite Islamists.

## Migration (*Hijrah*), the Call (*Da'wa*) and Holy War (*Jihad*)

The notion of Migration or Exodus (*hijrah*) or Hejira is often associated with that of *jihad*. It refers to a departure from territories ruled by infidels or a migration from the *dar al harb* to the *dar al islam*. In September 622, the Prophet left Mecca (called Yathrib, at that time), where he was being harassed by unbelievers, for Medina to work for Muslim supremacy and to return to reconquer the city when he was in a position of strength. This Exodus or *hijrah* has been interpreted in many ways throughout the history of Islam. It has been interpreted in a literal and strategic sense in wars and various struggles, and in a symbolic register by Sufis. When groups of Muslims feel that they are in a position of weakness, they often opt for a strategic retreat, returning to the fray later. One example is provided by the *Takfir wa-l Hijra* (literally 'Excommunication and Hijra') group which, under the leadership of the young agronomist Shukri Mustafa, came into conflict with the Sadat government in Egypt in 1977. The group took refuge in caves or in shared apartments, going into exile to find refuge in a world that was not ruled by unbelievers. The tactic has two objectives: leaving when one is in a position of weakness to seek protection against the more powerful forces of Evil; and gaining new strength in exile, returning in force, fighting the unbelievers, defeating them and re-establishing the faith.

These notions have found a new audience amongst Muslims in Western societies, where large new Muslim communities have become established since the 1960s. The vast majority of them eventually adapt and espouse the host society's way of life through secularisation, consumerism and individualism. A tiny minority become radicalised. Whilst the majority opts for peaceful acculturation and hybridisation in individual forms and a small minority rejects it, a third group opts for neo-communitarian forms. It then attempts to establish a peaceful Islamic community which withdraws more or less from society but still maintains non-antagonistic relations with it.[9] In this case, the logic of *da'wa* (a return to the faith or proselytism) prevails, whereas the logic of *jihad* prevails in the most radical groups. If the group feels that it can neither rely on *da'wa* nor launch a *jihad*, it can always opt for *hijra* (leaving the Christian country and choosing an Islamic one) and wait until it has the opportunity to implement one of the other alternatives.

All three notions give rise to various interpretations. Two of them are of particular importance. According to one, these notions can refer to an inner state: that of the believer who seeks self-realisation through spirituality. *Jihad* thus becomes an inner struggle to transcend the appeal of our baser instincts; similarly, *da'wa* is addressed to the elite souls of those who, unlike the vast majority, respond to it. The call is addressed to an elite living within more or less closed and elitist structures such as the new brotherhoods (*khânéqah, zaouia*). *Hijra*, finally, comes to mean the various stages an elite soul passes through in a hermetic Sufi group in the course of a purely spiritual upward journey towards the Absolute.

As well as having spiritual meanings, these notions can lead to concrete forms of social involvement. The literal meaning of *jihad* is a holy war against the Infidel, and that of *Hijra* is physical migration in order to escape repression or to face the impossibility of spreading a militant faith. *Da'wa*, finally, can mean proselytism in the literal sense of increasing the number of those who believe in Allah, and then forcing Islam upon non-believers or promoting it by publicising it.

The irreducible polysemy of these expressions and the diversity of the meanings they are given result from the existential positions of believers, but also from their political positions and their position in society. It is, then, not surprising that diametrically opposed modes of behaviour can be recommended in the name of Islam when it comes to dealing with social problems or concrete political modes of action. Unlike Catholicism, which has one institution that gives the sacred an official meaning, the many exegetical agencies in Islam that interpret the meaning of the faith and their polyphonic nature encourage diverse (and sometimes diametrically opposed) interpretations and modes of behaviour. The only brake on this infinite proliferation comes from tradition and from a certain homogeneity within the thought of *ulamas* belonging to institutions which may be hundreds of years old, such as the Al-Azhar University or the prestigious Zituna Koranic school. These help to reduce the number of possible interpretations but cannot unify them.

## MARTYRDOM IN ISLAM

In Sunni Islam, martyrdom is associated with, or even subordinate to, holy war. In Shi'ite Islam, which is a minority branch – one Muslim in ten is a Shi'ite – we find an affective structure centred upon martyrdom, and this gives the religion of Allah a particular meaning. Under the Umayyad dynasty, Islam was, in the eyes of the many who were opposed to the luxury and licentiousness of the Court, in danger of becoming depraved and distorted. Some fringes of Muslim society were quietly hostile to the Umayyads, but they lacked a leader who could lead a revolt against the Caliphate. Imam Hassan, who was the second Shi'ite imam, died without opposing Caliph Muawiyyah. According to some Shi'ite traditions, he was poisoned, or in other words martyred.

In the time of the third shi'ite imam – Hassan's brother Hussein – Muawiyyah died and was succeeded by his son Yazid. Yazid was known to have a taste for luxury and led a life that contravened in the eyes of many the principles of Islam. The opposition appeared to have found a real leader in Husain, who derived his legitimacy from the Prophet's family. He was his grandson by his daughter Fatima, who married Ali, the first Shi'ite imam and the fourth orthodox (*rashidun*) Caliph. He himself was the Prophet's son-in-law and cousin.

For reasons to do with the poor organisation of the struggle, Husain died in October 680 on the plain of Kerbala (in what is now Iraq) together with a handful of the faithful (72 according to Shi'ite tradition).[10] His martyrdom in tragic circumstances has become the emblem of 'twelver' Shi'ism. Every year, believers celebrate the anniversary of his death throughout the month of Moharram, when processions of flagellants and passion plays (*ta'zieh*) mark the stages leading up to his tragic death on the day he died (*Ashura*).

The twelver Shi'ites are particularly devoted to the Prophet's family: his son-in-law and cousin Ali, Hassan and Husain, who were the second and third Shi'ite imams and the sons of Ali and the Prophet's daughter Fatima. The line of descent ends with the twelfth imam, Mahdi, who went into occultation in 874. Shi'ites await his return, which will announce the End of Time. Husain has a special place and his martyrdom is remembered as a major event. Shi'ites take the view that, were it not for him, Yazid, like his father Muawiyyah before him, would have succeeded in adulterating the message of Islam. The purpose of the sacrifice of Husain and his handful of followers was to reawaken Muslims and turn them against this inauthentic Islam.

By dying as a martyr, according to the Shi'ites, Husain succeeded in discrediting Yazid, hastening the downfall of the Umayyads and establishing the Caliphate of the Abbasids, who were close to the family of the Prophet.

The martyrdom of the third Shi'ite imam provided an opportunity to denounce the usurpers so as to re-establish the true religion of the Prophet. In this case, the relationship between martyrdom and *jihad* is ambiguous, as the self-sacrifice was not made when victory was in sight. On the contrary, it resulted in a temporary defeat: the death of Husain in an unequal battle in which the 'Prince of Martyrs' (as Shi'ites call the third imam) died without having tasted victory. The victory was won post mortem because it laid bare the illegitimacy of an unjust government, as the Shi'ites contend. But its message is not unequivocal. For quietists who emphasise his sufferings, Husain's defeat means that this world is a vale of tears and that only the tears shed when his passion is celebrated in the month of Moharram can provide a balm for the countless ills reserved for the believer in this world. This is the dominant version which, with the exception of a few intervals, constitutes popular religiosity in the Shi'ite world. Shi'ites have indeed often been repressed by Sunnis, who regard them as deviants or even heretics. In such circumstances, the emphasis on suffering vision gave meaning to the permanent feeling of repression and at the same time consoled believers by promising them a happy afterlife in Paradise. Dissimulation (*taghieh* or *ketman*) of their true beliefs was a common practice amongst Shi'ite groups living on Sunni territory.

More rarely, the martyrdom of Husain has inspired rebellions and insurrections against repressive governments identified with that of Yazid. An activist version of the martyrdom of Husain came into being during rebellions against Sunni domination, when the repression became intolerable and, in Shi'ite lands, during anti-colonial struggles. From the nineteenth century onwards, we see the emergence of a resolutely militant version which transforms the death of Husain into a struggle against injustice, which is identified with the denial of the religion of Allah. Husain is said to have risen up against Yazid's illegitimate regime in order to emphasise the need to fight political and social oppression.

Even in the modern era, interpretations of the martyrdom of Husain give rise to many action-logics, and they are often divergent. On the one hand, the martyrdom of Husain can be an inducement to inaction, as it was predominantly in the past. The believer is afflicted by the spectacle of a world in which righteous men have no option but to die at the hands of unjust rulers and in which their only hope lies in the expectation of the End of Time. The martyrdom of Husain can, however, just as easily encourage the idea of a fight to the death as Shi'ism becomes secularised and the utopia of Mahdism plays a central role. The Mahdi (the Hidden last Imam, the twelfth) will come, that is, only if believers prepare for his coming by their deeds. They themselves must actively fight evil if the twelfth imam is to come and take up the struggle against injustice.[11] The eschatological vision helps build up a religiosity in which activism becomes the cornerstone of insurrectionary movements. Quietism is thus transformed into factional or even social activism.

Whilst Sunnis usually display great respect for the family of the Prophet and for his descendants down to the twelfth imam, they regard the Shi'ite attitude as excessive and, in some cases, ungodly or even heretical (*shirk*). According to Sunnis, they put the imam on a footing of equality with the Prophet and therefore give both the Prophet and his family a significance that makes them different from common mortals. As evidence of that, they point to the attitude of Shi'ites on their pilgrimage to the tombs of the imams: they observe the *tavaf* or circumambulation that Sunnites reserve for God during the pilgrimage to Mecca. That is why, when the Wahabites (Ibn Saud) seized Mecca in the 1920s, they destroyed the *zari'* (gilded or silver grills) around the tombs of the Prophet's family that allowed Shi'ites to observe their rites and take their vows.

The martyrdom of Husain does not have this foundational dimension in Sunni Islam, even though it is present and gives rise to many interpretations.[12] Husain's sacred death is still the subject of scholarly debates amongst Shi'ites and, to a lesser extent, Sunnis. Why did he accept death? What were his motives? Did he possess the innate knowledge (*elm e ladonnî*) that allows the pure to predict their own destiny? Did he wish to seize power and found a new political order, or was he simply trying to denounce Yazid's unjust and depraved regime? To what extent did his martyrdom have a mystic dimension? Was it a way of expressing his desire to ascend to Allah by literally 'annihilating himself' in Him (*fanâ fil lâh*) by becoming a martyr? These are controversial questions in Iran, Iraq and Lebanon, where Shi'ites are in the majority. Although they are of historical and religious interest, these debates then filter into society and, depending on socio-economic and political conditions and the international situation, the emphasis may fall on the activist or emietist version of his martyrdom. These interpretations are still of undeniable contemporary relevance.

In Shi'ite countries, the martyrdom of Husain remains the essential reference for young men who commit themselves to the path of martyrdom, and the event is therefore of great symbolic importance. During the Islamic Revolution in Iran, for example, Shariati's interpretation of the Ashura (the day the third imam died) played an important role in mobilising the youth of the great urban centres, as did, to a lesser degree the interpretations put forward by the cleric Motahhari and Ayatollah Khomeini.[13] Sunni societies do occasionally refer to martyrdom, but it does not have the fundamental significance it has for Shi'ites. That does nothing to preclude the possibility that advocates of martyrdom in Sunni societies (Palestine, Algeria, Egypt, Afghanistan) might die at the hand of other non-Islamic or Islamic social groups.

Martyrdom is a central issue in the struggle that young Kashmiris are waging against the Indian army, and in that being waged against the military government in the Algiers Casbah. Both Sunni Muslim societies and Palestinians are discussing whether or not the attitude of 'suicide bombers' is in conformity with Islam. Some take the view that it is a disguised form of suicide, which is forbidden in Islam as only God has the privilege of giving or taking life (except in the case of the Islamic punishments codified by *fiqh*, or Islamic jurisprudence). Others argue that suicide bombers are martyrs to the extent that they are defending Islam against an infinitely more powerful enemy who leaves them no other choice.

### The assassins

Modern forms of self-sacrifice have their historical precedents. One of the most important was a group of Ismailis who were willing to die for the sacred cause defined by their religious leader (*dai*). The Ismaili order known in the West as the Assassins represented one of the most complete forms of martyrdom (even though the word itself was not used). The order developed in Iran (and also in Syria) between the eleventh century and the thirteenth. It was a subgroup within Ismailism, a form of Shi'ism with seven imams, as opposed to 'twelver' Shi'ism with its twelve imams. Ismailism gave birth to the formidable order founded by Hasan Sabbah in the early eleventh century in an Iran ruled by the Seljuk Empire. The order spread across Iran as it acquired castles, mainly in the west and north of the country, and its distinguishing feature was its members' willingness to die for the sacred cause of Ismaili Islam, as incarnated by Hassan Sabbah. The goal of the assassination of the Seljuk Empire's dignitaries and Sunni religious leaders was to re-establish the rule of an Islam free of Sunni religious orthodoxy, so as to prepare the way for the End of Time and the Resurrection. Its followers were willing to die for the Cause and, when they executed their designated victims, they knew that they were sentencing themselves to death.[14] This was a form of martyrdom: putting to death an enemy of Islam defined by the *dai*, and then dying. What particularly impressed the Seljuk authorities in Iran, as well as the Crusaders in Syria, was the disciples' unswerving loyalty to Hassan Sabbah, the *da'i* and the hidden imam's lieutenant, who was himself descended from the Prophet's family. Dying in the service of the order was a source of great joy, and members of the order became servants to people who had been chosen to be killed. They devoted themselves to their masters until such time as they received the command to execute them with their daggers. Once that task had been carried out, the Assassin either took his own life or was put to death. The sect was based on a millenarianism which promised the End of Time and the establishment of a government that would clear the way for the Resurrection.

The Ismailis' fortresses remained impregnable for over two hundred years and their followers, who were found in the rural zones but also amongst the educated urban classes, were able to withstand the assaults of the Seljuks. It was only in the thirteenth century that they were wiped out by the Mongol armies. The group was characterised by its disciples' total devotion to the service of the religious order and its politic-religious leader, but also by its strict discipline and its members' ability to conceal their real identity by resorting to what Shi'ites call *ketman* or *taghieh*, or a religiously justified dissimulation of their identity in order to carry out their plans.

The same features can be found in modern activist groups. The example of the Ismaili Assassins demonstrates that many of the characteristics that we tend to attribute to modernity are in fact present in sectarian forms of Islam. Radical forms of action of premodern Muslim sects[15] and those of contemporary Muslim martyrs[16] differ, however, in one important respect. Members of premodern sects were usually willing to die and to kill their enemies because of their millenarian convictions (Hassan Sabbah's Ismailis believed that the Resurrection was at hand) and their positive image of the role they were playing. The Ismaili disciple who put to death a Seljuk dignitary believed that he was helping to construct a new *polis* in a new world.

Modern martyrs, in contrast, act out of hatred for a world in which, as they see it, they are being denied access to a life of 'dignity', no matter whether they are Iranian, Palestinian or members of a transnational network such as al-Qaeda. Whereas the sectarian martyrs of the Islam of the premodern age were convinced that their actions would bring about the advent of a new world and the destruction of the old, the actions of modern Muslim martyrs are intended to destroy a world in which there is no place for them as citizens of a nation or of an Islamic community. In most cases, they do not cherish any chiliastic ideal as a central theme in their motivations.[17]

## THE DIFFICULT SECULARISATION OF RELIGION

In traditional Muslim societies, anti-government insurrections were often justified on religious grounds. This resulted in the emergence of sectarian and non-orthodox forms of religiosity.[18] Although there was a wide variety of sects, one category was of particular importance. The sects in question subscribed to eschatological beliefs embodied in a Messiah known as the Mahdi. In some cases the Mahdi existed in flesh and blood in the person of a politico-religious leader; in others, he would not come until the End of Time. When these movements were successful, they formed governments which, to a greater or lesser extent, imitated those they had fought (as with the Mameluks in Egypt) by a change in the ruling elite and, in some cases, established new forms of orthodoxy. When they failed, they gave birth to deviant religiosities and to groups that used dissimulation (the Shi'ite *ketman* or *taghieh*) to go on practising their faith. Traces often survived in the collective memory, and could be revived or reactivated in other movements that rebelled against princes who were seen as unjust.

These types of socio-political protest and change were theorised by Ibn Khaldun, who saw this phenomenon as a transformation of *asabiya*, or the principle of group cohesion that cements a group's coherence and identity. A group that succeeded in establishing a powerful *asabiya* could seize power. Its *asabiya* was weakened by the passage of time. A new group with a strong *asabiya* would then emerge, challenge that of those in power and try to overthrow and replace them. This cycle was typical of power. A change in *asabiya* was often accompanied by sectarian forms of religiosity that denounced the ruling classes. That is why both Shi'ism and its variants, like the many forms of Ismailism, were able to challenge orthodox Sunnism, which was most of the time the religion of the ruling class. They then became a ruling class in their own right and adopted the same forms of government (the Mameluks in Egypt, the Safavid in Iran).

Similar protest movements could also develop when non-Muslim territories were invaded, but they did not necessarily lead to the emergence of sectarian groups. The Mongol invasion of Iran in the thirteenth century is a case in point.

The way to return to an 'unadulterated', 'authentic' and often puritanical Islam was to overthrow an established regime on the grounds that it was depraved and had strayed from the religion of Allah, and the new zealots preached strict obedience to the Koran. It was in this way that Wahhabism became established in Saudi Arabia in the eighteenth century. Wahhabism and the forms associated with it were one of the last avatars of a politico-religious transformation in traditional Muslim societies that had yet to be influenced by modernity.

Even when they make reference to a strict version of Islam, modern movements are not reducible to a change in *asabiya*. They represent a profound change in the representation of the community (*umma*) and of the people who are being individuated and becoming autonomous with respect to it, even when they explicitly claim to be at its service and prepared to sacrifice themselves to it. A new dialectic is now established between individual and community. The secularisation of religion is one of the major components of these movements, which are expressions of new tensions, and which put forward demands and exigencies that were not those of traditional Islamic movements.

When they took a non-modernised form characterised by *asabiya*, such movements presupposed the non-secularisation of religion. The Islamist movements of the twentieth century emerged at an advanced stage in its secularisation, and in conditions which their supporters often saw as tragic. Individuation works through the transformation of affects, relations with the body and its sexuality, with life, death, fear, the enemy, holy war, gender relations and the world at large. It also comes about thanks to a socio-economic challenge to regimes that have confiscated resources and blocked social development, particularly in the so-called rentier states, whose resources are based on oil revenues (Algeria and Iran for instance). It also relates to the ideal of a mythologised and united Islamic community that can heal the wounds of a modernisation that is breaking down social and cultural coherence without replacing it with new forms of sociability that look credible to wide sectors of society. That the sacred and the profane, the individual and the community, have undergone a profound transformation is acutely obvious in notions like martyrdom and *jihad*. Even though such expressions denote a semantic continuity with the past, they have a new content. In this form of martyrdom, sacrifice is certainly experienced as an act dictated by Allah, but the sacrifice is made by an individual who tries to leave his own mark on it. He is often an individual in despair, who has given up living and therefore feels that his life has no meaning in this world. There is a suicidal dimension to modern martyrdom. But unlike the anomic suicide who renounces life but has no connection with the sacred, he expresses his disgust with the world by mobilising the sacred and designating the enemy he wants to kill by getting himself killed.

The renunciation of the world is closely bound up with a vocation, with an aspiration that make religion, politics and the world closely related entities as a result of the secularisation of the religious.[19]

The new martyrs also abandon the elitist and aristocratic vision of religion. Any man, young or old, rich or poor, educated or illiterate, can become a martyr because all are equal in the face of death and because they therefore demand the same equality in the social and political field. This was not the case of the pre-modern martyrs that belonged to a spiritual aristocracy or a selective group of people, conscious of their being members of a tiny religious elite.

The secularisation of religion can be seen in the adoption of the modern tendency to resort to quantification to support arguments and to give a meaning to a logic of religious action. In my interviews with Islamist prisoners, the response to questions about how they could justify some three thousand innocent deaths caused by the attack on the World Trade Center on 11 September 2001 was inevitably given in statistical terms. I was asked how I could justify the deaths of hundreds of thousands of Iraqi children and old people amongst the civilian population as the result of the American embargo on oil sales, which led to a shortage of basic foodstuffs. If I produced statistics about innocent deaths, they invoked the even greater number of deaths that had nothing to do with the conflict. 'They did not mourn our innocent dead, and we are not going to mourn theirs,' was the answer I was given. The Palestinian struggle and the fact that there have been many more deaths on the Palestinian side than on the Israeli side were invoked in similar terms, to legitimise one cause rather than the other. The modern imaginary relies upon statistics to disguise its uncertainties and to back up its analyses. In humanitarian phenomena, we often hear actors invoking the possibility of saving the lives of hundreds of children and innocents at a time when, even in France or the West, only a few can be saved. The logic of devotion to the cause is translated into statistics and numbers that serve to legitimise the action. The same phenomenon can be observed amongst Islamists, but they refer to the number of deaths caused by one or the other side. The legitimacy of the war and the loss of innocent lives is measured in terms of the deaths caused on both sides. The act of *jihad* finds in this kind of argument a meaning that is directly related to a modern register inspired by statistical legitimacy and an objective assessment that can give it a meaning.

## REINTERPRETATIONS OF MARTYRDOM AND *JIHAD*

In Islamist movements, *jihad* is relevant in the fight against *jahiliyya* or ignorance. The word means the pre-Islamic period characterised by idolatry, which can reappear whenever believers stray from the true religion, as in present times. For Islamists *jahiliyya* is a characteristic of the contemporary period, in which the worship of idols has replaced the worship of Allah. When ignorance of the true God and idolatry extend their power over Muslims, it becomes necessary to call for a holy war or *jihad* to put an end to them. The powers that are exercised in Jahiliyya societies are godless and heretical (*kufr*) and they must be fought by the true Islamic faith in a holy war in which the believer must give up his life as Allah's martyr.

Two thinkers have been particularly influential in reinterpreting and modernising *jahiliyya* and *jihad* in the Sunni world: the Pakistani Mawdudi and the Egyptian Qutb. According to Mawdudi, nationalism is a form of godlessness and the traditional Islam that preaches respect for the five pillars of the faith – the profession of the Islamic faith (*shahada*), prayers (*salat*), fasting during Ramadan, pilgrimage to Mecca for those who have the means to make it, and Islamic charity (*zakat*) – stipulates that a *jihad* or war should be declared against those who have usurped Allah's power (*hakimiyya*). This war becomes a basic necessity because holy war is the dominant fundamental principle of Islam. This is a rereading and politicisation of the religion of Allah in the light of a new politico-religious mentality.

In order to legitimise this activist representation of religion, Islamist thinkers often refer to the period the Prophet spent in Medina, where he exercised both religious and political power. Whereas the Islamic tradition makes a de facto separation of power and religion (*dowla* and *din*), Mawdudi establishes a close link between the two by referring to an Islamic golden age, or the period that tradition declares closed because it is an *aurea aetas* and is therefore inaccessible to mere mortals. In order to do so, he introduces the twofold notion of sovereignty (*kakimiya*) and adoration (*obudiyya*), which did not exist in classic Islamic jurisprudence as a dominant view (*fiqh*).[20]

According to this vision, Allah alone enjoys sovereignty, and men are no more than his creatures. An authentic government rules a country in accordance with Allah's revelation. Sovereignty held by the people, the nation or some party is godless and contrary to Islam.[21] This tradition certainly existed in Islam long before Mawdudi, but it was, on the whole, a minority view. We find it in Ibn Taymiya, who was writing almost half a millennium before Mawdudi, and in Ibn Kathir (a *faqih* of the fourteenth century), but this version was still a minority view. The majority view recommended, like Ibn Khaldun, the separation of *shari'a* and state on the grounds that the golden age of the Prophet's time in Medina was quite distinct from later periods.[22] The dominant view held that the Islamic scholar should hold the function of the judge and not that of the ruler. The Islamist modernisation of Islam has entailed the extension of this view (Islamic jurisdiction, *fiqh*) into the realm of politics at large. In this way, politics and religion are inherently associated, be it through the shi'ite version of the *Velayat faqih* (the sovereignty of the Islamist jurist) put forward by Khomeini or in the sunni version of the *hakimiyya*, proposed by Mawdudi.

Qutb, who was influenced by Mawdudi, was the main inspiration behind the Muslim Brotherhood in Egypt. He radicalised Islamic thought by laying the foundations for a revolutionary Islamic government. He contrasts the exclusive political sovereignty (*hakimiyya*) of God with the illegitimate power based upon impiety (*kufr*) and ignorance (*jahiliyya*). This type of power is inspired by a modernity that can take the form of nationalism, socialism or any other kind of modernism. Its main features are the non-segregation of men and women, an exaggerated individualism and love of money. Recognising the exclusive sovereignty of God means accepting that one is a creature of Allah and submitting to Him. Anyone who does not do so rejects the omnipotence of Allah by confusing God's power with that of an autonomous creature. Legislating in a way that does not mean submission to God is tantamount to arrogating the attributes of God because all Islamic legislation must conform to His commandments.

The power of God must reign in every domain of collective life: recognising the sovereignty of Allah means rejecting the separation of religion as a ritual practice and political power at the level of the state. Whereas the majority tradition dissociates Church and state in an ambiguous manner, they are closely associated for Qutb. Most of the time in the tradition, this dissociation referred to the Golden age in which the close association of politics and religion was accomplished in the time of the prophet, particularly in Medina (the period of *Hijra*). But this age was regarded as not attainable, to be reached as the final stage at the end of time. The reality of the Muslim societies was that of the distinction between the ruler (sultan, caliph, shah, and so on) and the Islamic *umma*.[23] Qutb challenges the views of most Sunni Ulama, for whom the primary purpose of *jihad* must be defensive, and sees it as a matter of personal duty. According to him, *jihad* must establish Allah's authority on earth. Human affairs must be conducted in accordance with the commandments of God. Satanic powers must be destroyed and an end to the rule of men must establish the reign of Allah.[24] The defensive vision of *jihad* therefore does not correspond to the truth of the message of the Koran. Only orientalists and inauthentic Muslims restrict *jihad* to the defence of the land of Islam. It is not purely defensive, and is identified with the very movement of Islam, which must encompass the whole of the earth and all of humanity.

*Jihad* has, by its very nature, a universal vocation, and its function goes far beyond the function assigned it by traditional Islamic *fiqh*, which usually restricts it to the defence of the land of Islam. The war was first directed against the ruling classes in Muslim societies, starting with Nasser's Egypt. Qutb was hanged during the reign of Nasser in 1966.

In the work of radical thinkers like Qutb, Mawdudi and Khomeini, the denunciation of the hegemonic West and the Orientalists who are its authorised representatives often goes hand in hand with a radical critique of lukewarm Muslims or 'hypocrites' (*munafiqh*, or those who sow dissensions amongst Muslims, to use the Koranic phrase). These are Muslims who stir up ill-feeling in the community and who undermine its unity because of their cowardly attitude or their refusal to follow the path of God. These hypocrites refuse to fight the forces of Evil and often come to terms with them for fear of losing their privileges or simply because they are spineless. Mawdudi is critical of Muslims who are not willing to be actors in history and who accept Western dominance.[25] The true Muslim strives to realise his faith through war and sacrifice, and refuses to submit to a world that changes by endorsing the verdicts of the Koran, which do not change. Mawdudi contrasts the modern spinelessness of those who conform to a changing world and passively adapt to it as Muslims were taught to do by the colonisers, with the heroism of the authentic Muslim who tries to leave his mark on history, rather than submitting to its law. The praise of heroism, inflexibility and the bold attempt to establish *shari'a* presuppose a militant ability to resist the temptations of history.

These three thinkers are trying to give Muslims a new self-confidence. They lost their self-confidence as a result of the assaults of imperialism and the false prestige of a West that is depriving Muslims of their self-respect and devotion to their faith. Qutb and Mawdudi's equivalents in the Shi'ite world are Khomeini in Iran and Musâ Sadre and Fadlallah in Lebanon. Their ideas are close to the subject of power, or the notion of *Velayat-e faqih* (the sovereignty of the doctor of Islamic law) developed by Khomeini. Politics is subordinated to religion in the name of Allah. In Shia Islam, the origins of this notion go back to the nineteenth century and to clerics like Naraqi, who died in 1828, and Najafi, who died in 1850, or in other words to the period when the Qajar dynasty was increasingly being reduced to powerlessness by the imperial regimes of England and Russia.[26] It was at this time that a minority fraction of the clergy asserted its ascendancy over politics, which had previously been dominated by monarchs descended from nomadic tribes. The genealogy of this notion within Islam, and especially its Shi'ite version can obviously be traced much further back in time. Some see the premises of *Velayat-e faqih* in the notion of the just sultan (*sultan e âdel*).[27]

Khomeini's innovation does not lie solely in his qualities as a theologian, but above all in his qualities as a strategist and a politician. His version of Islamic activism is based upon the denunciation of the 'hypocrites' (*manafeghin*) who, after the overthrow of the Shah, tried to foment discord amongst Muslims in the name of an adulterated version of Islam. His main target was the People's Mujahedeen, a far-left Islamic formation, but he was also criticising those who lacked enthusiasm for the Islamic Revolution. The 'supporters of compromise' (*sâzech*) are in fact people who have compromised themselves through their allegiance to imperialism (*sâzech-kâr*), which Khomeini calls World Arrogance (*estekbar e djahani*). He uses a Koranic phrase, but changes its meaning. The word means 'imperialism', but as that term had been claimed by the Marxist and atheist left, he had to find an Islamic term that could denote the same meaning without arousing suspicions that he was borrowing from the very left he was denouncing. 'Arrogance' means excessive pride, and the forms of behaviour associated with it, and especially behaviour that leads people to forget God because of the emphasis they place on the self. According to the founder of the Islamic Republic, the West is arrogant because it enslaves Muslims and promotes a system characterised by a materialist and bestial secularism. In order to fight Western arrogance, Muslims must overcome their fear of the power of the West, which is based upon myths that are devoid of truth.

One of the main characteristics of Khomeini's discourse is in fact the extreme subjectivism we find in so many modern radical Islamic thinkers. He emphasises affects like fear, the strength of the soul, the feeling of honour, the will to sacrifice, and a Muslim identity that knows no doubts and is strengthened by turning to Allah. According to Khomeini, we are weak when we feel ourselves to be weak. In order to overcome our fear of our own weakness, we must make a heroic decision. When we do that, we can acquire the strength of God. Our feeling of weakness makes the enemy feel superior. Strength derives from an interiority which dictates, with the help of God, a decision that has no need of any external support.[28] This extreme subjectivism calls upon the outside world on the one hand and Muslims on the other to denounce America's intrigues. This radical discourse actually oscillates between a bipolar vision of the conflict between Good and Evil and a tripolar intersubjectivity in which the outside world is called as a witness to the machinations of the enemy.

Khomeini constantly appeals to the world, which he wants to convert to his version of history, and at the same time denounces the perfidious American enemy, who is denying Muslim peoples their rights. The status of the outside world is ambiguous in that Islamist discourse invokes a Manichaean universe which should not recognise that space of neutrality, but which is at times used to guarantee the legitimacy of the discourse.

Another dimension of radical discourse emerges when he addresses Muslims by praising, in keeping with the warrior tradition of the Prophet, the authentic Muslim's strength and combative qualities. In a speech to members of the Economics department of the University of Isfahan, for example, Khomeini extols the warlike resources of Muslim youth: 'We are men who fight, we are men who struggle. Our young people fought the tanks, guns and machine guns [of the Shah's army].'[29] The speech finally addresses the enemies of Islam (the West, as personified by America), inveighing against them, challenging them and symbolically humiliating them by invoking the notions of the honour and warrior virtues of Muslims. Khomeini's underlying Manichaeanism, in which Good and Evil can be clearly identified, generates a form of discourse with the self, Muslims, the enemy and the world as its backdrop. Khomeini uses his considerable oratorical skills to reduce this multiple polarity to a bipolarity in which the world and Muslims must ally themselves with the supporters of the Good against a Western enemy who has been weakened, but who still remains formidable.

The religious unity of hearts within a unified community that rises up against the 'satanic powers' and succeeds in defeating them gives Muslims a new strength. The most obvious example was the Shah's Iran, with its American-equipped ultra-modern army. The Muslim people of Iran were able to defeat it with their bare hands, with nothing but their raised fists and their faith in Allah. That Revolution was, of course, the prelude to a general uprising that would announce the End of Time and the coming of the Hidden Imam (the twelfth imam Mahdi, or the Shi'ite equivalent of the Messiah). In the meantime, absolute sacrifice and self-abnegation were required to demonstrate support for the cause of the Good. The oppressed (*mostadafine*, to use the Koranic phrase to which Khomeini, like Shariati, gave 'class' connotations) would succeed in taking their revenge on their oppressors (*mostakbirine*). Both expressions are strongly influenced by the ideologies of the Marxist left and Third Worldism: the oppressed are the excluded, the proletarianised masses, and the oppressors are the imperialists or ruling classes. The oppressed will emerge victorious from their struggle with their oppressors because they rely upon Islam, which is the religion that defends them. For that to happen, Muslims must accept martyrdom. A sacrificial community united by its willingness to cross swords with world imperialism will succeed in establishing the reign of Good by following the paradigmatic example of the Iranian Revolution, which has inaugurated a new world era.

Debates about these new versions of Islam raise the question of Islamism. In France, the term goes back to at least the eighteenth century and was used by Voltaire, albeit in an obviously different sense. If we take 'Islamism' to mean those currents that try to establish a close link between politics and religion, their history does in a sense go back to the first centuries of Islam. Minority tendencies have always tried to realise the ideal society of the Prophet, who was both a religious and a political leader. If we take 'Islamism' to mean a politic-religious current that tries to appropriate power and justifies a possible recourse to violence to install by authoritarian means a regime based on *shari'a* (religious precepts that have been codified to some degree), by ambiguously modernising Islam without exactly admitting it, and by Islamising – just as tacitly – modernity by placing particular emphasis on opposition to the West, it is a relatively modern phenomenon dating from the 1930s (the Muslim Brotherhood in Egypt) that reached its apotheosis in the last third of the twentieth century.

One of the important features of most Islamist currents is, as we have seen, the central role they give, in their doctrinal writings, to the notions of *jihad* and martyrdom.

In sociological terms, these currents are further characterised by the emergence of new categories of people, many of them from the universities, which began to proliferate in Muslim societies from the second half of the twentieth century onwards.[30] Many of the leaders of these movements come from a scientific background, and they seek to lay down the law about Islam and challenge the hegemony of traditional groups, which are in their view too quietist or have been corrupted by their complicity with illegitimate governments.

The challenge to tradition and its institutional mechanisms does not, however, come only from the new groups that have emerged as a result of the modernisation of Muslim societies.[31] We are also seeing the emergence of new clerics within both Sunni and Shi'ite religious institutions, and they are challenging the dominant interpretations. The example of Iran's Ayatollah Khomeini, who was a very distinguished religious dignitary (although not the most important before the Revolution), is symptomatic in this respect. So too were Egypt's Sheikh Abd Al Ghâffar Azziz, and Sheikh Omar Abdel Rahman, who were alumni of the Al-Azhar University. Each in his own way challenged the quietist interpretations of that institution's Ulamas.[32]

The radicalisation of interpretations of Islam and the desire to merge the political into the religious can in fact take two distinct forms. Some preach a return to an Islamic society that peacefully respects the norms laid down by Islamic canon law (*fiqh*) and attempt to promote Islamic education from below by convincing believers of the need for a return to a fundamentalist Islam, or in other words an Islam that can take in every aspect of life. They recommend Islamisation from below, and see no need for the violent seizure of political power from above before society has been profoundly Islamised. The Muslim Brotherhood in Egypt and the Refah party (subsequently known as Fezilet) in Turkey are cases in point. For others, the goal is to put an end to the reign of impiety and *Tâqut* (idolatry) by resorting to violence. Their model has many points in common with that of the European *gauchistes* or Latin American revolutionaries of the 1970s.

The new generations educated in non-traditional circuits such as technological or scientific universities often play an essential role in these protest groups. But the *Ulamas* intervene just as actively, at least on the fringes of their religious institutions.

After the death of Nasser, Sheikh Omar Abdel Rahman, a blind *alim* (religious scholar) who studied at Al-Azhar, inspired the radical Islamism of both the Jamaat-e-Islami and Islamic Jihad movements. He left for the United States in 1990 and following the first attack on the World Trade Center in 1993, he was sentenced to life imprisonment in 1996. His political theory is characterised by certain features found in various radical Islamist currents. He subscribes, for instance, to the theological Manichaeanism that rejects the traditional view that rulers can be placed on a graduated scale: *dhalim* (tyrant), *fâsiq* (sinner) and *kâfir* (infidel). In his view, these distinctions are reducible to that between a just Muslim ruler on the one hand and an unjust ruler on the other. The latter's reign is the reign of ignorance and idolatry, and Muslims have a duty to fight it. Whereas the traditional *ulamas* left it to God to pass judgement upon unjust rulers, and therefore saw no need to condemn them themselves, Sheikh Abdel Rahman – like Khomeini two decades before him – defends the need to condemn in religious terms governments that contravene Islam in the name of a totalising conception in which religion annexes politics.

A *takfir* (condemnation for impiety) is therefore a matter for an *alim*, and is bound up with politics. In the Islamic tradition, *takfir* applies mainly to mystics or deviants who are condemned by orthodox clerics. It was traditionally applied to individuals or groups within the community. The political dimension was absent or minor, and often concealed. The new conception of *takfir* makes it a political category out of one that was mainly religious and legal in the Islamic sense (*fiqh*). Although it can be legitimised by referring to certain minority currents within medieval Islam, this vision is still a challenge to the majority tradition because it changes the status of the *ulama* by declaring them fit to rule. This is especially true of Khomeini, who preached government by the Islamic Jurist or *Velayat-*

*e faqih*. An ungodly government must be fought with the weapon of faith, so as to establish an Islamic government that will apply *shari'a* law and fight the Westernisation of morality by resorting to the Islamic principle of imposing Good and forbidding Evil (*mar bil ma'ruf wa nahy an al munkir*).

The role of *jihad* now becomes essential. It is associated with the *alim*'s *idjithad* (giving religious opinions that conform to Islam) and politicises his role, which was originally restricted to the legal domain. A reinterpretation of Islamic laws that combines what are often traditional minority views with innovations in the conduct of human behaviour gives a legal vision a political extension. The political annexes the juridical by justifying itself in the name of Islamic jurisprudence (*fiqh*). The frontier between *dine* (religion), *dunyâ* (the world) and *dowla* (politics, state) becomes blurred. The end result is a holistic and rigidly unified version of Islam that was quite unknown to the tradition, at least its dominant tendencies. In Islamism, the relationship between politics and Islamic law undergoes a profound metamorphosis. Traditional Islamic law (*fiqh*), as defined by its orthodox tendencies, displayed the following characteristics:[33]

- Its nature was essentially technical: its notions and procedures were so technical that they were only distantly related to ethical or dogmatic considerations.
- It had a great capacity for innovation: the historical reality of its practice was characterised by great latitude when it came to pronouncing on specific points of law (*ikhtilaf*). This meant that it could change in times of social change.
- Islamic law was not a code. It was a corpus of legal precedents and principles, related to a highly developed corpus of hermeneutic and paralogical techniques.
- Islamic law was, by its nature, objectivist and took little interest in intentionality.
- Islamic law was, for the most part, private: it dealt with obligations, contracts, personal status and other aspects of customary life. These domains came within the remit of what was known as the *hoqouq al ibad*, or the rights of persons (creatures). There was a body of laws dealing with the public domain; this came into the category of *hoqouq allah* (the rights of God). It dealt with obligations relating to the property of the Islamic state. This body of laws did not apply to Muslims living in the territory of Infidels (non-Muslims). Muslims in that

position were *musta'min* and had to behave in an appropriate manner by obeying the laws of the country where he was living.

The authoritarian modernisation of Muslim societies results in a profound transformation of jurisprudence (*fiqh*), which comes to mean a relationship with the political that did not previously exist. *Fiqh* becomes politicised. This is a recent phenomenon, as compared to the function and nature of traditional Islamic law.

Whilst the Sunni world gives *jihad* a value that is disproportionate to its traditional weight, the characteristic feature of the contemporary Shi'ite world is its overevaluation of martyrdom, interpreted in a new and activist sense.

The Shi'ite interpretations of the 1960s and 1970s, or the period leading up to the Islamic Revolution, represented an attempt to reject the superhuman image of a suffering Husain who knowingly sacrificed himself to save the Shi'ite community. Every year, that community celebrates the spectacle of his passion throughout the month of Moharram. The traditional conception gives Husain qualities that are transcendental and therefore inimitable. He is *ma'soum*, or in other words incapable of committing a sin, and cannot be imitated by men. He must be venerated, and not taken as a model for concrete and immanent behaviour.

Unlike traditional conceptions, the new interpretations (and especially Shariati's) emphasise Husain's humanity. They are intended to enhance his image by giving him an immanent dimension and making him the actor of his own death, which occurred in an indeterminate situation: could he defeat Yazid's army by mobilising the town of Kufah, which had appealed to him for help? Sâléhi Nadjaf-Abâdi, for instance, argues that Husain felt that victory was possible in a historical conjuncture in which he thought he could mobilise part of society, and particularly the town of Kufah, against the Umayyad Caliph Yazid. When he realised that victory was impossible, he chose to die as a martyr because he was sure that, if he surrendered, Ibn Ziyad, who commanded Yazid's army, would put him to death with no mercy. That is why he refused to surrender, fought heroically when Ziyad attacked him, and thus achieved martyrdom.[34] The image of Husain that emerges from this narrative is certainly that of a being who is essentially superhuman, but whose knowledge of the future is no different to that of ordinary mortals. He had no innate knowledge (*elm e ladonni*), but sincerely believed that he would emerge victorious from his just war against the Umayyad Caliph. It was circumstances that made victory impossible. He preferred to die in glory rather than humiliation. In that sense, Husain was a human being and his behaviour is all the more praiseworthy in that he would not allow himself to be humiliated. According to Nadjaf Abâdi, Husain did not aspire to martyrdom, popular opinion notwithstanding. He wanted to seize power, and his death was the logical outcome of his failure to do so. The determining factor in the third Imam's rebellion was his eminently human dimension. When he rebelled, he gambled solely upon reason and experience, and certainly not upon some superhuman knowledge.

This representation of Husain breaks with the transcendence that is his in traditional Shi'ism. The humanisation of Husain means that ordinary mortals can take him as a model. Henceforth, he is imitable and immanent: his sainthood does not mean that he was immune to human fragility. The Prince of Martyrs comes closer to men and it is possible to follow in his footsteps by imitating him, even to the extent of making the supreme sacrifice. Salehi Nadjaf Abadi was not particularly well known to the young Iranis who took part in the Islamic Revolution, but he was well known in intellectual religious circles. Shariati mentions him in his interpretation of martyrdom,[35] and he therefore played a role in transforming religious themes in a way that made it possible, or even legitimate, for the younger generations to commit themselves to revolution in the name of Islam.

Morteza Motahhari, who was also a cleric, played a major role in creating an image of Shi'ite martyrdom that rejects the quietist tradition. He begins by describing the essential merits of martyrs who enjoy the gratitude of others because they agree to make the supreme sacrifice in the service of Allah. The martyr creates a milieu that allows others to live in accordance with the Good. He burns like a candle and gives others the benefit of a light without which they would remain in darkness. The body of a martyr is pure and does not, unlike other bodies, have to be washed before burial. Motahhari distinguishes between several types of death: natural death from illness or as a result of murder, suicide and martyrdom. A martyr agrees to risk death solely in order to realise sacred ideals 'for the sake of God' (fi sabil ellah), as the Koran demands. According to Motahhari, the martyrdom is based on two things. The martyr must, on the one hand, commit himself 'for the sake of God', and he must prepare himself by achieving a 'consciousnessized' (agahaneh) state of mind. The candidate for martyrdom must not commit himself for reasons pertaining to his personal interests or for reasons that might involve his egoism.

Good Shi'ite that he is, Motahhari defines *jihad* in relation to martyrdom. Unlike Christianity, he notes, Islam is not a religion in which the believer turns the other cheek when he is slapped by an unbeliever. This religion combines faith (*imân*), migration (*hijrat*) and holy war (*jihad*). Migration means leaving this life in order to achieve a sacred goal through martyrdom. To that end, the true believer is willing to sacrifice his life to save his faith in the service of others. Citing one of the Prophet's *hadiths*, Motahhari asserts that the Good lies beneath the sword and in the shadow of the sword. Islam therefore creates martyrs so as to advance its noble ideals.

In both Motahhari and Shariati, we see how the theme of martyrdom can be applied to ordinary mortals by inverting the exemplary and paradigmatic role of Husain. According to Shi'ite tradition, a holy death was meaningless unless it was related to the figures of the saints: the Prophet's uncle Hamzeh, who died in the battle of Uuhud, the first Imam, Ali, who was murdered in 661, and the many other Shi'ite *imams* who were put to the sword by ungodly Muslims working for 'corrupt' Caliphs. But these saintly figures are, in theory, inimitable. We can mourn their fate, but we cannot imitate them. It is only at a much later date that martyrdom becomes something the masses can imitate, thanks mainly to the Islamic Revolution, which opens up a vast field of possibilities, first in the struggle to overthrow the Shah's regime and then in the long war against Iraq between 1981 and 1988. The theme of martyrdom was appropriated by young people from the working classes. They asserted their willingness to die a holy death not only in rituals, but by staging their own deaths. In doing so, they created a version of Islam that was largely unknown to the dominant tradition.

The individualisation of the martyr's tragedy is another recent phenomenon. According to tradition, Husain was a superhuman being whose Passion had to do with his transcendent nature. The celebration of his death was a form of mourning, but as his death was almost predestined it was, paradoxically, a way of sharing in his glory. Sheikh Abbas Qomi records the words of Sheikh Koleini (sixteenth to seventeenth centuries), who repeated what he had been told by the sixth Shi'ite Imam Jafar Sadeq, who died in 765.[36] According to the latter, Husain never suckled at the breast of either his mother or any other woman. The Prophet took him in his arms, placed a finger in his mouth, and Husain sucked it and was thus miraculously kept alive for two to three days. The flesh of Husain was therefore born of that of the Prophet. The greatness of his martyrdom is a testimony to his superhuman dimension and he has a special place in the Shi'ite pantheon. He is not simply the Prophet's son-in-law. He is in a sense also his direct descendant because his superhuman flesh is receptive to the pain of a humanity that is in search of salvation. Husain's nature is not that of mortals.

In the work of Shariati or Motahhari, in contrast, we see the humanisation of Husain's affects and, by extension, those experienced by the martyrs who imitate him. According to Motahhari, Islam's roots lie in the joy of achieving martyrdom, which is why all the Prophet's companions wished to share in it. Similarly, he states that the first Imam, Ali, had a burning desire to die a martyr's death. We know how much influence this burning desire to die as a martyr had during the Iranian Revolution, when so many young men's testaments describe at length their inextinguishable appetite for death.[37]

New exegeses have transformed a Husain who was once inaccessible into a humanised hero who can be imitated by his disciples and followed by young men who want to fight the enemy. Husain is an *imam* who literally calls upon his supporters to follow him rather than to admire him and to mourn him in his inaccessible empyrean as someone transcendent who cannot be taken as a model.

For his part, Shariati goes one step further by turning Husain into a revolutionary. He describes a figure whose primary aim is to pursue the war waged against the supporters of Cain by the supporters of Abel, of Good against Evil. To do so, he calls for unparalleled devotion and for an abnegation that does any revolutionary honour. Husain is 'Adam's heir', the man who began an uprising and not the distant, timeless saint celebrated by the Shi'ite tradition.[38] He is inscribed in history and his epic is modelled on that of the heroes who fought Evil. It is the extent of his devotion that gives him the dimension of sainthood, and not his prophetic ancestry, which would divorce him from humanity and place him in a pantheon that is beyond the reach of the young. Candidates for martyrdom are legion in the new cities of the Middle East and the Maghreb. They are in search of dignity and are impatient to embark upon a heroic adventure that will let them escape the insignificance to which they are condemned by a dull and inglorious existence. Martyrdom gives them access to the dignity and respect that are so tragically lacking in cities like Teheran, Cairo or Algiers where, no matter whether they are Sunnis or Shi'ites, they are at best ignored and at worst despised, and condemned to a hurtful inferiority.

The humanisation and modernisation of Husain is of great symbolic importance in Shi'ite circles. It makes it possible to translate revolutionary abnegation into a religious idiom, to raise a banner of protest emblazoned with the prestige of a revolutionary and insubordinate Husain. Sunnis did not really need a Husain to supply a paradigm of martyrdom. They were shown the way by Lebanon's Shi'ites. Martyrdom on the grand scale was essentially a Shi'ite phenomenon after the Islamic Revolution in Iran, but it could be adapted to a Sunni environment when the emphasis on *jihad* replaced the paradigm of Husain. The backdrop to this *jihad* was the humanisation of Husain, who became an implicit model for Iran's young Bassidji martyrs, who volunteered en masse to fight at the front. When the Shi'ite vision was imported, via Lebanon, into Palestine it made it easier to organise the martyrdom of the young men of Hamas who declared themselves followers not of the Prince of Martyrs, but of those who had shown them the way by more or less imitating their brothers in Lebanon, who were themselves influenced by Hezbollah, which was itself directly influenced by the Bassidjis in Iran.

### Shariati on martyrdom

That Khomeini played an essential role in the Islamic Revolution of 1979 is undeniable, but Shariati played an essential role in the ideological changes that took place in Iranian society, and especially amongst urban youth. It is to him that we owe expressions like 'red Shi'ism' (*tashayyo e sorkh*: the colour red is a reference to the Shi'ite tradition's image of the bloodstained bodies of Husain and his companions as well as to 'red' leftism), 'Shi'ism, religion of protest (*mazhab e e'teraz*), and 'Ali's Shi'ism', which is militant and revolutionary, as opposed to the 'Safavid Shi'ism' that embodies the legitimacy of an oppressive government, as typified by the dynasty of that name that ruled Iran from the sixteenth to the eighteenth century.

Shariati constantly plays on two registers, and establishes a close connection between them. On the one hand, he makes a direct appeal to the individual, and to personal responsibility. The notions of 'constructing a revolutionary self' (*khod sazi e enquelabi*) or 'consciousness-raising' (*agahi*) are vital to his militant vision of religion, in which the role of the individual is essential. Second, he relates the individual whom he entrusts with the task of leading the revolution to victory, to what he calls a *maktabi* Islam characterised by the demand for self-sacrifice for an ideal that is more important than life. This notion has elective affinities with Qtub's *aqida*. According to Qutb, *aqida* is the spiritual link that binds young Muslims together and gives them stability and unity in a changing society tainted by idolatry. Because it establishes a link between the sacred and the new actors who are emerging on the social stage, *aqida* gives them the ability to prepare to fight for a true Islam with full knowledge of the facts. Unlike Shariati, Qutb stresses that Islam is not grounded in any class struggle. But both have forged notions (or given them new meanings) to make the younger generations aware of the need to build an Islamic society from scratch. And in order to do that self-sacrifice and martyrdom are necessary.

Shariati was probably the first to make a conscious distinction between holy war and martyrdom, between *jihad* and *shahadat*, at the conceptual level. In the Sunni tradition and according to the scholarly Shi'ism of most *marja-e taqlid* (the 'religious models' believers choose to follow), martyrdom is subordinate to *jihad*. Muslims must be prepared to die as martyrs 'for the cause of God' to ensure victory in the holy war. Now Shariati introduces two types of martyrs. On the one hand, there are martyrs like the Prophet's uncle Hamzeh, who fought the enemy at Uhud and died there on the field of battle; on the other, there are martyrs like Imam Husain: 'Hamzeh, who died in the battle of Uhud and who was given the name "Prince of Martyrs" (*seyyed ol chohadâ*), and after Ashura (the day of imam Husain's murder) Shi'ism gave Husain that name ... both are *seyyed* martyrs (they are members of the Prophet's families or his descendents): Hamzeh in the field of *jihad* martyrs, and Husain that of the martyrs of martyrdom.'[39]

Hamzeh is a hero, a *mujahid* ('one who makes *jihad*'). To that extent, he is unlike Husain: 'Hamzeh is a *mujahid* hero who fought to win and to defeat the enemy. He failed and died as a martyr. But he is an individual martyr ... Husain, on the other hand, is a different kind of martyr. He did not come to destroy the enemy by the might of the sword and in the expectation of victory... Although he could have stayed quietly at home and stayed alive, he arose and went to meet death quite lucidly. At that moment, he chose to die and to be destroyed, and he faced that danger so that he could die with the whole world watching. Hamzeh and the other *moujahedeen* came for victory and risked death, as their goal was to win. But the purpose of Imam Husain's martyrdom was self-denegation for a sacred cause which was itself threatened with defeat. Here, holy war (*jihad*) and martyrdom (*shahâdat*) are completely different.'[40]

The difference between Hamzeh and Husain is that one wanted to defeat the enemy but not to die, whilst the other knew perfectly well that he was going to lose the battle and perish. According to Shariati, that conscious death has much greater religious significance than one that tradition identifies with dying for the sake of *jihad*. In one case, death is a makeshift solution or the random outcome of a victory that was not really a victory; in the other, death was premeditated and therefore of greater significance because there was no possibility of immediate victory, and because the martyr was acutely aware of that. Shariati goes on: 'The "*moujahid*" philosophy of rebellion is not the same as that of the martyr.'[41] 'Martyrdom in the strict sense of the term', asserts Shariati, 'is a command that applies after the *jihad*, and the martyr takes the stage when the *moujahid* has failed in his task.'[42]

Divorcing the *jihadi*, who bases the legitimacy of his fight on an optimistic vision of possible victory in the fight with the enemy, from the martyr who is aware that he will certainly die for a desperate cause in which there can be no military victory in the here and now, has serious implications. According to the anthropology of traditional Shi'ism, the cult of suffering and the ritual celebration of martyrdom in the long month of Moharram are based upon the religious sensibilities of a minority persecuted by the Sunni majority. The cause of Husain is identified with that of Shi'ites, who are mistreated and repressed because of their faith. Husain is the embodiment of the desperate cause of the persecuted *mazlum*, who were caused infinite pain by injustice and unrelenting repression. They, like Husain, suffered a tragic fate whose cause can be identified with the fate of Good in this world. The rule of the Good will be re-established only at the End of Time, outside this world and not within it. Shariati's distinction is based upon the painful awareness developed by Shi'ism, but it inverts its meaning. The death of Husain is not imputed to an unjust but immutable world order; it is the result of his own decision to die in order to ensure that the voice of the oppressed will be heard throughout history and to demonstrate the righteousness of their cause. That is why martyrdom is, as he puts it, the 'heart of history' (*shahid qalb e tarikh ast*). Thanks to this mutation, a quietist cult of suffering can be transformed into tragic activism. A world in which the Muslim's only reaction can be the ritual display of his pain in ceremonies bound up with the poignant death of Husain becomes the world of a sovereign martyr who consciously chooses to die and who therefore teaches other Muslims a lesson in abnegation and self-transcendence. Dignity may be denied them in life, but they can achieve it in death, or in a struggle that rejects passivity and quietism and encourages the active commitment of individuals to a noble cause they have chosen for themselves in the full knowledge that it cannot prevail in this life.

Shariati integrates this vision of martyrdom into a conception in which a revolutionary eschatology allows the individual to rejoin society. Man, he writes, is both a being made of mud and a divine soul, a mixture of Devil and God. He has a propensity for both Good and Evil. The purpose of religion is to see to it that the divine half of man triumphs over the diabolic half: 'Martyrdom is an act whereby a man suddenly, and in a revolutionary mode, flings his vile being (the diabolic half) into the fire of love and faith and thus becomes completely good. That is why a martyr must not be washed in keeping with the Islamic ritual (*qosl*), and why, on Judgement Day, he does not have to account for his actions because the sinful and guilty man – this was his way of life before he was martyred – was sacrificed before he died, and because he is now "in the presence" ... Martyrdom is an invitation for all eras and all generations: "If you can, slay and if you cannot, die".'[43]

According to Shariati, the quintessence of martyrdom lies in that sentence. If it is possible, kill the enemy (this applies to the *jihadi*); if that is not possible and if the desired goal cannot be realised, the warrior must be prepared to die in a battle in which he does not reject violence against the enemy. Even though he knows the enemy is stronger, he must overcome his own weakness, sacrifice himself and thus demonstrate the righteousness of his cause to others and to future generations.

This message has been best understood by Palestine's Sunni martyrs, in part, perhaps, because of the example set by Hezbollah in Lebanon, where Shariati has become known thanks to the reappropriation of martyrdom in what is seen as an intolerable situation: the incomparably superior Israeli army makes any prospect of victory illusory. In that situation, self-assertion is possible only through the death of a subject who kills members of the enemy group by killing himself.

The Shari'a concept of martyrdom is a response to the new individual's situation in the Islamic world. In the absence of any possibility of self-realisation in the world, it holds out the possibility of self-realisation in death whilst remaining true to this Islamic representation of mutual violence. There is no acceptance of the violence of the other and no refusal to respond to it (as in the Christian version or the Buddhist notion of self-sacrifice by fire). The heroism of the act of self-destruction also destroys the other, even though he is known to be stronger and, for the moment, invincible. The new martyrdom uses the idiom of a radicalised Islam to express the despair of an embryonic individual who maintains his links with the sacred whilst striving to assert himself in a world that is deaf to his aspirations.

In its modernised and radical versions, martyrdom is an expression of an extreme situation characterised by the difficult advent of a process of individuation and by the failure of secular forms of modernisation, which have raised expectations of autonomy without actually satisfying them. Violent death is the result of a choice made because self-realisation is impossible, and it also results in the death of those the martyr identifies as the cause of his suffering. The act of martyrdom oscillates between suicide and the killing of the other, between resignation and self-assertion. There is at once a desire for self-assertion and a realisation that it is impossible. The dilemma is resolved through the destruction of both the self and those who are perceived as obstacles to self-realisation. There is both self-assertion and resignation, a will to fight and a will to die, and aspiration towards both self-realisation and self-destruction. The act of martyrdom is given a sacred status, and it therefore guarantees a happy end whereas life on earth is profoundly unhappy. Shariati has become the spokesman for a younger generation that is prepared to put its life on the line in a desperate attempt to 'slay, and if you cannot slay, be slain'. It gives a feeling of existing as an individual. That feeling is inverted, and death becomes a matter of urgency for both self and other. Both are swept away by a holy rage.

Seen from this angle, death by martyrdom offers a solution to the dilemma that Shariati describes so well when he imputes it to Imam Husain: 'Husain now [before he refused to pay bay'a or allegiance to the Umayyad Caliph Yazid] finds himself in a position where he cannot remain silent because he has a responsibility to fight injustice and oppression [zolm]; on the other hand, he cannot fight [with any prospect of victory] because he does not have the strength to face up to a mighty power.'[44]

Shariati raises the question of both responsibility and man's acceptance of his vocation. His decisionism overcomes both strength and weakness. We are responsible, but not in the communitarian sense. Our responsibility is not an immutable and intangible given. It is an appeal to the self, to an individual who becomes heroic by taking on this new identity, which is different to that of the communitarian past: 'He [Husain] is alone, but in this doctrine [Islam] even a lone man is responsible in the sight of an absolute power that defines destinies because the source of responsibility lies in self-consciousness [*âgâhi*] and faith, and not in power and ability. And who is more conscious, more responsible than Husain?'[45]

Shariati appeals to the conscious man (or man with a raised consciousness) who determines his own logic of action and refuses to yield to the banal and quietist realism that attributes the woes of life to an immutable and unjust order that will change only at the End of Time. The appeal to the individual is made by enjoining him to take responsibility for his own death whenever 'doctrine' [*maktab*] or in other words Islam demands it. This is not, however, the individual of the tradition against which Shariati is rebelling. This individual asserts himself through his willing acceptance of death, and in ways that make him a hero because he rejects the political and social injustice that has always crushed Muslims.

This conception – which appeals to responsibility and Islam to create 'an individual in death' – has, in the last two decades, become one of the constant features of Muslim martyrs all over the world, from the Middle East (Iran, and then Lebanon and the Palestinian territories), to Afghanistan and Pakistan (the Kashmiri struggle) and then Europe and the United States (the Islamists of the GIA in France, members of al-Qaeda throughout Europe and the United States). This individual cannot really emerge in the real world and finds it very difficult to live in a politico-social situation that he sees as hopeless (as in Palestine or Chechnya). He therefore accepts the twofold responsibility described by Shariati. Being unable to vanquish an incomparably greater power, he elevates the sacred above that power and, in order to achieve self-realisation by obeying the injunctions of the ideal he sanctifies, goes so far as to sacrifice his own life, and at the same time kills as many of his enemies as possible.

In this precise case, the sacred is not so much a theologically defined Islamic ideal as a desire to be part of the world, to be recognised as having a right to one's dignity. Thanks to a clumsy inversion, it is often transcribed into a deadly Islamic idiom. Shariati himself has been denounced by other clerics because his views have strayed from Islam and he has never been approved by the most committed Iranian clerics, such as Khomeini. Many have even denounced him in public. He has become the spokesman for a younger generation. Many of these young people have shaken off communitarian bonds that had already been loosened by the Shah's authoritarian modernisation, and are trying to rediscover their individuality and to assert themselves in new ways. But the political, economic and cultural situation does not allow them to do so. From their point of view, the Islamic Revolution in Iran provided an opportunity to emancipate themselves in ways that they could conjugate in the future tense.[46]

The Revolution's failure to meet these aspirations and the long war launched by Iraq, the brain drain, economic difficulties, and the feeling that the Revolution was in danger of falling apart because of the plotting of evil powers, and the United States in particular, were all factors that inspired a politico-religious attitude that might be described as a 'deadly' ('death-dealing', 'mortiferous') religiosity. Given that it was impossible to live in accordance with the aspirations they had cherished at the beginning of the Revolution, these young men concluded that they might as well die and take their enemies with them. The martyr's radical act was a response to both the impossibility of self-realisation and the fight against an enemy (the evil West in the case of Iran) who was perceived as being infinitely more powerful. In the case of Palestine, the twofold impossibility takes a different form. Israeli repression and the presence of settlers, and the corruption and nepotism of the Palestinian Authority make it impossible for the self to exist within a nation. The martyr finds it impossible to exist as an individual in a sovereign nation. The suicide bomber's goal is not so much to destroy Israel (young Palestinians are convinced of its undeniable superiority at the military and technological level), as to kill Israelis and to make his voice heard in a world where, unlike Israelis and Americans, he is denied the status of an individual with his dignity and decency.

Shariati unwittingly became the theoretician of 'the impossibility of being' for a generation of young people haunted by the dream of being part of the world. Given the despotic and corrupt political structures they are faced with (the Shah's Iran or the Palestinian Authority) and the global domination they resent because it is unjust and therefore profoundly ungodly (that of the United States in the case of Iran, and that of a US-backed Israel in the case of Palestine), they are espousing a new form of martyrdom, or a kind of neo-martyrdom, but they attempt to legitimise it by lending it the prestige of religion. In most cases, religion is no more than a pretext, even though Shi'ism finds it easier than Sunnism to justify death by martyrdom in a theological sense. The absence of a theological framework did not, however, prevent the young men who joined Hamas or Islamic Jihad in Palestine, the GIA in Algeria or the Taliban in Afghanistan from justifying their actions in religious terms.

### The martyr as 'individual in death'

Although arguments in favour of acts of martyrdom inspired by the model of Husain are, in affective and theological terms, less well developed in Sunnism, three phenomena are contributing to its expansion. On the one hand, the works of Shi'ite theologians and writers such as Shariati, Motahhari and Khomeini are increasingly accessible now that they have been translated from Persian into Arabic and other Islamic languages. Shi'ite Arabs (in Lebanon, Pakistan and elsewhere) who are discussing the question, the Arab world and, more generally, the Islamic world, also have direct access to their intellectual arguments. Intellectuals like Mawdudi and Qutb who emphasize the need for *jihad* and dying for the cause have been widely translated (Mawdudi's writings have been translated from the Urdu into languages such as Arabic, and even English) or can be read in the original (Qutb has been translated into English, Persian, Urdu and other Islamic languages). Shi'ite communities are also helping to transmit these ideas about martyrdom to Sunnis. The Shi'ites of southern Lebanon have introduced the Palestinians to them. The Iraqi Shi'ite community, which is Arabic-speaking, played a role both in opposing the regime of Saddam Hussein and in spreading the notion of martyrdom. Pakistani Shi'ites played a similar role in the struggle against the Soviet regime during the occupation of Afghanistan. One other factor is just as important, namely the development of the modern media, and of television in particular. Television viewers were able to watch the interventions of the Bassidjis during the Iraq–Iran war. Both the spectacle of Israel's invasions of Lebanon and the situation of the Palestinians during the First and Second Intifadas encouraged others to follow their example. The ethnic cleansing of Yugoslavs in Bosnia in the first half of the 1980s left its mark on the Muslims of Europe, where television viewers constitute a televisual virtual community. Some young people from the French suburbs joined the fight against the Serbs on the basis of what they had seen on television.

Finally, and as we shall see, martyrdom gives individuals who are modern but cannot assert themselves in the way they would like, a formidable ability to assert themselves in death. In the absence of any real individuality or political, economic and cultural autonomy, martyrdom has a remarkable ability to facilitate individuation in death. All the modern aspirations and desires that haunt a disoriented younger generation that is no longer protected by traditional communities and has been abandoned to a purely oneiric modernity can be realised through martyrdom. It allows young men to become individuals because it promises them that, when they die, they will have all the things they have been denied in life, namely a paradisiacal existence. Whereas tradition made martyrdom an exceptional, and above all painful, phenomenon designed to move believers to pity and to strengthen communitarian bonds in symbolic ways, a modernity in which there is no hope of self-realisation generates a type of martyrdom that is readily accessible to any young man who wants it. Dying a holy death allows them to accede to dignity through sacrifice, whereas everyday life is dominated by insignificance and lack of dignity. It gives meaning and dignity to those who have been dispossessed of them.

Martyrdom can give rise to two kinds of 'individuation through death'. The first is what might be termed an optimistic individuation: the individual risks death but has a positive self-image, whatever the outcome. Death is a possibility but the individuals concerned have no intention of dying as such and, if possible, try to escape death. The model for this optimistic martyrdom could be seen at the beginning of the Iranian Revolution, and again during the first Intifada. Those young people had no ambition to die, and wanted to fight an enemy (the Shah's regime) they thought they could defeat, or at least challenge in its bid for absolute hegemony (the Israeli army). Some of the young stone-throwers of the First Intifada were prepared to face the risk of death in their clashes with Tsahal, but the vast majority had no intention of dying. They were simply ready to accept the possibility that they might die in clashes with Israeli soldiers. The same remarks might be extended, mutatis mutandis, to the Chechens in their fight against the Russian army, the members of the Lashkar Taggiba present similar features against the Indian dominantion in Kashmir.

The counterpart to this optimistic version of martyrdom is a deeply pessimistic version. These martyrs are no longer concerned with life on earth. To be more accurate, they want to die and to take with them as many as possible of those they see as the enemy. Although directly descended from the first type, this type of martyrdom is anthropologically distinct and profoundly different in its affects. This was especially true of some young Iranians a few years after the Revolution and during the murderous war with Iraq. They saw tangible social evidence of disenchantment with an Islamic Revolution that they wanted to incarnate body and soul. The young men who enlisted under the banners of Iran's Bassidj (and who can be described as 'martyropathic' to differentiate between them and the martyrs of the first period of the Islamic Revolution[47]) no longer had any great interest in living. Their greatest ambition was to die and to destroy as many of their enemies as possible in doing so.

Whereas it was once a risk to be taken, death now became a 'burning desire', an 'unquenchable thirst' (as some Iranian martyrs put in their testaments), or a need to water, through death, the tree of Islam, which requires blood if it is to go on living. We have here a complex anthropological configuration in which incompatible elements come into play. This makes martyrs unstable. They need an institution (the Bassidj in Iran and Hamas or Islamic Jihad in the Palestinian territories) to accomplish their task and to make the transition from life to death. On the one hand, they are expressing a desire to assert themselves as individuals who have their dignity, who can come to terms with their situation and who can realise their ambitions. On the other, they no longer believe that they can realise them in a future, and have been seriously injured by the enemy who is the focus of their hatred. Such young men are constantly torn between a hatred that eventually takes over the whole of their lives, and a despair that no longer allows them to project their hopes into the future, and they find it difficult to gain their balance. This affect can be transcribed onto another register where the desire for life is transformed into a wish for death.

The underlying mechanisms of traditional Christian martyrdom stand in the way of this radical inversion. In the Iranian, Palestinian and Chechnyan cases, to cite only those examples, an irrepressible desire for modernity is combined with what is experienced as an absolute impossibility, and this inverts the vector of life into a vector of death. As martyrdom becomes more common, it becomes possible to build a ghostly community in death (in the very desire for death). What we are seeing is a form of contagion in which the very increase in the number of candidates for sacred death becomes a further factor. Candidates for martyrdom now know that their dead brothers who have gone before them are waiting for them 'on the other side'. The contagion has two anthropological effects: on the one hand, it has an effect on the living, who become a 'community of witnesses' to their glorious deaths; on the other, those who have died as martyrs form a 'glorious community' or a 'community of the chosen' that welcomes them with open arms and encourages them even more to take the next step and overcome their fear of dying.

Martyrdom is testimony to a religious feeling, but the death it implies is a very clear expression of social modes of action that are coded with a view to giving them sacred legitimacy. The code refers to tradition, to a collective memory and to all the things that bind together the members of a society, but also to forms of domination (by the clergy, the bazaar, political groups and parties). The way martyrdom is discussed in contemporary Muslim societies signifies both an appropriation of this code and its transformation, or even subversion, from within. New modes of codification are being introduced by those who claim to be adhering to a tradition. The meaning of martyrdom has undergone a profound transformation that can be seen in the new forms of holy death.

The traditional code denied individuality and imposed communitarian norms thanks to a practice centred on the celebration of the death of the great martyrs of Islam. It had three dimensions: first, the cult of Islam's 'saints' which gave members of the *umma* a feeling of social unity thanks to the reference to their holy deaths; second, death by proxy in order to save the Muslim community; third, the function of holy death was to provide an ideal model that was inaccessible to mere mortals, only a tiny minority of whom could aspire to it in exceptional circumstances. Martyrdom is now inscribed on the bodies of young men eager to assert themselves. The inaccessible dimension is declining in importance, and it is now the assumption of death and the desire to imitate the great martyrs of Islam that is characteristic of the younger generations born of the modernisation of Islamic societies, which has often been both authoritarian and regressive. Social change individualises these new actors in two ways. On the one hand, it is destroying the concrete communities familiar to previous generations, which instilled conformity to norms and rejected individuation. On the other, television and books give emigrant groups new aspirations. The media spread the Western way of life, often by mythologising it. The goal is now to build a nation or world or at least a new totality, and it is the articulation of the two effects that makes martyrdom possible. If this were nothing more than a frustrated aspiration towards individuality to the exclusion of all other social issues, the result would be at most suicide, but not martyrdom. When it becomes possible to die for a sacred cause that transcends personal desires in an imaginary totality, either national or global, then martyrdom is possible.[48] But for that to happen, there must be a tradition within which it can, when necessary, be legitimised, even if its meaning is inverted. The specific feature of Islam is that it legitimises sacred death in the service of the community or *umma* by making it part of the fabric of a war that enjoys religious legitimacy, namely *jihad*. It is because the aspiration towards individuality is articulated with membership of a real or imagined community that martyrdom can take on its new meanings.

### THE PARADOXICAL INDIVIDUALISATION OF RELIGIOUS DISCOURSE

Since the early twentieth century, the Islamic world has seen the emergence and intensification of a paradoxical phenomenon that finds expression in an individualisation of religious discourse and, at the same time, its growing rigidity. New intellectuals and *ulama* have emerged, and they are attempting to construct a type of discourse addressed not to the community, but to the individuals they are trying to 're-Islamise' or convince of the need for Islam. The tone of discourse now becomes modern, and it is addressed to creatures of flesh and blood, rather than to restricted groups of religious believers who have already been shaped by the religious tradition and who do not have to be convinced of Islam's legitimacy. The modernisation of Islam has resulted in the formation of a new middle class, the spread of Western habits and customs by diasporic groups, and the appearance of a new imaginary amongst young people. That imaginary is based upon a consumerist hunger and a desire to become part of what the media describe as a 'dream-like West' in which opulence, sexual freedom and political freedom go hand in hand. These mutations lead to a crisis in traditional communities, or even to their dislocation.

Islamist discourses take note of this. They offer to build a neo-*umma* whose frontiers will not coincide with those assigned to the old communities of the past. They do so in two very different ways. They may refer to an *umma* that transcends national frontiers and speak of a world shaped by the new distribution of populations, power and beliefs. Al-Qaeda is a case in point. It is partly based in the West and some of its members have lived there for ten or twenty years. Alternatively, they may refer to a specific society with specific national frontiers and argue the case for its radical transformation. Examples include the Islamic Revolution in Iran, the two Intifadas in the Palestinian territories and the FIS in Algeria. There is often little difference in the message of these discourses, as the reference to Islam is supposedly universal and neither national or regional. But the movements inspired by these ideologies can in fact take one of two forms, depending on whether they are addressed to a specific nation or to a neo-*umma* that has yet to be defined. All Islamist ideologies call for a neo-*umma*, but it can come into being either within a national framework thanks to a specific movement – in which case it must adapt to the problems and specificities of a particular society – or in a transnational community by an Islamic diaspora. The goal is to unite the Muslim world on a planetary scale. The one thing that remains constant is the reference to the individual, most of the time covered up by the secularisation of death (martyrdom) and references to a mythical Islamic community (*umma*), regarded as egalitarian and equitable in the modern sense of the word.

The example of Qutb is edifying. His commentaries on the Koran depart from the traditional exegesis of *tafsir* (literal interpretation) and *ta'wil* (allegorical interpretation), often refer to modern authors and avoid the ways traditional interpretations are constructed because they mean little to a modern reader.[49] He is attempting to transmit his interpretation of the Koran to his reader, and makes no attempt to conceal its individual dimension. Even if they did have a personal point of view, traditional authors tried to conceal it behind a system of references designed to legitimise the possible novelty of their views by 'traditionalising' them or claiming that their point of view was not particularly new or original, but corresponded to an authentic tradition that they were simply making explicit. The very tone was often impersonal, as their books were addressed to colleagues who were themselves well versed in Koranic exegesis and accustomed to that exercise in erudition. The vast majority of readers, including young Muslims, regard it as sterile and or at least incomprehensible. Qutb gives his interpretation of the sacred text, and does not conceal that fact. He cites modern authors like Mawdudi, Nadawi, Aqqad and Awda, and he does so in a way that breaks with what is seen as the traditional style by younger generations who have had a modern education and who have studied at universities and not *madrasahs* or traditional theological schools. His mode of approach to faith is personal, and relies much more upon intuition than on erudition in the traditional sense.

The same antithesis can be seen in writers like Shariati. Qutb is a Sunni, and Shariati a Shi'ite, but both want to rebuild the same Islamic society, despite their differences. They are not talking about a traditional community from which the individual is absent quite simply because he exists only in a mystical form, or 'apart from' or 'outside' the world, as Louis Dumont would put it.[50] They are trying to make room for an individual who is coming into being in an Islamic world at a time when traditional communities have been destructured by unregulated urbanisation, new forms of socialisation, the introduction of a market economy and authoritarian and modernising states. Such an individual is problematic. In a sense, individuality is a difficult issue in emergent new societies where the state's only response to individual aspirations is a heavy-handed authoritarianism. The new Islamic ideologies are in an ambivalent position: on the one hand, they have to make room for the individual; on the other, they subordinate the individual to the construction of a neo-*umma*, and ultimately that means rejecting the individual by putting him in a subordinate position. They mostly achieve this by making him an accomplice in the building up of a utopian Islamic community, to come as a result of their abnegation and willingness for the holy death. There is a manipulative dimension in this phenomenon that can be best achieved through an institution (Bassidje in the Iranian case, radical organisations in other Islamic societies). But the manipulative aspect should not cover up the fact that the 'enemy' (be it the Russian, Israeli or Indian army) plays a major role in polarising and radicalising the youth in these Islamic societies undergoing major political, cultural and economic crises.

The relationship between the Muslim *umma* and the individual is central to Qutb's political writings. He deals with this theme by relating it to the nature of Islamic power and the Islamic state and attempts to reconcile the rights and demands of the individual with the neo-*umma* he wants so badly. Sometimes he stresses the individual, and at other times the community.[51] He believes that an Islamic individual born in a Muslim community will be capable of 'an individualism that bears fruit' because the *umma* will prevent him from being trapped into the egotism that lies in wait for him in Western societies. Qutb solves the problem of the relationship between individual and society by locating it is a utopian community within a state that is striving to realise Islam.

Both Qutb and Shariati are haunted by the same problem: the presence of an imperialist and arrogant West that is perverting Muslim societies from within and dominating them from without. It is distorting Islam, breaking up Muslim communities and turning their members into pathetic creatures who have lost all self-respect because they have renounced their Islamic identity. His analysis of the West is illuminating. What he sees as the absence of any ethics at the heart of the Western system leads him to seek a community that has the meaning he finds in Islam. He therefore rejects the different and positive concept of emptiness that we find in discussions of Western democracy in the work of thinkers like Claude Lefort.[52] The void that lies at the centre of the political stage in Western democracy is, according to Lefort, an expression of the positivity of a system that sanctifies a centre that no one can occupy, and whose non-substantial nature is the very thing that safeguards the rule of the *demos*. Qutb wants a society in which the political and the social are substantially determined. The Western void frightens him, makes him ill at ease, and it seems to him to be a diabolical invention because material and technological progress go hand in hand with the Satanism that will pervert Muslim societies once it has brought about the moral destruction of Western societies.

Contemporary Muslim society is, in Qutb's view, a society of ignorance and idolatry. It is a society in which Islam has been pushed aside. The reason why reason and faith, and individual and community, are incompatible is that society has drifted away from the harmonious totality promised by Islam, where it will be possible to overcome the dichotomies of *jahiliyya* by having recourse to the laws of God. Those laws must be implemented by *jihad* or holy war, both at the individual level (this is an inner war that will lead to mystical enlightenment) and the external level (a revolutionary movement aimed at establishing the divine order opposed by the power of nationalist, communist or capitalist *jahiliyya*). Inside and outside meet when Shari'a is applied. If it is properly understood and duly applied, Islam can unite the world and the self, and government and society, in a form that is practical and not discursive. The same mystical drift in which revolution and inner enlightenment go hand in hand can be seen in the work of thinkers as different as Qutb, Shariati and Khomeini. According to Qutb, Islam reconciles opposites by its very nature. Opposites are only meaningful in societies that have repudiated Islam or in soulless Western societies that have been perverted by materialism.

The same point can be made with respect to Khomeini. Here too there is a mystical dimension, and like Qutb he is attempting to build a new Islamic order in which the new antagonisms born of the appearance on the social stage of new forces will be integrated into a reborn community. He had less contact with the West than Qutb, who spent prolonged periods in the United States. But his inner mysticism, like that of Qutb, overcomes the problem in a non-discursive and purely utopian way. Khomeini's initial dilemma was, as he was aware, that it is difficult to reconcile the freedom of the individual with the demands of a collective life dominated by Islam. His solution was not very satisfactory: the people certainly elect the government, but it is the Guide elected by a limited assembly of people with a competent knowledge of Islam who holds supreme power in *Velayat-e faqih*. Whereas Qutb's solution assumed that a voluntaristic *shari'a* would unite people and state, Khomeini's solution was shattered into pieces after his death. The people now have the vote, and their voice does have to be taken into account when the President of the Republic and Parliament are elected. Real power lies, however, in the hands of the Guide, who is not directly appointed by the people. The only way the system can avoid the dilemma of representativeness is by a magical recourse to Islam. The beautiful unity dreamed of by Qutb and postulated by Khomeini has not survived the test of reality. In Iran, there is no power where popular legitimacy rules (Parliament and President), and there is no popular legitimacy where real power does exist (the Guide and the structures around him).

Shariati's concern for the individual is voiced in an inflammatory discourse. He addresses the individual and speaks to him directly (most of his writings are transcripts of lectures), and challenges him to take up the heavy burden of an individuality that necessarily involves self-sacrifice for the sake of Islam.[53] Shariati's individual must teach himself to lead an Islamic revolution to a successful conclusion. He calls this the 'revolutionary construction of the self' (*khod sâzi e enqelâbi*). Its culminating point is consciousness-raising (*âgâhi*). The individual can then take his life into his own hands and agree, should the need arise, to sacrifice it for the Islamic cause. It is the sovereign individual who defines that cause, even though Islam came into existence long before he did.[54]

The heroic decision to achieve self-realisation through the voluntary sacrifice of the self for the revolutionary cause known as Islam is now the only thing to have a sacred meaning. Martyrdom realises the individual by making him the 'beating heart' of history.

And the individual who trains himself in this revolutionary way hastens the coming of the End of Time that will put an end to the history of injustice and spoliation. The individual is thus made to serve a revolutionary eschatology which ultimately denies him any autonomous meaning. At first he is recognised and flattered, but ultimately he is sacrificed on the altar of a history of collective salvation.

The individual defined by Islamists is fascinated by his enemy: Western man. He is trapped into an East–West dichotomy, and is wounded by the crushing superiority of *homo occidentalis* at the economic, material and mental level. The worm is in the bud: the West is no longer present simply because it is the dominant power, but because it has been incrusted in the imaginary of Muslim societies by a fifth column of Westernised Muslims and, at an even deeper level, by the emergence of new social strata that judge their identity by the standards of a modernity in which Islam plays an increasingly marginal role. Western values are no longer the values of an adversary who is incomparably more powerful in military terms or in terms of the foreign relations determined by classical imperialism. We are now in a different situation. The West is perverting Muslim societies from within as young people try to fulfil their ambitions in accordance with its ungodly model and its depraved imaginary. Shariati identifies the West with imperialism, and with the technological and military domination that makes Muslims stupid in cultural terms (*estehmar*, or 'reduction to the status of a donkey'; the word rhymes with *estemar*, meaning imperialism and colonialism).

The desire of intellectual Muslims, both religious and secular, to acquire an Islamic identity in the face of a multiform modernism that seduces the new individual with its consumerist needs and its liberation of all desires (and particularly sexual desires), became particularly obvious after the Second World War and especially in the last third of the twentieth century. Some, like Shariati, argued that Western dominance should be fought by adopting a model similar to that used in classic communist struggles, and invoked a historical vision defined in terms of the class struggle. Others, like Khomeini and Qutb, argued that *shari'a* should be applied through the seizure of political power and the establishment of a state Islam. Still others, like Mawdudi call for the education of Muslim societies so as to avoid the need for a future political order to impose diktats derived from a religion that is badly understood by society. Society must be Islamised long before the state can apply Islam.

In all cases, Islam is defined in terms of its antagonism to actually existing Muslim societies on the one hand and, on the other, to the West and its perverted norms, which are depraving Muslims by making them slaves to an immoral materialism and hedonism. A new generation of intellectuals is required if the definition of the individual is not to be dominated by antagonism to the West and if individuals are to be able to reclaim their membership of modernity within an Islam that is at peace and enjoys a more moderate relationship with the West. This is what we are now seeing in the work of intellectuals like Mojtahed Shabestari and Abdolkarim Sorush in Iran.

## MARTYROPATHY

The cult of martyrs can lead either to the conclusion that it is impossible to construct a self within an Islamic nation, or to the desire to establish a transnational Islamic community. Its adversary is either the West or particular representations of the West (Iranian revolutionaries saw Iraq as America's lackey, and members of the Islamic Salvation Front regard the Algerian military government as France's lackey). This hatred is very similar to the *ressentiment* described by Nietzsche and then Max Scheler.[55] *Ressentiment* involves two elements. On the one hand, things are inverted into their opposite: what looks like love is in reality hatred, and what looks like magnanimity is in fact cowardice. On the other hand, reflexivity takes the place of spontaneity. It is 'natural' to live one's life and to position oneself in relation to others. If one is determined from the outset by the gaze of the other, one can no longer live spontaneously. This basic dimension does not reject the influence of the outside world, and does not mean that everything is dictated by the self or that society has no influence. This is an affective dimension: when love is made reflexive by affects other than those that stem from a loving relationship, it becomes perverted. The same is true of inter-subjectivity. It cannot be subordinated to other goals.[56] In radical Islamism, the relationship with the other, and especially the West, is dominated by a hatred which makes destitute and demonises the other by denying the existence of the mechanisms of a neutral inter-subjectivity in which there is no *ressentiment*. This phenomenon is obviously not confined to Islamism and can be found in various forms of radicalism that pervert intersubjectivity by subordinating it to a sacred creed and hypercathecting it thanks to a Manichaeanism in which anyone who strays from the norm takes on the role of the evildoer.[57]

There is a second dimension to *ressentiment*, and it might be described as irrational. The hatred for the opposed group (the radical Islamist's hatred of the West, the anti-Semite's hatred of the Jew, or the radical Jew or Hindu's hatred of the Muslim, for example) is so great that it literally becomes an obsession and makes the believer unable to adopt anything other than a deadly strategy: killing the other at all costs, being killed, or both at once.

The supporters of radical Islamism are so obsessed with their hatred of the Western world that fighting it merely confirms its superiority, and their logic becomes deadly: death becomes a way of realising both self and other. It is no longer a matter of accepting the possibility of death in order to realise an ideal (as do many individuals obsessed by 'noble' ideals such as patriotism or the struggle against agents of absolute evil, such as the Nazi regimes or Stalinist communism). The obsession with death leads to a state of mind in which death is seen as a voluptuous incarnation of the ideal. It is an ideal that has a value in itself, and its realisation would fill those who believe in it with joy. The distinction between self-sacrifice for a human ideal and putting other men to death for love of death can sometimes become tenuous.

When the final step is taken, when death is no longer a subordinate means to a different end, and when the ideal itself becomes a source of death and is fascinated by death and destruction, we can speak of a perversion that is bound up with *ressentiment*. The ultimate goal is to destroy both self and other ('the enemy') thanks to a subjective metamorphosis that transforms life into death. This mutation of subjectivity can be called a 'mortiferous religiosity'. This phase is often reached in radical forms of religiosity and practically no religion is immune to it. It can, however, also be seen in extreme forms of nationalism or secular ideology. Some disciples of radical Islamism see life as something inferior to the happiness that can be found through the annihilation of self and other, or martyrdom. This type of martyrdom bears the brand of *ressentiment*, and its anthropological content is not the state of mind of a disciple who is willing to fight the enemy to the death and to accept the possibility of death in a battle whose outcome is uncertain.

At the level of both affects and the logic of action, martyropathy is a form of behaviour in which death, and not life, is seen as the goal. It cannot be fought against through classical means of intimidation or repression. This type of action may of course be justified by some 'noble' ideal. Martyrdom, just like heroism, means sacrificing one's life for an ideal that is more important than life. To that extent, martyrdom is no more irrational than other types of devotion and, in the eyes of its actors, the martyr's demands cannot be described as pathological. Martyropathy is the result of an inversion born of *ressentiment*. The goal is no longer to realise an ideal, but to take leave of life by destroying the enemy in an apocalyptic vision that will put an end to life. Acceptance of the logic of martyrdom subordinates the death of both martyr and enemy to the realisation of a goal that will put an end to injustice, establish fairness and bring happiness to the whole world (or community). There is no fascination with death, no luxuriating in death and no quest for happiness in and through death. Martyropathy begins with a change of meaning: a deadly logic takes over from the logic governing the struggle for life and the pursuit of a frustrated ideal.

When martyropathy springs from the denial of an individuality that cannot be realised within a national community, as in Palestine, Algeria and Iran, but also in Chechnya, the martyropathic subject blames those around him for his failure: they have failed to live up to his ideal of abnegation. In the case of Palestine, it is the Palestinian Authority that is identified as the cause, along with dissenters within different groups, either at home or abroad ('the men in Tunis'). Western or American complicity can obviously be invoked (with some justification) to explain the failure that is so resented. The important thing is that enemies can be identified. The martyropath makes his grievances absolute, gives the enemy the preponderant role and overstates the extent to which he and others are to blame. Despair then turns life into death and the inversion of values sees death as a form of plenitude. Religious feelings become obsessed with death and imbued with the sombre view that death is an ideal whose voluptuous fascination can be enjoyed by a living subject.

In the case of the mythical transnational neo-*umma*, the inversion lies in the amplification of the virtuality inscribed at the very heart of the project. Believers therefore have a great propensity to become martyropaths to the extent that the movement's ideal, from the outset and by definition, is out of reach. For members of a national group, martyropathy therefore takes on a tragic meaning: the self cannot be realised and the individual's demands are met with a blunt refusal. In the case of the mythical *umma*, it is the absence of tragedy that stands out. Death – slaying or being slain – is depersonalised.

This is not just a quantitative change. It is also existential. It is not inappropriate to use a computer metaphor, as many supporters of this transnational *umma* are familiar with the new communications technology. Just as a computer screen is emptied of its content when it is attacked by a computer virus, death is experienced as a situation that has no particular affect. Death means that the self is dissolved into a neo-*umma* characterised by emptiness. Death is in a sense a possibility (a blank screen) implicit in a project that has no specific content and which therefore cannot be realised. It has, as it happens, no specific content because it is a product of a network logic in which everything is exhausted in formal electronic communications (which have no cultural or social content) between group members who have no sense of direction and who embody no culture.

For al-Qaeda, the feeling of belonging is associated with Islam, but in a globalising version that is not shared by national martyrs. This is a movement that is designed to establish an Islamic Internationale, even though no existing Islamic society is involved. Islamic *societies* exist in the real world, but there is no such thing as *an* Islamic society. This purely mythical neo-*umma* is supported by an equally mythical enemy. The mythologised West has largely been constructed by Islamism's supporters. It is difficult to tell if we are dealing with a clash of civilisation in a work characterised by the end of ideologies, or with a very different phenomenon.[58]

Even though most of them are Arabs, al-Qaeda's members belong to a variety of communities. They live in a multicultural world, are involved in a plurality of cultures without belonging to any one of them. They can mobilise against the enemy but they do not have a coherent viewpoint or a project that is not defined solely by opposition to a principle of absolute Evil. That is why the inversion into a deadly logic occurs so much more easily. It is the logical outcome of hatred for the enemy, but the identity concerned cannot be supported by any positive self-assertion. It therefore cannot be said that this is a clash between two civilisations, one Islamic, and the other Western. It is the struggle of the at least partially 'Westernized' against a mythical West. The fighters borrow cutting-edge technology from the West and are mostly immersed in a Western cultural environment. Their attitude towards it is ambivalent and can become antagonistic. For most of them, Islam is a pretext, a support for a hatred of the West dictated by familiarity with the Western media whose news coverage is (like that of Al-Jazeera) inspired by a Western model.

In this particular case, there is no clash between Islam and the West, or between two civilisations, but an antagonism that is being promoted by broadly Westernised groups in the name of a mythified Orient or Islamic *umma* whose imaginary picture is itself a consequence of modernisation. They exist in all multicultural societies and, like with some radical cults, they define themselves in terms of their hostility to a mythological and demonised West. Neither the network's cultural content, its logic of action nor even the mentality of its protagonists have anything to do with an autonomous civilisation or an atavistic mode of existence that is irreducibly hostile to the West. It has much more to do with a split within the modern world, in which the West is, to a greater or lesser degree, the figurehead. The existence of cultist forms of antagonism towards the contemporary world is there to prove it. These antagonisms arise because our modernity no longer has a centre of gravity and because forms of individuality are being constructed along 'identitarian' lines. We worship conflicting ideals. These antagonistic ways of building a neo-*umma* on a planetary scale also reflect the existence of a community that has grown up around the media (and especially television), a reality that is becoming virtual in an increasingly complex world, and flagrant injustice (which is both real and exaggerated by the media). In the Islamic case, two phenomena exacerbate this still further. There is no solution to the Palestinian problem, which has become a festering sore throughout the Muslim world. Television allows Islamic diasporas all over the world to watch what are in effect live broadcasts of the humiliation and destruction in Palestine. Arab-Islamic people are then further offended when the West intervenes for strategic reasons, as when an American military contingent stayed on in Saudi Arabia after the Gulf War of 1991.

## DEATH AND FEAR OF DYING

Only those who can overcome their fear of dying can become martyrs. In order to ensure that they do so, certain organisations take in candidates and prepare them for a holy death. They use various modes of suggestion, indoctrination and supervision. In its traditional form, martyrdom has, as we have seen, a basically ritual dimension. Muslims (particularly the Shi'ites) mourn the martyrdom of saints, praise their warrior virtues and their ability to endure infinite pain and suffering in order to save the community of believers from deviation or corruption (as in the celebration of the death of Husain or the commemoration of that of the Prophet's uncle Hamzeh). The death in question is that of a saintly figure (the Prophet's companions, members of his family or his descendants) and not that of an ordinary person. Mourning martyrs is a matter for the whole community and does not concern individuals as such. The role of individuals is to commemorate the martyrdom of exceptional persons to whom popular devotion gives a superhuman dimension. The senior hierarchy of *ulamas* and clerics is dubious about, if not opposed to, the conferring of superhuman status on saints and martyrs, but popular devotion demands it. That is why martyrdom only occurs in exceptional circumstances in these societies.

Collective martyrdom, or systematic martyrdom that does not obey a sectarian and heretical logic, is a modern phenomenon. It is from the nineteenth century onwards and with the modernisation of modern societies that the idea that there is a link between personal martyrdom and *jihad* becomes important. But it is really after failed attempts at modernisation on the part of regimes that have attained national independence, or following crises in societies that were on the point of winning their independence or autonomy (Palestine, Kurdistan, Chechnya) that this notion, which is bound up with *jihad*, takes on a new importance. Once marginal and purely ceremonial, martyrdom becomes central and leaves its mark on Muslim societies that are in crisis. The relationship with holy death is transformed in three ways. First, it is individualised, posed in concrete terms and not in an abstract form in some empyrean to which mere mortals cannot have access. It is politicised, secularised and takes on a contemporary meaning. It relates to a new representation of the religious that does not simply commemorate an immemorial past. Individualised martyrdom corresponds to a secularisation of the religious. Religion now relates to this world and its preoccupations, and not to a transcendental and inaccessible world that will restore justice only at the End of Time. According to this conception, death is not something that is experienced simply through ritualisation and commemoration, but through the enactment of an individual's death by that individual. Hence the fear of death and the fear of succumbing to that fear, which has to be overcome through the spiritual transcendence of life, by taking one's fate into one's own hands in an irreversible act.

In their testaments, or in interviews, the martyrs themselves speak of a dissymmetry between themselves and their enemies. They are not afraid of dying, but their enemies are terribly afraid of it. Even in death, the martyrs feel that they are involved in a confrontation, defying the other and demonstrating their own superiority. As these martyrs act within established structures (Hamas and Islamic Jihad in the Palestinian territories, the Bassidj in Iran, al-Qaeda in the case of the attacks on the United States), one of their essential tasks is to help members overcome their fear of dying by having recourse to prayer, reading the Koran, delegating a cleric to watch over the candidate, and allowing them to mix with other believers who are also awaiting death. Together, they will form a restricted '*umma* in death'. They obviously expect to die, but it is as though they had already left life behind them. Death also implies purification and an act of repentance. The martyrs ask their families to forgive them for any offence they may have caused them, to take care of their debts, and ask them not to commit acts that might tarnish their image in the eyes of God.[59]

The fear of dying is neutralised by recourse to a religious vision that holds that the moment of everyone's death has been predetermined by Allah. In his *Neglected Duty*, Abd al-Salam Faraj, for instance, asserts that we all live an ephemeral existence on this earth and will die when the moment comes. Iranian martyrs recited ad nauseam the poem that decrees the predestination of all by God's determination of the moment of their deaths. Martyrs use this image of a preordained death to overcome their fear of dying.[60] Martyrdom takes place only if death occurs, of necessity, at a specific moment, regardless of whether or not one opts to die a holy death. The martyr therefore proclaims that it is better to embrace a holy death than to die the cowardly inept death of those who die in their beds.

Several symbolic registers of the Islamic and Mediterranean world can be invoked to overcome the fear of dying, and especially the sense of honour. In order to defend a Muslim honour that has been besmirched by the incursions of American imperialism (in Iran), Russian imperialism (in Chechnya) or Israeli imperialism (in Palestine), the fight must be waged to the death, and this now becomes a leitmotiv in the *jihad* against the enemy. In their testaments, martyrs constantly refer to honour to justify their commitment to death, both in order to legitimise the choice they have made in the eyes of their parents, who are often opposed to the idea, to overcome their own doubts, and to confirm the righteousness of their choice in their own eyes. By dying young, martyrs break one of the pillars of a society based upon intergenerational mutual aid, especially given the absence of any welfare state to take care of the problems of the elderly, as happens in the West. By putting their sense of honour first, they attempt to compensate in symbolic terms for their failure as sons to help their parents.

It is not only his own life that is devalorised by the martyr. He also devalorises the lives of those around him. Whether or not Islam permits the killing of innocents is debatable. According to Mafhoud Assoouli (Abu'l Munthir), who is one of the GIA's Algerian leaders, there are three categories of Algerians: those who fight Islam, those who wage *jihad* on behalf of the religion of Allah, and those who support Islam through democracy and elections. He declares the latter to be impostors who must perish together with the first category. According to the version of Islam that claims to represent the cause of God, regards dying for His cause as a reward in itself and which strives to impose its image of the enemy on the whole of humanity, those who shirk the struggle are traitors and killing them is justified in religious terms, be they Muslims or not. This goes against the Islamic tradition which recommended that old men, women and children should be spared. The majority tendency forbade the killing of non-Muslims who were not involved in the fight. According to some, even Muslims found on the battlefield should be spared.

The subject of desire also gives rise to a mystical relationship. The only desire worthy of that name is the desire to die for the cause of God, but also for love of God. The only fascination *sensu eminenti* is a fascination focussed on Allah, and not the material things of this life. As the martyr's desire crystallises around Allah, his ties with this world, and even with his closest relatives, are loosened. In the case of al-Qaeda or the Palestinian martyrs, parents often know nothing about their sons' decisions to die. This is for security reasons. Then there is the fact that the martyr must distance himself from everything that reminds him of his attachment to this world, and his family is no exception. The organisation isolates its future martyr and its members, and tolerates no interference. It is essential that preparation for death take place behind closed doors, and the martyrs must be rooted in that isolation. Even when that is materially impossible, as during the preparations that were made in the United States for the attacks of 11 September 2001, it is possible to write a sort of testimony or vade mecum that subjectively recreates this isolation within an imaginary *umma* that legitimises the decision to die as a sacred act. The putative testimony of Mohamed Atta provides one example. It is full of references to Koranic *surahs*, and speaks constantly of the sacred character of his act and of the need to immerse himself in the Koran before taking the final step.[61] Moral cleanliness must be accompanied by the physical cleanliness achieved through ablutions (*qusl*) that purify the believer for his meeting with God in the next world. The secularisation of the religious is radical: martyrdom sanctifies the close relationship with this world and the profoundly political nature of the sacred. Thanks to the absolute transcendence of the sacred, the domain of this world and that of the next are no longer divorced. The sacred becomes secular and leaves its mark on the political and the social.

Death is a central category in modern martyrdom, not only because it means the death of the subject, but also because of the nature of the issues involved. The small groups leading Islamic uprisings against established governments have, of course, always referred to justice and accused them of being unjust. A *hadith* that is traditionally cited states: 'Power endures despite impiety, but it does not endure despite injustice' (*al mulk yabqâ ma al kufr wa lâ yabqâ mal al zulm*). But the notions of justice and injustice here referred to the traditional vision that posited a relationship between prince and people based upon that between the shepherd and his flock. It was based upon recognition of the supremacy granted the shepherd in exchange for the protection he gave the flock. That relationship precluded politics, gave the people no share in government and, in exchange, required the shepherd who wielded power to protect his subjects from the mighty.

The purpose of death by martyrdom is no longer simply to depose the unjust ruler and to replace him with another who leads his people as the shepherd leads his flock. A new type of subject is coming into being, and the individuation of that subject makes death a political issue of a new kind. This implies that a new relationship is being established with politics, culture and society. That relationship may not be of a democratic kind, and it may even be undemocratic, as death now has to do with a desire for self-assertion and not a demand for a new ruler, as the traditional model would have it. Martyrdom is a manifestation of a desire to be a self, and that desire is constantly frustrated, denied and rejected in a situation that is experienced as being inexorably oppressive. It also has to do with the desire to build a new community whose content will be different to that of existing communities, which do not conform to 'true Islam'.

This new *umma* is something excessive, and it breaks with tradition even though it masks its novelty by referring to a mythologised past. Even when it claims to be reproducing an immemorial past, it reshapes it into something that has nothing in common with the real history of Muslim societies. The idealised past justifies the legitimacy and respectability of the new aspiration towards living in a newly fraternal world, whereas day-to-day reality is a realm of individual egotism in which there can be no unity of hearts. The community that the martyr wishes to bring into being is a sanctified version of the desire to live in a fraternal society, as opposed to a world in which the destructuring of the communities of old has given birth to a world of egotism in which there is no possibility of effective, objective and real self-realisation.

Two kinds of death are possible. In the cases of Palestine, Algeria and Iran, martyrdom is an expression of self-realisation in death because the national cause cannot facilitate it. It has not been possible to build a nation that conforms to the martyr's aspirations. That nation could support a project that ought to give meaning to the wishes of the new martyr.

In the case of al-Qaeda, death is the sign of a different form of dereliction. Those who live the despair of others 'in virtual reality' experience a loss of self. They take on the role of the righter of wrongs, not so much so as to return the world to an equilibrium it has lost or to create a new humanity or a new nation, as to extend the meaning of their struggle to the whole world. We are seeing a 'globalisation' of holy death, and its anthropological and sociological content is different to that of martyrs whose goal of self-realisation within a nation that cannot come into being. In this precise case, death establishes a new articulation between self and community. Most of those who choose this type of martyrdom are suffering from an identity crisis. They are young men who are stigmatised in European countries (such as France and England), converts who are seeking a part to play, and immigrants whose life in the West has convinced them of its profound immorality.

Whatever its nature, martyrdom always expresses a death wish born of the same concrete questions: how can I overcome my fear of dying, how can I programme that fear, and how can I successfully carry out an operation that results in my own death? There are other questions too: how can I inflict death on the enemy, how can I cold-bloodedly kill people who have no direct involvement in the war and who are not in a position to defend themselves? How, in other words, can I put others to death without feeling guilty and without being affected by transgressing the basic taboo on killing?

Quite aside from the forms of auto-suggestion mentioned earlier, it is common to evoke Paradise in order to overcome the fear of dying that might assail the future martyr. The emphasis is now placed on the next life, which is eternal, in a world that is infinitely better than the world in which the future martyr is living. His act has such great merit in the eyes of Allah that it washes away all his sins and promotes him to the ranks of the chosen.

He must, finally, be helped to overcome the taboo on killing other men in a situation in which they are seen, by both parties, as being only indirectly and not entirely responsible for the martyr's situation. There are two ways of doing this. On the one hand, theological opinions (*fatwas*) expressed by the religious authorities declare that it is permissible to put to death people who are, either directly or indirectly, involved with powers that repress Muslims. These religiously motivated opinions also state that it is permissible to kill Muslims who help to enslave their brothers in religion.

Another way to combat the taboo on killing is to train the candidate's mind to see murders and massacres as religious rituals in which 'enemies' are killed. Video cassettes available in England at least up to 2002 –and in France before 1995 – show Muslim fighters waging bloody battles in which they put their enemies to death. One of them, which was recorded by the radical Algerian group 'Prédication et combat' is entitled 'L'Algérie'. It could be bought for £10 in London in early 2002. The video begins with the divine command: 'Fight them until God's sentence is carried out on earth.' The commentary goes on: 'Our enemies fight in the name of Satan, you fight in the name of God.' The *mujahedeen* set an ambush for the Algerian army. A military convoy comes along the road and we see an explosion that destroys the truck and the soldiers it was carrying. The militants approach the scene of the explosion. The camera shows the carnage. We see the bloody bodies of the young Algerian conscripts: one has been decapitated and another has been blown to pieces. Suddenly, one of the guerrillas gives a shout. One of the soldiers is still alive. The fighter draws a knife and cuts the dying man's throat on the spot. There are five shots of blood spurting from his carotid. They then do the same to the dead soldiers. Another video cassette entitled 'The Mirror of Jihad' shows the Taliban in Afghanistan decapitating a Northern Alliance soldier with a knife. These cassettes are designed, on the one hand, to dehumanise the enemy, even if he is a Muslim (the murdered Algerian soldiers were Muslim conscripts, and many young Algerians are conscripted by force) and, secondly, to provide an apprenticeship in murder. Killing is shown as an extension of the sacred act of cutting a throat (the throat of a sheep) to the enemies of Islam. The enemy is, as it were, an animal sacrificed in a holy action. The use of knives is intended both to reinforce that idea, and to recall the feats of arms of Islam's heroes.

# 2
# The Impossible National Community

The impossibility of building a national community gives rise to two distinct forms of martyrdom. In the case of Palestine, the origins of martyrdom lie in the crisis of nation-building (the first Intifada) and the feeling that nation-building is impossible (the second Intifada). In the case of Iran, the nation certainly existed but it was threatened by the war with Iraq. The war was experienced as an imperialist manoeuvre designed to destroy the new Muslim nation. Martyrdom was the result of the realisation that it was impossible to build an Iranian nation that corresponded to political Islam's virtuous and heroic model. Iran's martyrs began to organise holy death on an unprecedented scale: hundreds of thousands of young men were involved, through an organisation: Bassidj.

## MARTYRDOM IN IRAN

The phenomenon of revolution in Iran dates from the late 1970s and the 1980s. During this period –which stretched roughly from the year 1979 to the death of Ayatollah Khomeini in June 1989 – the phenomenon of martyrdom developed with an intensity that had never been known in Iranian history in general and in the history of Islam in particular. In the struggle against the Shah and then in the war against Iraq, which was one of the longest (1980–88) in the second half of the twentieth century and which left more than half a million dead and wounded on both sides,[1] martyrdom was everywhere. What was originally a cultural phenomenon became a political phenomenon affecting young Iranians, most of them 'disinherited' (or oppressed, *mostadafine*) men from lower or middle-class groups that had been urbanised over one or two generations. This political Islam was initially regarded as being specifically Iranian and Shi'ite. Shi'ite radicalisation in southern Lebanon, where some groups launched suicide attacks on the Israeli army, corroborated that idea. It was only in the 1980s and with the emergence of organisations like Hamas and Islamic Jihad in Palestine, and of the radical currents (GIA and others) that emerged from the disintegration of the FIS in

Algeria, that it became apparent that this vision of martyrdom was not specific to Shi'ites.

### The revolution adrift

The Iranian Revolution began amongst popular rejoicings and was fought in the name of ideals that were social and political, as well as religious. Its main slogan was 'Freedom, Independence, Islamic Revolution'. But the euphoria did not last very long. It could not survive the worsening of the political situation, the disputes within the new elites fighting for power, or the war with Iraq, which lasted for more than eight years.

This state of affairs was in flagrant contradiction with the hopes that had been raised in the dawn of the revolution, when everyone was promised a right to the oil that had been stolen by the Shah's regime.

Scarcely a year after the Revolution, the state of society was in complete contradiction with the dreams that had been cherished in the early days of the revolutionary movement. The economy, which had remained relatively undamaged in the first year of the revolution, was gradually slowing down and visibly regressed because of the war launched by Iraq – mainly in the oil-producing areas of Iran (Khuzestan) – and political uncertainties relating to the radicalisation of the revolutionary movement. At the same time, and despite the ideal of justice promised by the Revolution, the foundations were being laid for a hyper-speculative economy in which parasitic groups quickly grew rich, whilst inflation and unemployment eroded the living standards of the middle and lower classes.[2]

The nationalisation of whole sectors of industry and the expropriation of industrialists who had fled the country, post-revolutionary negligence, and the emigration of a large proportion of the middle classes from which technological and scientific personnel were recruited, threw society into a tragic situation. A sullen atmosphere combined with a feeling of having been betrayed – by the counter-revolution for some, and by the supporters of the revolutionary government for others – came to dominate a society traumatised by the successive failures of the revolutionary movement. It was a social failure because of the increase in poverty, and especially the growing gap between rich and poor, or between the emerging new elites and the poor. The speculative economy was a failure because it had transferred resources to non-productive activities. The war made the situation more difficult still, put the lives of young men at risk, and threatened the oil-producing area that provided the state with most of its income.

Scarcely two years after the Revolution of 1979 and in the middle of a war, society found itself caught up in a deadly struggle as the new Islamic government began to repress its opponents and tried to gain legitimacy by invoking the wartime emergency and the need to unite against the anti-Islamic Iraqi aggressor.

The *Bassidji* model made eminent sense in the context of backdrop of a Revolution that had gone adrift, an increasingly tense social situation and an economy that was in regression. It expressed both the feeling that the End of Time was at hand and the despair of the present day. For one category of young people, life no longer had any attractions or any meaning. 'Meaning' was something to be conquered by dying a dignified death that presaged an irenic post mortem future, and not in a life that was by definition not worth living. The Islamic task par excellence was now to do everything possible to die as a martyr and to persuade others, by force if necessary, to embrace death. It is of course only a tiny minority of revolutionary youth that thought along these lines. But that minority was not just any minority: it was the spearhead of the Revolution. Its ambition was to fight its enemies and to expel the Iraqi adversary from the national territory, but it was also manipulated by the state, which looked to it to provide a principle of legitimacy for its version of Islam. It was therefore given all the means at the government's disposal, especially the print media and television, which devoted long hours to 'stories from the front'. Propaganda and the cult of heroes made young men in search of a holy death the 'stars' of an absent modernity. The post-revolutionary state glorified the martyrs who had died at the front and the 'living martyrs' (*shahid e zendeh*) – the badly wounded and the survivors of the massacres carried out by the Iraqi army during chemical bombardments – to gain a repressive legitimacy. It directed its repression against an opposition that was challenging its mode of action by simply reminding it of the promises the Revolution had made about social justice and freedom.

## Shi'ism and the revolution

The Shi'a Islam that was the ideological mobilising force behind the Iranian revolution was not just a reproduction of traditional Shi'ism. The many transformations that took place within it made it a weapon that could be used by many sections of the population. Its secularisation began in the late nineteenth century and it became radicalised from the 1970s onwards, thanks mainly to Shariati, who became the revolutionary movement's chief ideologue.[3] His expressions 'revolutionary self-construction' (*khadsâzié engh'elâbi*), 'red Shi'ism' (*tachayya'e sorkh*) and 'Ali's Shi'ism' (*tachayyo'é alavi*) became the common currency of the Iranian Revolution. The secularisation of Shi'ism radically transformed the role of the believer.[4] Shi'ites tended in the past to be rather quietist and ritualistic, and to seek consolation for the injustice of the world in a cult of suffering and to place their hopes in the Messiah (the hidden twelfth Imam). Muslims often adopted a passive attitude and mentally projected themselves into an End of Time that left oppressive and unjust regimes free to dominate the people in this world. True believers now transformed their passive expectations into active expectations, and the inauthentic Shi'ism of the ruling classes or Safavid Shi'ism (*tachayyo'é safavi*) into a truly revolutionary Shi'ism or 'Ali's Shi'ism' (*tachayyo'é alavi*), the Shi'ism of the first Shi'ite Imam. They did so by launching the revolutionary struggle against their oppressors. According to Shariati, this attitude was in keeping with Shi'ism's original vocation and would hasten the coming of the hidden Imam.[5] For the first time, the youth of a modernising Iran came to see themselves as the subject of history rather than the passive, weeping victims of an unjust world. This politicisation of the sacred remains to this day one of the essential characteristics of the Martyrs of the Revolution or 'Bassidj'. After the Revolution and the beginning of the war with Iraq, the resources of Shi'ite ideology were exploited to justify the martyrdom of young men at the front and, above all, to boost the fortunes of a government which, throughout the war, could do no more than organise the socio-economic decline of Iranian society.

As we have seen, martyrdom plays a much more important role in Shi'ism than in Sunnism. The life histories of the Shi'ite Imams are marked by their actual or supposed martyrdom, as almost all these saintly figures succumbed, either in reality or in the imagination of believers, to the cruelty of Sunni governments. Its eschatological nature leads some modern interpreters of Shi'ism to emphasise its supposedly revolutionary aspect.[6] Yet ever since it was established as Iran's state religion under the Safavid dynasty from the sixteenth century onwards, Shi'ism has always been predominantly quietist. The expectation of the coming of the Mahdi (another name for the hidden twelfth Imam) discredited all temporal power (which had been usurped because it was not the power of the twelfth Imam). But because all temporal power was discredited, it did not need to concern itself with legitimacy. Believers waited for the End of Time and often tolerated autocratic political regimes without challenging them directly.[7] This gave governments great latitude, and they skilfully exploited the Shi'ite cult of suffering and, if need be, organised it and gave it material aid.[8] Religious authorities and political regimes arrived at a modus vivendi which, except during periods of crisis or instability (changes of dynasty, competition for power between various pretenders) gave the state great latitude.[9] As the influence of foreign powers grew in Iran (Great Britain in the south and Tsarist Russia in the north of the country) from the early nineteenth century onwards, a gradual revival occurred within religious ideology. The clergy, sections of the bazaar and of the urban population attempted to give a concrete meaning to the expression 'illegitimacy of power' by secularising religion. Throughout the twentieth century, Shi'ism became one of the main poles that allowed the construction of a new relationship with politics, the others being nationalism, which became increasingly important from the 1930s onwards, and Marxism, which had a great influence on Iranian intellectuals until the Islamic Revolution.

The Islamist tide washed across Iranian society after a period of intense socio-economic modernisation and after the Shah's closure of the political field, which excluded the new social classes born of modernisation. In the early 1970s, the movement opposing the Shah – or at least its main components – ceased to be democratic because the supporters of political pluralism, leftists and Islamists all fell victim to the repression.[10] What is more, the Islamic opposition was radicalised after the repression of the 1960s, and especially after the repression of the 1963 rebellion, which led Khomeini to go into exile in Iraq. The Shah's regime succeeded in suppressing all democratic opposition, and extreme forms became the only ones capable of mobilising people in the name of an ideology that could replace a nationalism that had been discredited by the imperial regime.

Iran found itself in a paradoxical situation on the eve of the Revolution. On the one hand, the country had experienced a period of high growth[11] and a real modernisation that extended to new social categories, end especially the middle classes, and made them more sympathetic to the West. On the other, the closure of the political system after the agrarian reforms of the 1960s denied these new groups access to the political stage. That gave birth to a protest movement which fed on the crisis in the imperial regime. The regime was badly affected by the illness of the Shah, the election of Jimmy

Carter to the presidency of the United States, the attendant rise of the ideology of human rights, and the discrediting of a political system that was increasingly based upon repressive apparatuses, led by SAVAK. The revolutionary movement was born of a temporary alliance between the traditional bazaar,[12] a faction of a radicalised clergy led by Khomeini, left and far left intellectuals and new urban classes that were experiencing modernisation but were frustrated by the Shah's regime.[13] This incoherent coalition gave birth to the united movement of the Iranian Revolution, in which the urban population rose against imperial power. It had only a vague vision of the future, and the most contradictory slogans coexisted: justice, freedom, equality and Islam. The groups that seized power when the imperial regime fell were heterogeneous: figures like Bazargan, who was Prime Minister in the provisional government for the nine months following the overthrow of the Shah,[14] rubbed shoulders with members of the clergy, representatives of the bazaar, people appointed by Khomeini, some of the exiled intellectuals who (like Banisadr) went back to Iran after the fall of the Shah, former members of the nationalist movement of Mossadegh's day, and the leaders of Islamic fundamentalist movements (the *fidayeen eslam*, who were Iran's equivalent to the Muslim Brothers in Egypt).

Real history was being made outside the circle of the legal government. One pole was organised around Khomeini, a second around Bazargan, and a third around Ayatollah Becheti. Other groups were formed in the provinces and succeeded because they had local roots. Leaving aside the group supporting Bazargan, the others, disparate as they may have been, shared the same anti-democratic creed and the same allegiance to Khomeini. They formed the hard core of Hezbollah. The name comes from the Koran ('Party of God') but rapidly took on pejorative connotations for those who suffered the assaults of a loosely structured group that was financed by the state and took the form of a paramilitary movement designed to intimidate, if not liquidate, its opponents by establishing the puritanical Islam demanded by Khomeini with his desire to create a radically Islamic Iran. The group acquired an institutional reality under the name 'Party of the Islamic Republic'.[15] It took in hand young people of modest social origin, peasants who had been forced off their land, and members of the local organisations responsible for security at neighbourhood, factory and town level during the Revolution. These organisations were known as *Komité*. They were gradually 'purged' (*pak sazi*) and integrated into the new state's repressive apparatus.

This heterogeneous population was generically described as 'the disinherited' or 'the oppressed' (*mostadafine*).

Like all forms of populism, Khomeini's populism attempted to acquire an identity, first by manipulating the hopes of various groups, and then by designating a common enemy, namely American imperialism, which was referred to in Koranic terms as World Arrogance (*estékbâré jahâni*). It was a target for the anger felt by everyone in a situation where a scapegoat was needed to explain the Revolution's failures. Conversely, Khomeini was personally able to embody both the political and the religious dimensions because he was the great Ayatollah who, since the Revolution, had been promoted to being the country's greatest religious representative.

### The Bassidj

Shortly after the overthrow of the Shah and the establishment of the revolutionary regime, the new government created a popular organisation to defend the Revolution against the assaults of its enemies. The Bassidj was born of a desire to defend what was still a fragile revolution against the supporters of counter-revolution and especially the 'Taqutis' or rich supporters of the Shah. The Bassidj, whose literal meaning is 'mobilisation', was created to allow working-class youths to serve the Revolution.[16] At the start of the war with Iraq, the organisation was integrated into the Pasdaran army, another military organisation that came into being just after the Revolution. Together, the two formed a people's army independent of the traditional army, whose hierarchy was suspected of being sympathetic to the Shah.[17] The Bassidj was made up of voluntary recruits. When the war was at its most intense, it was some four hundred thousand strong. The Bassidji distinguished themselves by their devotion and lack of fear in the face of death.[18]

The war with Iraq, which lasted more than eight years, posed a threat to the very existence of the Revolution and especially, in its initial phases, the evolution of the revolutionary movement. The democratic tendency led by the Movement for Freedom (*Nehzaté âzâdi*), which was already extremely weak, did not survive the war. Using the pretext of defending the Muslim fatherland and revolutionary Islam, the pro-Khomeini group known as Hezbollah took a firmer grip on power, exploiting the threat of an Iraqi invasion of the country to silence the weak demands for the self-determination of a society that had only recently been freed from the imperial dictatorship. It was against the background of the threat of invasion, and in the context of a revolution that was itself in danger that the Bassidji actor came into being. The Bassidj was the revolutionary government's spearhead not only in the war against Iraq, but also in the struggle against the opposition inside Iran. It operated on two fronts. On the one hand, the Bassidj was directly involved in the physical repression of oppositionists; on the other, it helped to legitimise the Khomeini regime. The fact that young men were prepared to sacrifice their lives to defend it provided a society that had no defensive capacity, and which was exhausted by its mobilisation during the Revolution, with startling proof of the 'legitimacy' of the Hezbollah government.[19]

### The Bassidji model

In the context of a revolution threatened on all sides by war and counter-revolution, as represented by both the royalist right and the far left, the Bassidj mobilised men who were either young (between 18 and 30) or very young (from 14, and in some case twelve, upwards), and willing to sacrifice themselves for the sake of the Revolution. Those known as 'God's madmen', who identified Khomeini as the personification of the ultimate saint, savant and political leader, joyfully accepted martyrdom to protect a revolution that had gone adrift.

The war with Iraq and the invasion of part of southwestern Iran made them feel that were living under a threat. Both the integrity of Iran's territory and the Islam promoted by the Revolution were in danger. National feeling fused with religious affect: the danger threatening the Islamic Revolution was also a threat to the country's territorial integrity. The same phenomenon occurred during the French Revolution, and it now produced the same reaction: the French Revolution was in danger and the whole of Europe had formed a coalition against France, just as revolutionary Islam was under threat of death and just as Iran had been invaded. The nation united and rallied in the face of the enemy.

Revolutionary organisations took in young men who wanted to defend the Islamic fatherland and the threatened Revolution. Conscripts were enlisted in the traditional army, whilst young volunteers willing to sacrifice their lives joined the Bassidj. They made up the bulk of its forces.[20]

Studies of the subjectivity of these young revolutionaries show that it was not homogeneous and that at least three types of actor can be identified. First, there were those who felt quite helpless because of the critical state in which the Revolution found itself. The revolution was the incarnation of Islam. Their views had undergone a radical change: at the start of the Revolution, they had been optimistic but they now became pessimistic and radical. Their radicalisation was, in a way, the result of the feeling that the future of the Revolution was under threat as it became bogged down and as the economic paralysis worsened. These young men felt they were looking into the abyss. Their feeling of helplessness explains why they adopted a type of religiosity that saw martyrdom as the only salvation. These radicalised martyropaths were motivated by hatred and despair, and constantly oscillated between the two affects.[21] They were hostile to those they regarded as enemies of the Revolution, be it the Iraqi army, the opposition inside Iran or Muslims who were reluctant to defend a revolution that was coming more and more under threat. But at the same time, they did not believe they could save the Revolution in this life. They therefore began to compete with one another to become martyrs.

Two other types of actors coexisted alongside the martyropaths. Some adolescents enlisted in the Bassidj and Pasdaran armies to assert their autonomy from their parents and to be recognised as adults. For them, the war was almost a rite of passage from adolescence to adulthood. The playful dimension of the war played an important role in their decision to join the Bassidj. The manner in which Bassidj-affiliated organisations in the schools manipulated their religious affects was an important factor in their mobilisation.

A third group also joined the Bassidj. It played an important role by acting as a springboard for those who took part in the war. It allowed them to enjoy a rapid socio-economic upward mobility in a society that was becoming impoverished and in which social mobility was becoming increasingly difficult.[22] The Bassidj and the Pasdaran army gave these young men important positions in the army, but also in other state organisations and in the public sector, which was greatly expanded as a result of the nationalisation of the assets of the 'Taqoutis' or the Shah's elite. The vast majority of the young men in the Bassidj belonged to this group of 'opportunists'. They rallied to Khomeini out of conviction, but also because he was head of state and could guarantee their social promotion.

In financial terms, the Bassidj was the Pasdaran army's responsibility, but it also benefited from the 'gifts' that various public and private organisations were forced by the government to make, and from the financial generosity of organisations such as the Martyrs'

Foundation.[23] Other institutions whose finances were not under ministerial control also gave contributions to the Bassidj and the Pasdaran army.[24]

Some young men were unable to reconcile the utopia of the early Revolution with an increasingly difficult post-revolutionary reality. Young men who had, in the first years of the war, been smitten with the revolutionary dream and then disillusioned with the actual development of the Revolution, came to be motivated by feelings of hatred and despair. The future they had dreamed of when the Revolution dawned seemed very far away.

In terms of age-cohorts, the composition of this state-supported and state-financed organisation was heterogeneous. The vast majority of those who joined it were young, but its membership also included adolescents and a minority of old men. Their motives were not all the same. Their social origins were mainly in the urban lower classes (and in some cases the middle-lower classes). The majority of its recruits were schoolchildren, post-adolescent young people or people in their twenties. In some cases, young people from the same family joined different or even antagonistic groups.[25] Individual attitudes towards the Revolution and its future were of crucial importance. Rural youths joined the Bassidj, but not really out of conviction. They were more interested in finding a way into the urban world, and wanted to live their adolescence to the full, surrounded by abundance and far away from the needs and the boredom of the rural world. Most of those who joined the Bassidj for ideological reasons came from the towns or the large cities. Only those who had already experienced modernisation and destructuring were in a position to become 'radicalised and despairing revolutionaries'. Only those young revolutionaries who felt that they had an established Ego could feel guilt, and that meant that communitarian structures had to have been broken down. Most of those affected had lived in the great urban zones before the Revolution.

Young people in the Bassidj were systematically manipulated by the state. Everything was done to encourage them to join. The government did not do so simply to provide the Bassidj with cannon fodder, but also to acquire a certain legitimacy. It argued that a regime for which the young were prepared to die could not be illegitimate. The martyropaths certainly chose to die to defend their Islamic country, but they were mainly motivated by their feeling of desperation at seeing the collapse of the revolutionary utopia. It could not be realised in this world and therefore had to be realised in death. For them, this was an existential issue. But the revolutionary government gave their desperation a political meaning and manipulated it because it was a source of strength. It used it as an instrument to consolidate its own power in a society that was both traumatised and intimidated by the extreme commitment of its young people. The despair of some was manipulated to repress others.

The Bassidj was, for some years, the crucible where the register of society was fused with that of the state. This would have been inconceivable in a traditional Shi'ite community, where everything to do with the state was identified with a logic of violence and fear.[26] Most people joined the Bassidj of their own accord. Similarly, the martyropathic group's wish for death was obviously exploited by the Bassidj, but the Bassidj did not create it. Both the state and the group of volunteers who saw it as an expression of their own aspirations to martyrdom colluded in the exploitation of this martyropathy. The reason why it now became possible to 'confuse' below (society) with above (state) was that communitarian structures had already been largely destroyed and were gradually being replaced by individuals who were becoming partially autonomous.[27] This was a society that was making the transition towards a new form of social organisation, and the fact that young men volunteered to join the Bassidj was a sign that a 'quasi-individual' was emerging.[28] At the same time, the Bassidj was also an expression of the confusion of young revolutionaries who could no longer make any distinction between the registers of state and society. The mental confusion brought about by the effervescence of the early days of the Revolution, which was artificially sustained by the Bassidj, led them to confuse the respective domains of government and society. The confusion arose mainly because of the destructuring of the old society and the chaotic emergence of a new society in the course of a revolution that paid more attention to utopia than to reality. The dynamic of the Bassidj drew its strength, at least during its early years, from the living source of a revolutionary society in ferment. Its mode of organisation was a matter for the state, but the martyropaths did not perceive the Bassidj as a state organisation. They chose it as their new 'family'. They 'married' it. They felt themselves to be the brothers (barâdar) of other martyropaths who were also in search of death. The Bassidj was, they believed, made in Khomeini's image, and he had sanctified it with his blessing. That is why a new and repressive government could manipulate the Bassidj.

For youngsters who wanted to play games, the Bassidj was an adoptive family. They left their natural families and joined it to find a new identity. Their new identity was a voluntaristic construct forged in the face of death. In this period of war, upward social mobility was blocked and for young people coming on to the labour market, the Bassidj was the only place where they could gain promotion. Eager to climb the social ladder, they found its atmosphere conducive to self-assertion. They could assert themselves through their prowess as warriors. What was more important, the Bassidj also provided many opportunities to live life to the full. By joining the Bassidj, they also fulfilled their ambition to save the country, the Islamic nation and a religious revolution that was being threatened by the Iraqi invasion. The national feeling experienced by others, and which they shared, could be combined with a desire for upward mobility and youthful enthusiasm.

In order to be effective, the Bassidj required an organisation that could both police society and encourage young people to join it. The Islamic associations were some of its most effective instruments. They were formed during the Revolution. They were neighbourhood or local groups entrusted with the task of running things on a day-to-day basis (preventing theft, maintaining order, and so on). After the Revolution, these associations were gradually infiltrated by the state and its various repressive apparatuses.[29] They then played a major role in purging 'counter-revolutionary' elements in the administration and in inciting young volunteers to join the Bassidj.

Schools were these 'associations' best source of recruits. They were able to establish themselves within a hierarchy that was independent of the schools' administration (they reported to a special section of the Ministry for National Education) and won over certain secondary school students who became, de facto, the government's interlocutors. The very fact that they were involved with the Bassidj also guaranteed them an academic success they did not always deserve.

The Bassidj attached great importance to ideological propaganda. A special clergy was appointed for the purpose and played upon these adolescents' feeling of invulnerability and their heroic aspirations.

The Bassidj gave young people the feeling that they were part of a revolution *against* the rest of society. They were encouraged to see themselves as a 'pure caste' that was not part of an increasingly impure society: the day-to-day reality was that people were turning away from revolutionary slogans whose inanity was being revealed as the economic situation worsened. The twelve to 17-year-old adolescents in the Bassidj were accorded a quasi-adult or even super-adult status. They were praised for having risen, thanks to their voluntary commitment, above adults and parents who refused to enlist.[30] The adolescents and other Bassidji all wore the same uniform. They became equal to the adults and sometimes enjoyed greater prestige.

The Bassidj also took in non-martyropathic young people, and it did so in very positive ways. It paid the unemployed and gave them an opportunity to use their creativity while risking their lives. Battles provided the young Bassidjis with an opportunity to demonstrate their creativity by improvising and finding makeshift solutions. Handling mines became a form of 'self-fulfilment'. The decision to join this group of youngsters was not motivated by a death wish, but by a need to work, and work gave them a new status. They also wanted to save the threatened Islamic fatherland and, in the case of secular members of the far left, to save the fatherland and the people. For their part, leftists joined the Bassidj because they thought they would be able to establish links with and indoctrinate working-class youths. In the first years of the war, everyone could find a reason for fighting the Iraqi army. For those on the left, it was the vanguard of Western imperialism. For nationalists, it represented an Arabism that aspired to conquering the Arab-speaking provinces of Iran for nationalists (parts of Khuzestan, which had been invaded by the Iraqi army, are Arab-speaking).

As the martyrs' enthusiasm faded as the war dragged on, compensatory mechanisms were gradually introduced to encourage young people to go back to the front. Both material incentives and coercion were used. Those who remained at the front for a certain length of time were given fast-track admission to the administration's 'intelligence' services. They played a role similar to that of SAVAK under the Shah. Admission requirements were relaxed for Bassdjis who wanted to go to university, and for young members of their families. Access to martyrs' cooperatives, where prices were far below those in the markets, was restricted to wounded Bassidjis and their families, and to the families of Bassidji martyrs who also enjoyed other material benefits.[31]

The Bassidji who went to the front to fight the Iraqi army were all men. They were usually young and very rarely old. There were certainly groups of young women Bassidji (Bassidji 'sisters'), but their role was restricted to providing medical care, caring for the young men who were directly involved in the fighting, repressing 'badly veiled women', and even intimidating the parents of martyrs who protested the way the Islamic government was manipulating their sons. The 'sisters' used ceremonies to celebrate the death of martyrs as a pretext for silencing the protests of their parents or friends.

Bassidji women were not directly involved in the war. This was not because some girls refused to carry guns, but because of the attitude of an Islamist government that rejected the equality of men and women. The women martyrs were those who were killed during Iraqi bombardments, whilst doing their jobs as hospital nurses, or for other reasons to do with the war.

## Opportunism and play

Throughout the war, the main motive for martyrdom was a desire to protect the threatened Islamic fatherland and to fight an Iraqi enemy supported and aided by Western imperialism. Martyrdom took many different forms. As we have seen, a very small minority within the Bassidj were martyropaths, but they played a major symbolic role both in the government's legitimation strategy and in encouraging other Bassidjis, who regarded them as superior beings who had renounced life and its pleasures to achieve a mystical perfection by dying a holy death. The non-martyropaths were, it should be recalled, made up of two distinct groups. On the one hand, there were the opportunists who were looking to the Bassidj to provide them with a springboard that would give them upward mobility in a society whose poorest members had no other way of moving up the social ladder. The 'game-players', on the other hand, were mainly young boys and adolescents who wanted to live life to the full and to want for nothing. They risked their lives so as to make the transition to adulthood in a warlike atmosphere of reckless heroism. For them, the war provided an opportunity for entertainment and thrills. They became free in the ranks of the Bassidj because the hierarchy had been inverted: the young commanders distinguished themselves by their bravery, and that gave them greater prestige than their elders. They demonstrated their heroism by risking death and thus transcended their adolescence. They were well fed, and given board and lodging by a society from which the state was extorting funds under the pretext of being charitable to the young men who supported it.

The martyropaths died because they despaired of a world that was a cemetery for revolutionary ideals, whereas the young adolescents in the Bassidj were willing to put their lives in danger because they were playing a reckless game and wanted the intense experience of the bloody festival known as war. It allowed them to relive the festival of the Revolution's dawn and transcend the morose life of the post-revolutionary period. Their actions were a denegation of the gloomy atmosphere that prevailed in a society where there had been no joy since the war began and where shortages had destroyed dreams of prosperity. This is why the 'playful' martyr's relationship with death was totally different to that of the martyropath. On the battlefield, 'playful' martyrs could escape the institutionalisation of the revolutionary utopia. For them, the sacred was something they could find in effervescence, excitement and communion, and they contrasted that with the cold logic of the rich traders on the bazaar and the mean, prosaic calculations of their parents, who were not too sure about making ends meet. Any stabilisation was seen as a challenge to their Islamic utopianism, and it led them to raise the stakes in battle. Death was not the result of a sullen hatred, but of a desire for ecstasy and effervescence, of an aspiration to challenge the monotony and deadly boredom of a life in which the disinherited were worse off than ever before, even more vulnerable and frustrated than before in their desire for consumer goods. This death had none of the gloomy nature of martyropathy. It was a rejection of institutionalisation, a longing for the effervescence of the start of the Revolution, and not a desire to die at all costs. The manipulation of the desires of immature young people eager for intense pleasures gave considerable weight to an Islamic order whose legitimacy was in fact based upon a neo-puritan vision of social and cultural relations.

For their part, the opportunists used Hezbollah's Islam to join the new regime's middle class. They formed a new elite which, thanks to the new revolutionary networks set up by the Islamist state, replaced the old ruling classes and which, in exchange for its venal loyalty to the regime, guaranteed itself a life free from need. The new institutions that came into being during or after the Revolution were their springboard: the Construction Crusade (*jahâd sazandegi*), which had a monopoly on rural development projects (it was later transformed into a ministry), the Martyrs' Foundation, an economic colossus with financial and industrial resources of its own, the *Astane ghods*, which managed the estates of Imam Reza in the northeast of Iran, and which is one of the richest institutions in the country,[32] the various revolutionary committees (Komiteh, which were subsequently integrated into the Ministry of the Interior), the Pasdaran army, and so on. These revolutionary organisations were a means to social and economic upward mobility for young people who were eager for consumer goods and who joined Bassidj for ulterior motives. Their reward for exposing themselves to danger was admission to a state apparatus which allowed them to share in the oil wealth. Part of the urban population became upwardly mobile, thanks mainly to the committees (Komiteh) and the Pasdaran army that intimidated their neighbourhoods. When necessary, its members intervened to protect their friends and acquaintances from the regime's repressive apparatuses, where they had personal contacts. The state was able to establish a new form of nepotism thanks to these young people who, at neighbourhood level, were both feared and respected because of the far from negligible help they could provide in emergencies.

### Archaeo-Islam

In societies subject to authoritarian modernisation, the concrete appearance of the individual comes about as a result of the destructuring of the traditional communitarian order on the one hand, and the self-assertion of a being who is becoming at least partially autonomous on the other. That being experiences a bitter discontent as his desire for liberation comes into conflict with his sense of belonging to the group he is betraying by becoming autonomous. The Revolution attempts to link the two dimensions by introducing a third term, namely the revolutionary utopia personified by Khomeini. The utopia cannot, however, stand up to reality for very long. It gradually breaks down. To remedy that, the young revolutionaries became martyropaths. In order to compensate for the Revolution's loss of grip on reality, they attempted to enhance Khomeini's charisma. As the revolutionary movement lost its grip on reality, the martyropaths strove even harder to give the Revolution's Guide (Khomeini) superlatively charismatic attributes. In order to do that, they turned the Guide into a figurehead not only at the level of their individuality and subjective feeling of existence, but also in relation to their families and the communitarian order, which were simply replaced by a Guide who was now absolute.

At the same time, Khomeini's prestige was enhanced by the nature of his message – a death-obsessed Shi'ism that sanctified death by using the vocabulary of martyrdom and denying the legitimacy of life on earth during a period of war and crisis in which, for these disoriented young people, everything was seen in apocalyptic terms. The martyropaths retreated into the Bassidj and cut themselves off from society. The breaking of social bonds now became a source of anxiety. The young people who had chanted 'Freedom, Independence, Islamic Republic' at the beginning of the Revolution no longer knew what to do with their own independence and freedom. No longer able to take responsibility for their own actions, they abdicated their autonomy and fell prey to anxiety and bad conscience. They came to resent their own freedom because it transgressed 'revolutionary' norms, and they explained the Revolution's reversals in terms of their own failure to live up to its ideals. As a result, they felt profoundly guilty. New individuals who have only recently shaken off their communitarian ties undergo a crisis when the revolutionary movement in which they have invested their identity destroys that identity as it goes off the rails. The exaggerated puritanism of the Bassidji was a 'moralised' expression of their feeling of guilt: they believed they had betrayed the revolutionary ideal, had invested too little of themselves in the service of Islam and had therefore driven the Revolution off course.

At the beginning of the Revolution, young people had attempted to modernise Islam by moralising modernity, but modernity now became synonymous with sin, depravity and a failure to live up to the revolutionary ideal of abnegation, because it is 'egotistical' and implies a quest for individual happiness. Hence the exaggerated archaisms and the inflexibly stubborn insistence on the reformulation of tradition which was itself reified, deformed and mythologised in a despotic and sometimes even totalitarian way. We now see the emergence of what might be called 'archaeo-Islam'. This is a counter-modern invention presented as an authentic image of tradition, but it is in fact nothing more than an inverted modernity in which life becomes death, consumption becomes self-destruction and community becomes an inversion of modernity for individuals in crisis. They literally consume themselves through their martyrdom which, in some exaggerated cases, takes on the appearance of homophagy, or the ingestion of their own flesh. Archaeo-Islam is an inverted modernity in which freedom is transformed into a logic of absolute taboos. Cultural openness turns into an attempt to withdraw from the world, and it takes a paradoxically exhibitionist form; exhibiting that closure was an inverted way of being part of (rejecting) modernity. The taboos pronounced by Hezbollah and applied by authoritarian means within the public space were not traditional communitarian taboos, but politicised expressions of regressive forms of Shi'ism that were themselves excessively rigid because they were based upon inflexible interpretations. In this context, the hatred and *ressentiment* were directed against the world and the body. A religion that had been made to conform to their demands for repression and their denial of the rights of the embryonic individual supplied the pretext.

Even the category of the political now took on a dubious meaning. For the martyropaths, it was no longer either a bond between autonomous beings in a public space (democracy) or a way of managing collective life by referring to sacred texts interpreted by doctors of the law (institutionalised Islamic theocracy), but a way of compensating for their own disquiet. A martyropath is an individual in crisis who no longer knows how to control his individuality and who tries, by resorting to a repressive category of the political, to rid himself of his individuated being and to embrace death. The quasi-individual who believed that the Revolution would give him the support he needed to accede to modernity, lost both the community that once supported him and the revolutionary utopia that was supposed to replace it. Martyropathy became the ultimate expression of the political and, at the same time, a legitimate way of constructing an individual-in-death. We have here a combination of an exaggerated puritanism (a moralised expression of the taboo on living), archaeo-Islam (the sacred invested in a deadly religiosity), and the absolutist charisma of Khomeini (the 'Islamic' voice proclaiming the vanity of this world and preaching that martyrdom is the way to the sacred).

The young revolutionary's aspirations towards modernity could take two major forms: consumerism as a festive way of partaking in modernity, or productive development as a promethean way of participating in modernity. With Iran at war, and with industrial production falling, both proved impossible. In one sense, they were too prosaic for some young people, who were in love with the Absolute. The Revolution turned the quest for the Absolute into a morbid neo-mysticism in which anything to do with life proved to be insignificant or even insane. The promethean feeling of self-realisation induced by modernisation turned into the lethal creation of a self. Revolutionary consciousness became a deadly force and led to the production of a self-in-death. Demolished by the war economy and social chaos, consumerism became fixated on the body. Those who could no longer be consumers began to consume themselves. The desire to consume was projected onto a deadly form of the sacred. The outcome was a necrophile neo-asceticism.[33]

The young martyropaths who joined the Bassidj displayed several distinctive features. In their own minds, they were living under siege and were obsessed with their ubiquitous enemies, both at home and abroad. In their view, all other considerations, including family ties, were meaningless. Their self-image was marked by a deep feeling of guilt.[34] Guilty of impurity, they lived in a society that was even more 'impure' and corrupt than they were, and in their view that was a justification for repression to 'purify' it by suppressing all men and women who opposed their intolerant version of Islam.

Martyropathy is a movement whose dynamic presupposes, at least in its early stages, that 'below' (revolutionary youth) can fuse with 'above' (the post-revolutionary state) in a crisis situation in which the threat that the Islamic fatherland will be invaded by the enemy coexists with the despairing feeling that the revolutionary utopia is collapsing. Its roots lie in a post-revolutionary society and in its basic instability, as well as in the threat posed to the Islamic nation by an Iraqi invasion.

The Bassidj did exhibit one essential feature of the new individuality that was emerging: the egalitarianism of its symbolism, its recruiting methods, the way its leaders were addressed and its ability to ensure that there was no social differentiation and heirarchy between its members during the first years of the war.

Inside the Bassidj, all the divisions of post-revolutionary society were symbolically denied and abolished. Its young members masked the social divisions between rich and poor, 'oppressors' (*mostakbirine*) and 'the disinherited' or oppressed (*mostadafine*), superiors and inferiors, and observant and non-observant Muslims. The outside hierarchy was abolished and replaced by a 'hierarchy of the heart' in which differences were dissolved into a unitary and egalitarian feeling of belonging: the leaders were Bassidjis too, did not demand the distance that army officers traditionally keep between themselves and their soldiers, and did not hesitate to be in the front line. The absence of any hierarchy or strong discipline added to the feeling of unity, even though there was indeed a hierarchy in which considerations as to 'reliability' (identification with the Islamic Republic) counted for a great deal in all but the lowest ranks.

Individual martyropaths, 'playful' ones and opportunists had a different relationship with the hierarchy. Martyropaths surrendered their identity for the greater good of an organisation that granted them plenitude in death, and literally handed themselves over to the hierarchy because they wished to rid themselves of their desire to lead autonomous lives. The Bassidj satisfied the martyropaths' desire for heteronomy. The game-players and opportunists, in contrast, were drawn to the absence of any hierarchy, the egalitarianism and the feeling of fraternity. Whereas society was non-egalitarian, these young men experienced the fraternal equality of an organisation in which an egalitarian ideology prevailed in the face of death. For all these young people, the possibility of dying a martyr's death created a 'We' that was both egalitarian and pure ('without dishonour'), and offered an alternative to a non-egalitarian and perverse (impure) 'They', namely post-revolutionary society.

The one thing that united the various groups within the Bassidj was the struggle against the enemy who had invaded Islamic Iran. These young people were certainly mobilised in the name of Islam, but their religion was based upon the threat of invasion and occupation hanging over the Islamic country that was the cradle of revolution in the name of Allah.

The Bassidj succeeded in playing on two registers that are incompatible in the real world. It gave the martyropaths a feeling of hierarchy, total order and sanctity. For the young game-players who were trying to escape a non-egalitarian and unjust daily life, it satisfied the need to escape poverty and the degrading situation of the disinherited by creating a society in which everything was available to all, in which there was no hierarchy and which gave them access to goods and services. That it could do so in a context where the Islamic nation was under threat gave it great legitimacy. It succeeded in reconciling all these different registers by turning to the charismatic figure of Khomeini. He guaranteed its legitimacy by giving his blessing to the struggle against the enemy of a Muslim people and country. For young martyropaths, the Bassidj was not an organisation like any other, but an organisation in which the Ego of each of its members was taken care of by Khomeini in the context of a personalised and intimate relationship. The Guide of the Revolution prepared them to meet the Imam of Time and made them worthy to come into contact with the Messiah who would open the gates of Paradise for them.[35]

Thanks to its symbolic manipulation of its young members and the fusion that arises from an unreal fraternisation behind closed doors, the Bassidj was able to artificially preserve the unitary ambiance of the early Revolution. But it was because the post-revolutionary situation allowed it to do so that the state could manipulate them. This state was neither what it would become within a few years (domination without legitimacy) nor what it was at the beginning of the Revolution (an expression of the unanimity within society). It was an intermediate form of state which concealed and hid the breakdown of unanimity by uniting various categories of the population in the struggle against the Islamic nation's enemy. Inside the Bassidj, young people could still dream of the unanimity of hearts, but it had disappeared from society itself. The war allowed the Bassidj to reject reality by recreating the effervescence of the early Revolution by channelling it into the struggle against Islam's enemy. It would rather die than have to renounce the dream-logic that inspired the Revolution, even though reality had turned against the Revolution and had now come to see it as hostile. Revolutionary martyrdom helped to conceal despair in the face of a cruel reality, but in another sense it also sustained that despair by giving it a sacred content.

There was a morbid dimension to the religiosity of the Bassidj's martyropaths, and it stemmed from a deadly religiosity. It was different from traditional communitarian Shi'ism as it was from the Shi'ism of the dawn of the revolution, which was inspired by the utopian hopes it placed in the new Islamic society of the future. This morbid Shi'ism was an ephemeral phenomenon born of a tragic situation characterised by the collapse of the revolutionary utopia, a war that posed a threat to the Islamic Revolution and a crisis in a society that had believed it could restore justice, plenty and freedom, and which was now seeing the inversion of those ideals. Living conditions had been expected to improve, but both poverty and wealth were growing. People had once idealised a life of peace and justice, but the social scene was dominated by war, daily injustice and the arbitrary exercise of fragmented power. In the religiosity embodied in a fraction of the revolutionary youth, death had an irresistible fascination, but it was inspired by despair at living in a society abandoned by hope and not the hope of building a new society.

The subject gradually came to feel himself a foreigner in this world and expressed his distress by committing an act it sanctified by calling it martyrdom. There was, however, one crucial difference between this sacred death and traditional Shi'ite martyrdom. On the one hand, death was the result of a deliberate choice, whereas in traditional martyrdom, the warrior of the faith was striving to accomplish a religious ideal and succumbed unwillingly to death by sacrificing himself for the sake of an ideal. Secondly, this neo-martyrdom meant self-realisation through the death of an embryonic individual, whereas traditional martyrdom experienced as an archetypal event and, ultimately, one that could not be reproduced by mere mortals.[36] Any Muslim could now become a martyr. Martyrdom had been 'democratised' just as religion had been secularised.

Martyropathy, *homo islamicus novus*'s desperate means of self-expression, was the product of the subject's entry into a traumatic modernity in which the mediating structures that once prevented suicide had broken down. Which brings us to the third characteristic of this type of martyrdom, namely its suicidal dimension. Young men turn to martyropathy and take their own lives by having recourse to the sacred out of hatred and despair because they are living in what they see as an intolerable situation (the moment the utopia collapsed in the case of Iran, the moment when a young Palestinian admits that there is no concrete solution to the problems of life under the Israeli occupation). They take their own lives but conceal the suicidal dimension of their actions. They sanctify their own deaths by attempting to build a real community in death. Unable to experience a modernity but knowing that it exists in other parts of the world, they acquire it by denying the legitimacy of life, painting a black picture of the modern world from which they are excluded and erecting the obverse of modernity into a necro-community that has nothing in common with the traditional Islamic community. There is in martyropathy a real fascination with death (paradoxically, it is the subject's one remaining hope) and with the Other. There is an individualised aspiration towards death because it is the one means of self-expression left for an Ego that is intent upon realising itself in death because it believes it cannot do so in life. The Ego needs to blossom in a collectivity, but it cannot be the collectivity of 'normal' living beings, and must be a collectivity of individuals with mortiferous ambitions that they try to fulfil in death. The Bassidj was one such community. This 'community in death', which the Bassidj gave made him feel that the task he had set himself – taking his own life whilst fighting the enemy who had destroyed his utopia – had a religious legitimacy. Just as the existence of a destructured individual imbued with a deadly eschatology is a sine qua non precondition for the realisation of an ambivalent act that oscillates between self-realisation and self-destruction in death, there must also be a group, small or large, to socialise these young men, if they are not to lapse into a despairing torpor and if they are to agree to take the final step. A morbid religiosity has the ability to make individuals fight the enemy by taking their own lives, and that is what makes it different to anomic despair. In his radicalised despair, the individual has no intention of dying quietly, and wants to take the world with him. Just as his death is 'vital' to him, so he must leave his mark on a world that is hostile to his desire to perpetuate the revolutionary utopia.

A further distinctive feature of Iran's martyropaths was their great instability. They oscillated between several contradictory principles. On the one hand, a revolutionary Ego asserted itself by defending the Islamic utopia and fighting those who were against it (this is the classic revolutionary consciousness); on the other, they abdicated from life and took flight in suicide because they despaired of being able to fulfil their ambition in this world. Hence the urgent need to escape life, which is the last vestige of 'impurity'. This dimension is deeply imbued with death: the young martyropath is drawn to his own death and intends to die by encouraging his brothers to follow his example and by bringing about the death of the enemy. This 'lethiferous' dimension was an expression of the 'new' Iranian revolutionary mentality: his goal was to kill both himself and his enemy, who were equivalent from the viewpoint of necrophile Bassidjis for whom life in this world no longer had any meaning. Death was also, finally, a warrior virtue: dying was a way of asserting one's superiority over the enemy in a hostile world by destroying both themselves and the enemy.

The martyropath's ambivalence means that he sees life in this world as a form of impurity and that he is convinced that he must die a martyr's death to purify himself. This attitude is based upon the heteronomy of the revolutionary Ego. Having become unstable, it oscillates between self-assertion in the relentless fight against the enemy, and the flight into suicide. Attachment to life offends the morbid convictions of the martyropath. As a result, he mentally leaves behind a society in which the desire to go on living at all costs is exacerbated by a climate of war and shortages. When, for example, he has a few days' leave with his family, he often cuts short his stay and leaves his parents and friends, or even his wife and children, to return to the front. He is profoundly disgusted by the spectacle of life in the city and amongst people who are 'cowardly' enough to cling to life – these expressions are frequently used in the testaments of martyrs.

The relationship between martyropathy and sacrifice is crucial. The martyropath believes he is sacrificing himself for the sake of Islam; he is in fact abdicating in the face of his own instability. The martyr's sacrifice still had its natural meaning early in the Revolution, to the extent that this feeling of abnegation was shared by others. When the revolution in Iranian society was at its height, the young martyrs were seen by the vast majority of the population as 'sacrificing themselves' for the sake of Islam. Scarcely two years later, the Bassidjis still thought they were 'sacrificing themselves', but their parents and others thought their attitude was incoherent in itself and repressive where others were concerned. The martyrdom of young Bassidjis was used by the government to give itself legitimacy at the political level, and to prolong a war that was becoming more and more bloody and more and more of a burden, even though no real advances had been made after three years. The feeling of sacrifice was therefore no longer shared by others, and it was this 'blindness' that allowed them to act as though they represented others when the vast majority had already rejected the revolutionary utopia and no longer followed the Hezbollah that defended it. The martyropath was a revolutionary who was behind the times, and who still acted as though the unanimity of hearts still existed, whereas it had shattered into pieces by the second year of the Revolution. He claimed that his actions were intended to realise the revolutionary utopia, but his role was in fact to signal the failure of the Revolution by doing away with himself in hatred and despair.[37]

The 'individual-in-death' incarnated in the martyropath was the creation of a minority of young men whose necrophile religiosity was of great importance throughout the war: the Hezbollah government turned them into its vanguard in order to legitimise its repressive ascendancy over society and to promote a neo-puritanism tinged with a strict moralism. The fact remains that the vast majority did not subscribe to this necrophile view of life but did not openly oppose a government that ruled through terror. The majority chose to lead a double life. In one life, they surrendered themselves to the Islamist regime, and appeared to submit to its ideology within public space; in their other life, they fulfilled their ambitions in a place that was not under full government control, namely the black market. The regime might well call for a struggle to the death against American imperialism (the Great Satan), but the dollar reigned supreme in the black market that now extended throughout society. Official ideology was based upon the sombre abnegation of the martyropath, but the black market was a place of unbridled egotism that blatantly ignored the government and its promises. The result was galloping inflation, and the appearance of money-grubbers who exploited a war economy and shortages to rapidly enrich themselves with the complicity of government agents. This was an increasingly divided, even schizoid, world. On the one hand, martyropaths were preaching martyrdom and aspired to it; on the other, large sections of society were involved in more or less shady and illegal activities on the black market. The martyropath found this duality extremely painful. He could not tolerate the fact that the ideals of the Revolution were being flouted so easily, that the real world could, only two years after the Revolution, have abandoned the Islamic utopia that should have established justice and fraternity in this society. The growing gulf between these aspirations and reality led him to despair and death.

After Hezbollah's seizure of power, the Iranian Revolution was characterised by an exaggerated puritanism. Whilst all revolutions are puritanical to some degree, the puritanism was taken to extremes in the case of Iran. This had something to do with Hezbollah's hegemony, as it used its strict representation of religion as a means to repress and intimidate society. The Hezbollah government imposed puritanical norms on society, made the repression of political opponents an Islamic precept and thus created a space in which any opponent was of necessity immoral and in which anyone immoral was a 'political' opponent. Iran's Hezbollah in fact condemned hedonism because it was an expression of wish for autonomy from its totalitarian concept of power.

There was another component to this post-revolutionary puritanism, and it was bound up with the consumerism introduced by the imperial regime in the early 1970s. Under the Shah, consumerism meant affluence for the middle and upper classes, and a dream of affluence for the lower classes; post-revolutionary neo-puritanism was characteristic of a period of shortages (the war, the failing economy) when consumerism had to be symbolic because it could not be real. The subject was haunted by the same immoderation, the same desire to appropriate things and the same unquenchable thirst. And yet Hezbollah's neo-puritanism was not simply a product of the symbolism of consumerism. When a desperate revolutionary youth totally rejected consumerist modernity, it trapped itself in the myth of an archaic community. Its puritanism dictated a mode of behaviour that wanted to put an end to the reign of a modernity that was impure because it was consumerist, and consumerist because it was impure, so as to embrace purity by forbidding things and, if necessary, in death, which was the supreme taboo on living and which could therefore be sanctified as martyrdom. Modernity was seen as an impurity, as something that transgressed an already puritanical Islam that could be used as a shield against it.

This post-revolutionary puritanism was, however, also bound up with the crisis in the new society. The neo-puritan attitude adopted by so many young people after the Revolution did not simply reproduce traditional modes of behaviour towards communitarian honour (*namous*) and female modesty. In the past, such modes of behaviour were internalised, and customary law or Islamic jurisprudence sanctioned norms that were respected by the vast majority of Muslims. The sexual promiscuity implicit in new modes of urbanisation and the upheavals brought about by social change represented a challenge to traditional Islamic norms. In the past, communication was something that occurred mainly on the man-to-man level, as male–female relations were governed by a code which, for the majority tendency, precluded intimacy and love.[38] Relations between young people were now the source of a latent sensualism that could not be expressed in broad daylight. It could, however, exist in a disguised form, such as ideological indoctrination sessions in far left groups in which men and women established mutual relations with a crypto-sexual content. That is why Hezbollah's puritanism found a fertile breeding ground amongst the new working classes that had recently been modernised and deracinated by the Shah's agrarian reforms of the 1960s. Hezbollah's exaggeratedly strict moral standards were therefore given a fairly favourable welcome by new groups that were undergoing modernisation in an urban space. The existential discontent of the martyropaths was matched by a feeling of self-dispossession on the part of peasants who had been driven from their land into depraved cities that threatened to defile their daughters and dishonour their men.[39]

### Family authority in crisis

The traditional family was disrupted by the succession of actors who appeared on the Iranian political stage. The authoritarian modernisation of the imperial period broke down some of its solidarity networks as the state took the place of the old community in many domains, such as education and employment. After the agrarian reforms of the 1960s, the influx of landless peasants into the towns created a new kind of family that made the transition from villages to towns with an economy that was becoming modernised and industrialised. Families then suffered the repercussions of the Revolution. The post-revolutionary state briefly introduced a higher principle of authority: Khomeini was the 'superlative father' who usurped the role of the *pater familias* in every domain where the defence of political Islam was at stake. The young martyropaths also played a role in transforming their families, as they abandoned them to join the Bassidj, often against the wishes of their parents. Whilst the revolutionary state challenged the authority of fathers from outside, the martyropaths undermined from within those pillars of the anthropological order of society by preferring Khomeini to their biological fathers, obeying his orders and disobeying those of their parents, who usually wanted to prevent them from going to the front. The loss of any family feeling is one of the obvious signs of martyropathic subjectivity. The martyropaths gradually abandoned their fathers, mothers, friends and brothers by sacrificing them to a morbid passion which, as it grew stronger, became their sole obsession.

Under the growing influence of the Bassidj's necrophile ideology, the sermons of the mullahs and the general atmosphere inside the organisation, the martyropaths became incapable of conceiving life outside this closed world. The Bassidj was like a quasi-cult or a closed community sustained by the effervescence that was reproduced and amplified by the isolation of martyropaths, who saw death as the ultimate stage in their spiritual purification. In this exclusive relationship with a death that was seen as the only source of meaning, the images of fathers, mothers, families and friends faded. The martyropath's passion could lead him to try to destroy his own family and that of others. Initially, his major concern was to ensure that, when he died, his family did not behave like a family in mourning, but like one that was rejoicing. As his passion for holy death grew, he might ask his close family to follow his example by joining the Bassidj. If the male side of family agreed, the result was a martyropathic family. Should that happen, what he demanded of his family was not that it should behave as a dignified martyr's family when he died, but that it should die and forget its responsibility to preserve the lives of its members. Being an 'individual in death', he might go so far as to reject a family that wished to preserve his life by frustrating his wish to die, by force if need be. The support he received from the state meant that a family faced with these exorbitant demands had little room for manoeuvre.

According to the martyropaths' worldview, they had not sinned by leaving the family (they felt no guilt at abandoning their old parents, or in some cases their wives and children, by going to an almost certain death at the front) but had sinned against the Islamist order. The martyropath feared that he was insufficiently devoted to it even though he was giving his life for it. In his psyche, the Islamist order replaced the family.

Put to the test by the upheaval of the Revolution, families did sometimes agree to the demands of their martyropathic sons. The male side of the family, or most of it, left for the front. This type of family, which might itself be described as martyropathic, was statistically marginal but sociologically significant. It was a particular configuration that emerged amongst urban families during the war. The martyropathic family differed from the vast majority of families in three respects. First, whereas the average family did not want its young sons to volunteer for the front, the martyropathic family strongly encouraged them to do so, not for financial or nepotistic reasons, but because of its martyropathic convictions. Second, it was not only the young sons who left for the front. Fathers and even uncles and nephews followed them. Third, women themselves often shared these mortiferous beliefs and intervened to persuade their sons, brothers or fathers to join the Bassidj and leave for the front.

Several different configurations can be found in martyropathic families. In some cases, the phenomenon concerns only the father and some of his sons. This is a first-degree martyropathic family. In other cases, up to three generations of men (grandfather, father and son, father and nephews or great-uncle, father and son and all possible combinations) joined the Bassidj in order to die as martyrs. In some cases, women sent their men folk to join it. All social taboos (the intolerable character of the death of a son and the head of the family) were swept away by an enthusiasm for death. A revolutionary unanimity was reconstructed within the family thanks to the male line's collective departure for the front (father and son). Inside the Bassidj, they discovered a unanimity that transcended the generation gap, as it allowed everyone to escape the breakdown of revolutionary unanimity in an atmosphere of morbid fraternity that denounced the world and its turpitudes in the name of a purity that could never be attained in life.

In psychological terms, members of martyropathic families were much more out of touch with reality than families where only the son joined the Bassidj and broke with his family, which still had strong links with real life. In general, families remained in touch with reality by preserving life in their midst, whilst simultaneously mourning the death of their sons. In martyropathic families, in contrast, it was not just the sons but almost all the men of the family who left. Their collective martyrdom allowed their parents to overcome the generation gap and to collude with their young men in a shared world they experienced as a reconstructed family unit untouched by the traumatic destruction of society.[40]

Just as some families were particularly prone to martyropathy, certain regions produced many young men with a vocation for martyrdom. They included Nadjaf-abad in the province of Isfahan, where many families 'gave' the Revolution several martyrs and, in some cases, most of their sons. Several explanations can be put forward to account for this phenomenon, which affected towns near Isfahan, which was itself a pole for development and industrialisation under the Shah's regime. In historical terms, the province of Isfahan was the official centre for the propagation of Shi'ism in Iran, after the Safavids established it as their capital in the seventeenth century. Many towns in Iran define themselves in terms of the symbolic differences between them and neighbouring urban agglomerations, and the rivalry between Nadjaf-abad and the city of Isfahan is notorious. The inhabitants of Isfahan were suspected by those of Nadjaf-abad of being calculating hypocrites, whereas they regarded themselves as being honest and generous. The town of Nadjaf-abad therefore used its martyrs to prove its superiority over the regional capital of Isfahan. What was in everyday life a matter of symbolism became an actual fact during the period when martyrdom was in vogue. What is more, Ayatollah Montazeri, who was Khomeini's dauphin before he was deposed, originally came from a village of Nadjaf-abad and many young men from the town and the surrounding area joined the Bassidj because that was their way of demonstrating their loyalty to Montazeri, and therefore the regime.

In the great urban centres, the Bassidj was essentially an important means of channelling the mental confusion of the young into a culture of morbidity, as opposed to the polis or even society. Revolutionary youth took their revenge on what they saw as a profoundly unjust, cynical and 'egotistical' society by joining the Bassidj. In small towns, in contrast, communitarian cohesion had not been undermined to the same extent. Their young people felt no hatred for society and remained part of it, because their communitarian solidarity had not been challenged by the deracination and the sullen class antagonism seen in the great urban centres. The Bassidj played an important role in the socialisation of the young in towns where they had been left to their fate, or in other words in the great cities where there was no longer any feeling of solidarity with the rest of society, and where the young felt excluded because they had been 'disinherited' and oppressed. In those zones, the

Bassidj gave them an anti-social sense of identity. In small communities with a high level of cultural homogeneity, in contrast, the Bassidj became an extension of the community, giving it the blessing of both Islam and the state, and sanctioning young people's commitment to defending the Islamic fatherland.

In regions where the Shah's modernisation had already undermined communitarian structures, the emergence of martyropathic individuals signalled the weakening of the communitarian order and the advent of the 'individual-in-death'. It was a wild and uncontrolled way of managing identity. The subject took responsibility for his own death and, at the same time, used the state to construct a neo-communitarian identity. It appears to have been great urban centres like Teheran and Isfahan that produced martyropathic individuals. Relatively unmodernised regions that had been spared the transformations brought about by the imperial regime kept their distance from the Revolution in general, and from martyropathy in particular. This appears to have been the case in Baluchistan and Sistan in the southeast of Iran, and of Kerman in the south. In these regions, young candidates for martyrdom were much less zealous than elsewhere.[41]

### The new body and its discontents

The martyropath's relationship with his own body and blood reproduced the schizoid relationship that existed between a real society in which the Revolution had become bogged down, and his subjectivity, whose greatest ambition was to create a utopia. As there was no possibility of realising that utopia in this world, martyropaths concluded that they might as well go into exile to get away from it. This renunciation of the world was the result of a specific form of violence: rather than renounce the Islamic utopia, the believer renounced life, which he regarded as an obstacle to the realisation of Islam. The relationship between body and blood followed the same logic. His blood must leave his body and must be spilled, just as the true Muslim left the world and lived outside it throughout his martyrdom. Blood was to the body what the Ego was to the world: they had to separate, consummate their rupture and free one another from the impure confusion of life.

The nature of the body and blood of the martyropath, who had been driven to despair by the disintegration of the Revolution, changed as the revolutionary movement's model fell apart. Everything that had been kept in a state of cohesion and fusional unity during the revolutionary dawn became dissociated and disintegrated. The relationship between body and blood, which was once incarnate, became distended as its atomised elements took on a morbid meaning that was in perfect keeping with the necrophile religiosity of martyropaths who had been adopted by the state, as personified by Khomeini.

The body of the Iranian martyropath was affected by a deep feeling of sinfulness. A ternary relationship was established between body, blood and sin. If the body was to be purified, it must rid itself of its blood. Similarly, the subject had to part from his body if he was to redeem his sins. So long as it was inside his body, his blood was a burden just as his sins were a burden to his soul. Salvation meant casting off that burden. This was in reality an act of dissociation: the body evacuated its blood and dissociated itself from it; in doing so, it cast off its sinful burden and became pure because it was lighter. The Ego's burden of sin and the body's burden of blood were of the same nature: sin weighed down the soul, and blood weighed down the body. War provided an opportunity to cast off the burden of sin thanks to the bloody suppression of the body. Why was the blood that poured from his body associated with the salvation of the martyr? Because his blood sustained him and gave him life so long as it circulated through his body, and it was therefore a source of impurity. But as soon as it escaped the body, it put him to death and thus became a source of purification. Purification could come only from death, from a violent break with the world. Blood could therefore be given two diametrically opposed meanings, depending on whether it was associated with life or with death. If it was associated with life, it took on a negative and sinful meaning; associated with death, its meaning was positive and salutary.

Blood was transformed into a morbid principle by using the cultural schemata of Shi'ism, in which the blood shed at Karbala by Husain, his family, his half-brother Abbas, his sons Ali Akbar and Ali Asghar provide a model for martyropaths. But these schemata were in fact detached from the cathartic meaning they once had, and were then re-ritualised and restructured in morbid ways. The young revolutionaries initially wanted to spill the blood of the Iraqi enemy who was trying to invade their Islamic country and to overthrow the revolutionary order. But that stage was left behind when the Revolution became bogged down, when the hope that the utopia could be realised began to fade, and when a mortiferous religiosity replaced the optimistic religiosity of the early Revolution. The thirst for blood was now unquenchable but had no specific object. It no longer differentiated between self and other. Everything began to look the same: being slain and slaying, killing and being killed, taking one's own life or that of the Other, self-annihilation and the annihilation of the world in the same apocalyptic movement. Reality became one-dimensional, identity became heteronomous, and that made it easier for the Islamist state to indoctrinate and manipulate its young martyropaths.

### The vogue for martyrdom

The vogue for martyrdom can also be analysed in terms of fashion: the wish to imitate the other in death was a constant feature of young people in the revolutionary movement because it allowed them to take on a collective identity, to look different to others, and to establish a new hierarchy of the heart rather than a social hierarchy. The principle of imitation was a reflection of a culturally unified and homogenised society in which traditional hierarchies based upon distinct and well-defined identities were being called into question. Iranian society was experiencing a painful birth, and new social relations were being defined in terms of the individual's ability to imitate its young martyrs. A new 'individual-in-death' was being constructed.

Fashionable figures were sanctified in a rigid form which was neither ephemeral, as they are in disenchanted societies, nor immutable (or perceived as such), as they are in old societies that are dominated by tradition. One of the holiest figures was that of Khomeini. In the past, he might have been a saint, or the founder of a sect or schism. As it was, he became a figure of the Sacred, as defined by the notion of a 'quasi-sainthood'. He became the 'Imam', which was a neologism in his specific case as the term's meaning alluded to the implicit and ambiguous sainthood of the historic leader of the Revolution. The expression 'imam' once meant 'prayer leader' (*imam jamat*), the chief official appointed by the state to lead a town's main mosque (*imam jome*), someone descended from the Prophet's family (one of the twelve *imams*) or the descendant of an *imam* (*emâm zâdeh*).

Khomeini was recognised as a being who partook of both this world and the next, and who connected the two in a way that precluded the traditional transcendence of the sacred. Because he was a quasi-saint, he secularised religion by creating an exceptional and ambiguous form of mediation between the two worlds. Unlike the traditional *ulama*, he spoke directly to the 'people'. His charisma differed from the *baraka* of the traditional Shi'ite holy man.[42] He was part saint and part man of the law, but not, unlike the twelve Imams, an exclusively holy being. He was, however, descended from them in some ambivalent way which his followers refused to make explicitly clear. He could therefore be many things at once: head of state, doctor of the law or guarantor of a Revolution that had gone adrift. He helped to create a world that was making the transition to modernity and therefore operating with mental categories in which a new type of fashion – a destabilised form of the sacred – became an essential dimension of the affective life of the young. He became the model they imitated, even though the distance between him and his young imitators was, in their eyes, incomparably greater than that between fashionable stars and their fans in the West.

The destabilisation of the sacred could be seen in young bodies inscribed with the 'fashion' for martyrdom after the Revolution. The worsening war and the violent way in which some actors renounced the world led to a real vogue for martyrdom. This occurred in a specific situation. The Revolution had failed to achieve its utopian goals, but young people were not ready to admit that it had been a failure. They concealed its failure and it was their rage – half obvious and half hidden – that gave birth to martyropathy. For their part, the martyropaths went on pursuing the revolutionary utopia of an Islamic society in which inflexible justice and the unity of hearts would prevail, and despised the real world in which those ideals were falling apart day by day. Being unable to realise them in this world, the martyropaths would realise them in their death, and in the expectation of the world to come. This gave rise to a principle of morbid individuation that spread throughout a collective movement. The vogue for martyrdom spread because it was so widely imitated. For its part, the government did all it could to stage it in the form of ceremonial displays of mourning and repentance and encouraged its imitation by dramatising it. The martyr's self-destruction became a model that could be imitated by many young people who were trying to construct their identity in a tumultuous context in which the certainties of the past no longer existed.

Working-class youths took on a 'disinherited identity' that degenerated as the movement fragmented into a tyrannical Hezbollah identity that saw the repression of deviants and 'the Westernised' as the cure for their impossible social promotion. Emulating and imitating those who denounced 'counter-revolutionaries' also became something of a vogue.

As revolutionary effervescence gave the failure of the Revolution an apocalyptic tone, young people began to acquire a truly morbid *habitus* and, for a few years, the craze for martyrdom knew no bounds.

In this context, the fashion for martyrdom became a collective phenomenon in which individuals participated in death by emulating, imitating and outbidding one another in a way that was reminiscent of fashion phenomena in general and the fashion for certain clothes in particular. There were, however, two differences. First it was not really to do with clothes and was the product of a semiology in which the body was the support for signs of death and not clothes. Second, society was living through the tragic situation of revolution and war, and the fashion for martyrdom did not have the deliberately non-serious simulacra that characterise fashion in non-revolutionary societies that are at peace. On the contrary, it was a 'deadly serious' fashion because there were no simulacra.

There was one difference between men and women. In terms of clothes, the female equivalent to the somatic aspect in men found its field of application in the veil. This was because women's bodies were not admitted to martyrdom: they could die a martyr's death as they cared for the wounded on the field of battle, but they could not join the Bassidji brigades and physically fight the Iraqi enemy. Women's bodies were specular, whilst men's were incarnate. With their headscarves and veils, women's bodies were supposed to reflect men's desperate rage and desire to fight. They became fighters by proxy.

For those, mostly adolescent or post-adolescent, who really wanted to play games, fashion had a specific meaning. They started a party in which the game of exposing themselves to death gave rise to joyful emulation and a frivolity as everyone tried to outdo everyone else. Their state of mind was not dissimilar to the simulated and artificial seriousness of ordinary followers of fashion. In their case, martyrdom was almost a celebration of danger, and accepting danger was a form of self-assertion. Both imitating others and adopting a frivolous attitude towards death were ways of taking this to extremes. The angry despair of the martyropaths was replaced by the joyful unconcern of playful martyrs for whom the heroic act of confronting death was a way of increasing their youthful vigour, their feeling of immortality and their foolhardiness. It was this superabundance of life that led them to imitate others. Martyrdom was a way of defending the Islamic nation against the enemy, but it was also a way of playing a game in which ordeal by death became a joyous fashion in a time of war and crisis when life was not worth very much anyway. Gambling with death fused with the joy of living in a collective shared excitement. Imitating others encouraged them to raise the stakes and they put their lives at risk as though they were playing Russian roulette.

Just as the function of the phenomena of fashion is to allow members of a group to recognise one another and to construct an identity of their own, these angry but disconcerted revolutionaries found their martyropathic identity in the Bassidj, and acquired a special status by dying for the cause of Islam. Martyropathy thus created a new elite by inverting the subaltern status of the disinherited who had been pushed to the bottom of the social ladder. They became superior beings who were different from the rest. They were the vanguard of a warrior aristocracy that traced a line of demarcation between those who were afraid of dying and those who wanted to die. They were different from the rest of society, which was doomed to be impure, because they had acquired an elite identity defined in terms of their deadly purity.

The phenomenon of imitation played a major role in the Bassidj, where the wish to follow the example of the martyropaths and to 'take their path' was constantly present. As with the phenomena of fashion, the ceremonial aspect was of prime importance. A symbolic dimension that was endangered in the towns, and amongst young people who were the victims of destructuring, was given a new lease of life. Being unable to invest their ardour in building a new world because revolutionary war and disorder made that impossible, the actors invested the field of holy death. The fashion for martyrdom became a way of standing out from the crowd because it was based upon collective passion and particularly despair for many young people. That despair was its tragic breeding ground.

### Avatars of violence

The violence generated by martyropathy was indissociable from its inscription in the Bassidj, even though post-revolutionary despair existed before the organisation was founded. The Bassidj channelled the rage of the young martyropaths, the playful young martyrs' desire to join in the party, and the opportunists' quest for social promotion into anti-social violence. It used them to intimidate and neutralise anyone opposed to the puritanical and repressive turn the Revolution had taken.

We can identify three moments in the unleashing of the violence. Initially, it was the feeling that the revolution was under threat from the enemy that prevailed. The enemy was everywhere and could take many different forms. Supporters of the United States and more generally the corrupt West, the selfish, who wanted an easy, comfortable life (the *mostakbar* or the rich and arrogant), and non-revolutionary Muslims were all enemies. The list grew longer as the gradual failure of the Revolution had to be ascribed to external factors. There was something paradoxical about this enemy. On the one hand, it was the fact that the enemy was all-powerful and could appear anywhere that made the failure of the revolutionary utopia plausible; yet as the enemy took more and more different forms, the more the true revolutionary had to renounce his ideals so as to attend to the most urgent things first to save the Revolution. Ultimately, saving the Revolution came to mean renouncing revolutionary ideals on earth. There came a point when, because it had to limit its ambitions and postpone the realisation of its utopia, the Revolution no longer had any vocation here on earth: all concrete achievements had to be postponed indefinitely. At this point, death became the only thing capable of proving that the Revolution would last. It was the only thing that could prove that the revolutionary subjectivity could survive the destruction of its utopia. It was as though death were the void left by the gradual disappearance of everything that once gave a meaning to the Revolution. It was the only plausible project in a revolution that no longer had any vocation upon earth: for the young martyropaths, the world had become uninhabitable. At this third stage, both Self and Other were guilty. That legitimised the project of annihilating the group in order to achieve 'self-purification'. In this apocalyptic situation, which lasted for most of the eight-year war, destructive acts against the world became the true believer's only hope of salvation. Revolution no longer had any constructive vocation in this world. It now took the form of a desire for destruction that extended to Self and Other alike. Being part of a worldly totality, life itself was subject to obloquy. The struggle against life itself became as important as the struggle against the enemy because life was an insidious form of impurity. The violence that was once focussed on the enemy and the counter-revolutionary now targeted the subject: there was no distinction between the revolutionary actor and his neighbour, or between friends and enemies.

## The Bassidji model breaks down

Two major events formed the prelude to the breakdown of the Bassidji model. The end of the war denied the martyropath faction the ability to die a martyr's death and to go on confusing suicidal wishes and beatification. When Khomeini died shortly after the end of the war on 4 June 1989, the last groups of martyropaths lost the support of a charismatic leader who allowed them to use their deaths to mask the tragic bankruptcy of the Revolution.

The length of the war had given the martyropath's passion a free reign and it had spread through mimetism, but it gradually faded as it came into contact with a reality in which there was no room for utopias. The real world gradually gained the upper hand and the Revolution lost its energy as it came into contact with the parallel economy and the black market, or in other words with an everyday life in which revolutionary abnegation inexorably cooled. It now came into contact with the usury of a new elite that proved to be as venal and as 'out of touch with the people' as the elite of the Shah's day. Young people originally rose up against the down-to-earth realism of their parents and strove to preserve a revolutionary Islam by joining the Bassidj. Their enthusiasm for holy death was gradually transformed into a cynical detachment. Everyday life taught them to adopt an ambiguous attitude towards the new government. The ideology of sacrifice and abnegation that gave it its legitimacy came into conflict with the boundless egotism of an individualism that had 'gone wild'. Individual ends were the only legitimate ends, and revolutionary slogans, which were increasingly devoid of any substance, were used to pursue 'basely material' interests. During the first years of the Revolution Hezbollah's young members wore revolutionary 'half-beards' or badly shaved stubble to distinguish themselves from both the long, bushy beards of traditional pietists and the clean-shaven faces of Westerners. Their stubble now made them look devout even though they were involved in illegal forms of commodity speculation (dollars, frozen meat, electrical appliances). Those who had left the Bassidj exploited their past membership to find sinecures by specialising in the supply and distribution of goods in a society where shortages and the difference between official prices and those on the open market allowed them to make big profits. A businessman who had the support of the Bassidj or one of its many revolutionary organisations had a major advantage over his competitors. An increasing number of individuals owed their economic success to their membership of the Bassidj, the Pasdaran army or the Construction Crusade and private enterprise. In the long term, this neo-nepotistic exploitation of the post-revolutionary state led to the frustration of the majority of young Bassidji, who could not use their abnegation as a means of getting rich. Marginalised and reduced to economic exclusion, the majority of the young people left to their fate by the Bassidj when the war ended formed a group of malcontents. As time went by, their grievances found expression in spontaneous and sporadic revolts that the government was able to put down without any difficulty.[43] As a result the government lost its legitimacy in the eyes of many of those people who had once spearheaded the Revolution, some of whom had joined various radical groups affiliated to Hezbollah because they rejected the 'realists' who were demanding that Iran overcome its timidity and open itself up to the outside world.

Many who had fought in the Bassidj or the Pasdaran army went on to work for the state, either in the administration, its industrial structure or in the private sector. Few of their revolutionary ideals could stand the test of time: freedom ('post-Islamist' intellectuals gradually gained a form of freedom under surveillance and with some room for manoeuvre after the death of Khomeini), economic independence (Iran is still largely dependent on oil at every level of its economy), Islamic purity (private space became a place for the transgression of all the taboos that were respected in public but were infringed when the government's vigilance was relaxed for a moment), the Islamic revolution's vocation for worldwide export (a pro-Iranian Hezbollah militia was created in Lebanon, but the experiment failed everywhere else). All that remained of the revolutionary slogans was the repression of women, who became a scapegoat, and ostentatious, but increasingly meaningless, demonstrations and parades organised by the government's new clients.

### Conclusion

The origins of the various figures of martyrdom in Iran lay in the war and the progressive collapse of the Islamic utopia. Impotent and frustrated, the first revolutionary generation witnessed economic regression, the brain drain, the destruction caused by the war, and the appearance of a new and venal elite that was the embodiment of the antithesis of the revolutionary virtues of abnegation and devotion. The death of Khomeini sealed the fate of those actors who were prepared to die for the Revolution. A new generation appeared on the scene, and it was no longer fascinated by martyrdom. Less than

20 years after the Revolution, the reformist cleric Mohamad Khatami was elected to the presidency of the Republic in 1997. He represented two generations: a revolutionary generation that had become cynical after two decades of an ideology that had no real basis, and that of the children of a revolution in which they played no part but who still suffered its negative effects on the economic and social levels.

The new generation's major concern was individual freedom in the face of constant repression on the part of the organisations that maintained Islamic morality (the militias of the Bassidj, the Monkerat), freedom of speech in the face of a hierarchy that had confiscated freedom in the name of fidelity to the Revolution, and upward social mobility in a situation where the economy had no dynamism and was suffering under the weight of privilege and state interference.

In this conjuncture, martyrdom was at best a marginal theme in society. No one was interested in it. Notions such as Islamic civil society (*djâmé; éyé madani e eslâmi*), the separation of religion and society, social tolerance (*tasâholl, tasâmoh, modârâ*), freedom for men and women, the rejection of puritanism and a desire for individual emancipation were becoming more important. Three major movements were active in society: the student movement, the women's movement and the intellectuals' movement.[44] Each demanded, in its own way, an end to the ideology of martyrdom and demanded the opening up of the political stage. In its turn, the new society called into question the image of the diabolical West, and the representation of the self as the positive pole in a Manichaean relationship in which the West was the negative pole.

Theocratic Islam (*Velayat-e faqih*) was in turn challenged by the intellectuals, some of whom spent several months in prison. A new conception of Islam emerged and challenged revolutionary subjectivism, its extremism and its radical and strict version of Islam. Yet this new society found it difficult to put forwards its new ideals. In the political system bequeathed by the Revolution, those who enjoyed democratic legitimacy, like the President of the Republic, Parliament and the municipal councils, had no power, and non-elective institutions (the Guide of the Revolution, who is elected by a group of clerics, and the Council of Guardians which verifies the Islamic nature of the laws passed by Parliament and the juridical apparatus) held most power.[45] Political stagnation and the privileges associated with theocratic power helped to perpetuate a system whose legitimacy was increasingly contested by the younger generations.

The vast majority of people in Iranian society now reject radical ideologies that attempt to promote a closed and theocratic society, and an Islamist activism based upon martyrdom and its tragic and heroic vision of life. We are now witnessing the gestation of new forms of individuation and the emergence of a new generation that knows nothing of the pathos of martyrdom and its political and religious radicalism.

## MARTYRDOM IN PALESTINE

Martyrdom in Iran, Algeria and Palestine obeys an internal logic born of the frustrated ambition to have a nation whose existence has been denied. As we have seen, the Iranian martyr was primarily defined by his relationship with a nation that mobilised Islam in order to bring the revolutionary utopia into existence. The utopia could not hold out against reality and the disenchantment of its actors for very long. As it fell apart, the utopia led to martyrdom, which was the form taken by revolutionary subjectivity during a crisis in a context of war. Palestinian martyrdom does have some similarities with the Iranian version. Islam is harnessed to the task of nation-building in both cases. But unlike the Palestinian nation, the Iranian nation did exist, albeit in the utopian and Islamic form lent to it by Iranian martyrs in the course of a war that called into question both the survival of the Revolution and its political meaning. In the case of Palestine, by contrast, the issue confronting the movements that preach martyrdom is a nation that can only be conjugated in the future tense. When secular organisations like Al-Fatah failed to mobilise the youth of Palestine, Islamic groups like Hamas and Islamic Jihad took over the task of building the nation.

There is a second difference between the Iranian and Palestinian cases. In Iran, the state played a vital role, whereas the embryonic state that exists in Palestine has been more or less marginalised by movements that are in conflict with it, and which challenge its monopoly on violence. What is more, the meaning of holy death changed between what is conventionally called the first Intifada during the period lasting from 1987 to 1993, and the second Intifada. The latter began in October 2000 and has caused many more deaths.

There are noticeable differences between the two movements.[46] The first combined the theme of nation-building with that of self-assertion as a Muslim. Martyrdom played an important symbolic role, but it remained subordinate to the broader goal of building a nation that sought to assert its political and cultural autonomy with respect to an Israeli state that was incomparably more powerful but that had been forced to recognise the independence of Palestine by the pressures exerted by its young people, according to the Palestinian perception. The young stone-throwers, who were the emblematic figures of the first Intifada, testified to the possibility of a Palestinian victory over an Israel that opposed the building of a sovereign Palestinian nation. The self-image of the young people who were challenging Israel's hegemony was basically positive. In the first Intifada, a number of things were combined: the challenge to Israeli power went hand in hand with a challenge to the patriarchal structures of the great Palestinian families and, at least at the beginning of the movement, with feminist demands on the part of the women involved in it. The latter dimension was quickly suppressed for complex reasons that had as much to do with the crisis in Palestinian society as with the way families were structured.[47] Women were, moreover, excluded from the movement's decision-making processes from the outset. Women's autonomy would have been an obstacle to national unity and the permanence of a communitarian vision in which the ideal unified society was a mirror image of the patriarchal family.

The first Intifada gave everyone the feeling that they had recovered their honour. The many forms of humiliation experienced by Palestinians had created a debased self-image: annexation by Israel, Israel's crushing economic and military superiority and its more open society made the enemy an inaccessible ideal. Palestinians felt ashamed because they could not emulate it. Israeli television and radio showed a society that was not simply based upon anti-Palestinian feelings. They also showed a society that was producing, creating and inventing new modes of being, whilst Palestinian society, which had been shaken by so many crises, had adopted a rigid posture and a vision of both itself and its Other dominated by bitterness, whilst the pain of having lost ancestral lands had been a trauma for which there was no cure. The only weapon Palestinians could use against their superior and pitiless enemy was a feeling of offended dignity and a wounded identity. The first Intifada allowed Palestinians to overcome this crushing sense of inferiority and deep shame. It sometimes crystallised in violent flareups or outbreaks of terrorism, but these expressions of protest never lasted very long. Young people who had lost their self-esteem redeemed their honour by defying the incomparably more powerful Israeli army. They acquired a new dignity in their own eyes. That is why recourse to martyrdom was much more episodic than in the second Intifada that broke out almost ten years later.

The second Intifada (Intifada al-Aqsa) was the result of the setbacks and failure of the Oslo Accords. They created a Palestinian authority that was not a real authority in a fragmented, even shattered, country and gave birth to a schizoid society.[48] Those in power were venal and, for the most part, devoid of scruples. They allowed themselves to do what they forbade others to do, and made nepotism and clientelism the basic principles of a fragmented and heterogeneous government. In doing so, they ensured that they had a monopoly on lucrative trade. In the eyes of Palestinians, the same unscrupulous leaders became the Israeli army's lackeys and did its dirty work for it by arresting Hamas militants and anyone who challenged Fatah's hegemony, which was believed to be its reward for its subservience to Israel. The period between the first and second Intifadas saw the unfolding of the tragedy of a society being established in a peace that was not its peace by a government that did not represent it, and which was perceived to be dissolute and greedy. The outcome was economic decline and, what was more important, moral despair. The dream of a nation in the land of their ancestors had been no more than a parody. The land had been mutilated by Israeli settlements. Palestine was an aborted nation dominated by a semblance of a state whose leaders' main concern was to refuse to allow society to have a political role and to help its authorised representatives get rich.

Both tensions between Israel and Palestine and the nature of the Palestinian leadership meant that there was no political solution to Palestine's problems in the eyes of the Palestinian youth, and martyrdom therefore became a way of totalising life. In a context where Palestinians did not have the means required to enjoy even elementary forms of citizenship, and where the land had been broken into pieces and reduced to a multiplicity of localities, each with a different political status, and therefore could not crystallise the national feeling that presupposes a homogeneous territory inhabited by one people, building a nation was impossible. Martyrdom, in contrast, did have some of the attributes of a non-existent citizenship. Because it functioned as an act of witness, it engendered a shared feeling of belonging to one nation. Its sacrificial rites gave a feeling of abnegation in the context of war against a foreign state, and its Islamisation made the absent fatherland the one place where the sacred could be invested.

This totalisation was characterised by an inversion: life becomes death. The inversion was bound up with the realisation that the Palestinian nation could not be built in this life. This was experienced subjectively and then amplified by a society that was in turmoil during periods when the tensions were at their highest between the Israeli army and the Palestinians. This feeling made the difference between the first and second Intifadas. During the first, it was believed that the nation could be built if the young were mobilised and if the traditional power structures of Palestinian society itself were challenged. The second was increasingly marked by a pessimistic worldview which more or less implicitly admitted that the nation could not be built. At this point, a holy death that both guaranteed the martyr a place in Paradise and destroyed part of Israeli society became the only tenable solution. It was this political impasse that gave rise to a new form of radical martyrdom amongst the Palestinian *shebab* ('young people'), as well as in other sectors of the population that had not been directly involved during the earlier period.

If we look for the link between the different configurations of martyrdom in Palestine, Iran, Algeria or Egypt, to limit discussion to those cases, we always find an element of defiance. In the case of Palestine, the defiance can take a number of different forms. It is, first of all, a way of showing Israelis that they too are vulnerable, despite their superior firepower and military capabilities. Second, the defiance takes on an introverted dimension. It is directed at the family and at relatives, and is intended to persuade them to support the martyr. As his act brings them glory, families can scarcely criticise the behaviour of a young man who has sacrificed his life for the Islamic fatherland. The challenge is also addressed to Palestinian society: holy death will make it possible to build a nation that cannot be built by the living. The defiance also has, finally, a sacred dimension. Martyrdom is compatible with Islam and therefore purifies the martyr by guaranteeing him a place in Paradise. A martyr's death does not signify the end of his existence; it is a prelude to a new life, and this greatly attenuates the terrifying nature of death and the horror of dying for the nation. The challenge is an act of witness addressed to a specific world. It is not addressed to America or to either the friends or enemies of Islam. It is addressed to a sui generis community the martyr is trying to convince thanks to the fascination of the tragic and heroic nature of his act. The challenge also has a reflexive dimension, and is addressed to the Self: it is an Ego that is dying and giving its personal aspirations a meaning at the extreme point of death. Holy death therefore has four constituent dimensions: a relationship with the Self, with the Other (family, society or Israeli enemy), with the world, and with the sacred.[49]

Martyrdom is the result of several intentionalities and not just one. Martyrs' testaments and various eye-witness accounts reveal the explicit reasons that lead Palestinians to embrace sacred death. One reason that is often invoked is the feeling of 'having had enough' of a situation in which economic decline and political heteronomy result in a growing loss of dignity. In some cases, the factor that triggers the decision is the death of a friend or family member who has either died a martyr's death as a suicide bomber or has been killed in a clash with Israeli soldiers. In others, a sudden decision might be linked to a family crisis or to the rejection of what is seen as a life of degradation. Although the vast majority of martyrs are members of political organisations, there are also isolated cases in which individuals take the decision to die on their own, and without consulting any particular group.

It is the historical circumstances surrounding the establishment of the Hebrew state that make the case of Palestine so distinctive. The foundation of Israel was profoundly traumatic for the Palestinians, many of whom had to go into exile. The predominant Israeli view is that the Jewish state was born of the massive collective trauma of the Shoah. Both sides interpret history through the prism of their respective traumas, and cultural forms of interpretation and dialogue based upon an understanding of the other become inoperative. Israelis place the emphasis on the authority of the Bible, the establishment of a new state and the forms of violence that followed the occupation of their new land, which was theirs long before the Palestinians took it over. Palestinians place it on the theft of their land, and the feeling that the Israeli enemy has the West and especially America on its side.

### Everyday life

One of the main causes of the repeated uprisings and the increasingly radical attitude of a fraction of Palestinian society lies in day-to-day living conditions. The state of Israel dominates it in economic, political, military and symbolic terms. Everything reminds Palestinian society of its inferiority and heteronomy. The subaltern societies of the age of European imperialism recognised the superiority of their colonisers but symbolically neutralised it by strengthening their communitarian ties and keeping a physical distance between themselves and their colonisers. Colonial cities, ways of life, administration and management were divided into segregated zones, each with its own norms and ways of managing day-to-day life. European social cohesion and specificity on the one hand, and the strong cultural identity of the colonised on the other, meant that the *ressentiment* could to some extent be absorbed by social regulatory measures and by the support offered by communitarian structures. Those elements that once guaranteed the stability of colonial life no longer exist. The communitarian forms that regulated the Palestinian population have lost the strength they had two or three generations ago, and the process of individuation prevents it from turning to a collective armature. Spatial segregation has been broken down by both social and symbolic mechanisms. Television means that the imaginary is no longer confined within a closed world, and modern individualism means that submission to Israeli superiority is no longer possible, as it was when a colonial mentality convinced the colonised that their rulers were their superiors and became the psychological prop that legitimised colonialism. Both Israelis and Palestinians are fully caught up in modernity and, at that level, their mentality is that of modern egalitarianism, even though racists on both sides claim to be able to prove the superiority of their own group. They live, in short, in a world that is imbued with modern egalitarianism, whereas social relations between the two sides are governed by a neo-colonialist model.

This phenomenon does not in itself explain the forms the conflict takes on both sides. Certain aspects of the day-to-day lives of Palestinians and Israelis alike fuel the hatred, stir it up and at certain moments make it the element that structures relations between them.

Mental, if not physical, proximity is another important factor. Many young Palestinian men have spent part of their lives in Israeli jails. They have been subjected to beating and even torture, but they have also learned to live and collude with their oppressors. Time spent in prison destroys Israelis' superiority by turning them into enemies who can be ill-treated in the same way as Palestinians. The longer these young men spend in prison, the more they lose their fear of incarceration.

Palestinians watch Israeli television. They sometimes watch it in preference to their own, and secretly admire the freedom of its political debates and the democratic way in which Israeli public space is constituted, and contrast Israel with a Palestinian Authority that is rife with nepotism, clientelism, corruption and authoritarianism. Although Al-Jazeera is their favourite news channel, and Lebanese channels their favourites for entertainment, Israeli television is also consulted and often watched.

Israeli consumer goods also play a far from negligible role in bringing the two populations together. Both the Palestinian leadership and Palestinians in general are often greatly tempted to boycott goods from a country that represses them and denies them the right to self-determination. These attempted boycotts have had little impact. There is too great a disparity between the superior quality of Israeli products and those from the Arab countries and local suppliers. What is more, consuming Israeli products gives Palestinians the feeling that they are on equal footing with Israelis in symbolic terms, that they too are part of a world on which Israel has an exclusive claim, that they too can live like Israelis and therefore become their equals.

Although jobs are increasingly hard to find and therefore increasingly valued, working in Israel also brings Israelis and Palestinians together. Jobs are becoming scarce because of the restrictions on movement and the repeated sealing off of Palestinian territory. For anyone who does not belong to one of the great families, to Fatah's client groups, or who is not one of the 'men from Tunis' who came back from Tunisia with Yasser Arafat in 1994, one of the 'Palestinians abroad' who have come back from exile in Egypt or the Maghreb, or a member of the local mafia, the only alternative is to find work with Palestine's embryonic state sector, where wages are lower and where they are often given thankless tasks. Someone working for the police force takes home the equivalent of US$240, whereas a job in Israel can pay anyone with the right permits between US$800 and US$1,400. The sealing off of the Palestinian territories makes it difficult if not impossible to move around. The identity checks that are made after terrorist attacks and the curfews all make working in both Israel and the territories an uncertain business. When the territories are sealed off, travel to both Israel and the other Palestinian areas is disrupted. Because they cannot reach Israeli markets, perishable goods rot where they lie, and the vicissitudes of Palestinian–Israeli relations mean that trade is always liable to disruption. The authorities often turn a blind eye to informal, and often illegal, trading with Israelis (cars stolen on one side of the road blocks and sold on the other, drug-trafficking, the sale of weapons and alcohol, currency transfers) and this too brings the two sides closer in some senses. Although there is a degree of psychological closeness, it is increasingly impossible to travel, to work or to get through zones where there are more and more checkpoints. Getting authorisation to go through them can mean waiting for interminable hours.

The Israeli army's arrests of young men during their ever more frequent incursions mean that it is impossible for the majority of the *shebab* to lead a normal life, as the slightest hint of activism leads to arrest. The long periods they spend in jail also mean that young men become radicalised in prison, where they fall under the influence of their elders. It was not so much a specific ideology and indignation or the feeling of humiliation that made young Palestinians militant.[50] The explosive mixture of prison, exile, living on the run, the instability of life and the constant need to keep moving to avoid being arrested by Israeli forces give rise to an extremism that can even overcome fear.

The segregation of the Palestinian territories increases as the Israeli army refuses to allow people to move between their different areas, or between them and Israel, by introducing curfews.[51] The feeling of humiliation and worthlessness has therefore become a constant feature of everyday life. After the second Intifada, a combination of this feeling of impotence and the Palestinians' feeling that they were being denied both justice and their rights created a breeding ground for extreme forms of action, and especially for 'suicide bombers'. For men, everyday life was a domain in which there could be no honour. On the one hand, they could no longer provide properly for the economic needs of their families because of the perpetual worsening of the economic situation; on the other, they were constantly impotent in the face of an Israeli army that made them physically aware of their military inferiority. Thirdly, they could no longer move around freely and had no control over their relationship with space. They were reduced to passivity and immobility on what they regarded as their own land. As public space had become a place of dishonour, the home became the place where they could defend their honour against their wives and children, with varying degrees of violence. Men who have been humiliated outside the home will make up for it inside the family. The secular nationalism embodied by Yasser Arafat and his Fatah party have been unable to unite society, if only because of the corruption inside the new government. Islam can restore a feeling of symbolic honour that compensates for loss of face in real life. Arafat's death in November 2004 might open up new vistas in the political field after the Palestinian presidential elections in 2005, but this is far from certain given the deep suspicion between the two societies.

Daily life also plays an essential role in encouraging martyrdom. Because it cannot meet young men's expectations, life both radicalises them and drives them to despair. The fact that Israeli settlers are everywhere, that there are always soldiers on the crossing points they have to use to get to Birzeit University in particular (there are at least three) and that the territories are systematically sealed off makes Israelis a crushing presence for Palestinians. In colonial India or Algeria, it was possible for much of the population to live and die without ever meeting an English or French settler in vast expanses of their land. The Israeli presence in the Palestinian territories rules out that possibility, partly due to the exiguity of the land. The many roads that have been built under Tshal supervision since the Oslo Accords are designed to guarantee the safety of settlers in the Occupied Territories. Palestinian-owned land bordering the settlements is often occupied by the army, and its Palestinian owners cannot work it.[52]

In an economy with an extremely high rate of unemployment (up to 60 per cent or more in the Gaza Strip), the most widely spread feeling is boredom. Between humiliation, anxiety about Israeli attacks (and Israelis have their own form of anxiety about suicide bombers) and the boredom of day-to-day life, there is not much room left for feelings of tranquillity. Love cannot be freely expressed because of Islamic censoriousness, which is emphasised in order to reinforce the sense of unity in the face of the enemy threat. Unlike women, men cannot cry for fear of losing face and looking 'effeminate'. They go out to meet their friends and spend whole days playing cards, smoking hookahs, and then go to bed as soon as they get home. Sleep is preferable to this boredom. Sleep is the best way to forget day-to-day life, the nightmare of punitive Israeli raids and the immobility of time in the absence of any economic or social activity. The news that a young man has been martyred interrupts the stagnation of time and drives away the boredom for a moment, but it also heightens the fear of Israeli reprisals. So they watch television, and especially Al-Jazeera, which shows pictures of Israeli tanks moving into Palestinian towns all day. The only alternative is to watch Lebanese television, which shows programmes sometimes bordering on the obscene. Their lasciviousness and frivolity allow them to alleviate the boredom of a day-to-day life in which there seems to be no future.[53]

Israeli Palestinians introduce an even more ambiguous degree of proximity. They live in an extremely difficult in-between position. They feel themselves to be Palestinian but they possess a nationality about which they feel ambivalent, if only because of the privileges it gives them. When they travel abroad, their Israeli passports give them incomparable advantages and greater freedom of movement. Being Israelis, they are entitled to the same state benefits as other Israelis, with some exclusions and exceptions, including being conscripted into the army and having the right to live in the occupied territories. But in psychological terms they still experience the pain and tribulations of their Palestinian brothers and sisters, even though their attitudes and behaviour are not the same, or at least not for those of the second, third or even fourth generations.

## The vicious circle of violence

The humiliation experienced by Palestinians goes far beyond the symbolic order, even though there is no denying the importance of that dimension. Objective factors give the subjective feeling of humiliation an objective substratum. Water is a major issue in the Occupied Territories. The unequal way it is exploited does Palestinians a great injustice.[54] The Occupied Territories bristle with Jewish settlements, and their numbers continue to rise. The Territories are fragmented into three zones. Zone A, which is Palestinian-controlled, makes up less than 4 per cent of the West Bank, but is home to some 20 per cent of its population.[55] Almost all Palestinian villages and 23 per cent of the West Bank are in Zone B, where the Israeli army is in charge of security and has the right to intervene. Zone C, finally, includes 73 per cent of the West Bank's surface area, uninhabited areas and 'strategic' Israeli settlements. This zone is under Israeli control. The fragmentation of the land is reproduced by the blatantly discriminatory status of its inhabitants, depending on whether they live in one of these zones, in Jerusalem or are part of the diaspora (those who became refugees in 1948, those who were 'displaced' in 1967, and those who have lost their right to lives in the Occupied Territories for administrative reasons all have a different status). It would be impossible to build a viable Palestinian state on such a fragmented territory where Israel has appropriated most of the resources (water is an important strategic issue) without dismantling the settlements. Rather as though they were fortified villages, the settlements are often on hill tops and their inhabitants enjoy the same standard of living as the middle classes of the West. They overlook the Palestinian villages lower down the slopes. The symbolic domination (above/below) is mirrored in an economic superiority that stems from Jewishness and not class relations: Israeli Jews are granted rights denied to Palestinians, who are reduced to a form of neo-colonial inferiority within an apartheid-like system.[56] It is not only Palestinians who reach this conclusion; so do the supporters of the 'Moral Camp' in Egypt.[57]

No matter whether they are the vanguard of a nation whose existence is denied (Palestine) or, as we shall see, of an impossible transnational community (al-Qaeda), the martyrs all have one thing in common: they have a utopia. That utopia can never be completely realised, and the problem is to find a compromise between it and a stubborn reality.

The idea of a national community gives rise to at least two utopias. It may have been impossible to establish a nation because of the presence of a much more powerful enemy, whom the martyrs see as being resolutely opposed to its establishment. That is the case with the Palestinians. Alternatively, there may be a nation whose socio-political system does not correspond to the wishes of the martyr. That was the case in Iran before the Revolution and when Iran was attacked by a Western-backed Iraq in the 1980s. This was also the case in Algeria after 1992, when the elections that had been won by the Front Islamic du Salut (FIS) were cancelled by the military regime. In all these cases, a certain social configuration was being challenged by the proponents of holy death.

The roots of Palestinian martyrdom lie in three independent utopias: the return of all Palestinians to what was their land before the state of Israel was founded; the establishment of a new Palestinian state in Jerusalem; the feeling that the only language Israelis, and especially their army and politicians, understand is brute force, and that they cannot be trusted. Jews are dehumanised and given an inferior status. The point of reference is not the anti-Semitic ideologies of Europe, but the crushing superiority that makes them inhuman because of their excessive use of illegitimate violence. At the same time, some Islamic tenets of the 'impurity' of other religions (and particularly Judaism) are reinterpreted and reinforced in the symbolic struggle against Israel in terms of the absolute antagonism between Muslims and Jews, which is something rather new in Islam. There are three utopian visions on the Israeli side too. The first is that of a Greater Israel, and it has led to the building of more and more settlements in the Occupied Territories. The second is the idea that there is, if American aid is forthcoming, a military solution to the Palestinian problem. The third is the dehumanisation of Palestinians, and Arabs in general, by invoking European colonial prejudices or the attitudes of Jewish communities in North Africa. These prejudices are reinforced through the almost ceaseless antagonism between the Palestinians and the Israelis since the foundation of the State of Israel. Muslims do precisely the same thing.

The difficulties of this situation are exacerbated by the United States' support for the state of Israel and by the way American Protestant Zionists subscribe to the myth that Greater Israel is the Promised Land. Both they and some Jewish Zionist groups claim that there is a theological basis for annexing all of the Occupied Territories in the name of some primal identity. According to this a millenarian view, such annexations will hasten the coming of the Messiah.[58] For similar reasons, the Al-Aqsa mosque must be demolished to allow the third Temple of Solomon to be built. That will pave the way for the Apocalypse, as the Bible foretells.

Palestinian martyrdom is largely the result of a utopian logic that feeds on its own failures. The utopias of the Israeli enemy reinforce Palestinian utopias in a never-ending antagonistic interaction.[59] The outcome is a deadly logic that operates in a vacuum, irrespective of how much death and destruction it might cause. Many Israelis and Palestinians are of course aware of the dangerous nature of this interaction, but their lucidity is powerless against the cycle of mutual violence and counter-violence. René Girard's theses notwithstanding, the vicious circle of rising extremism has not completely blinded the actors involved.[60] The tragedy lies in their inability to reject an action-logic in which passions have the upper hand. Palestinian martyrs fuel Israeli extremism, which in its turn corroborates the deadly premises based upon Israel's refusal to accept the Palestinians' right to existence and to political and territorial independence in a viable state. The outcome is a spiral of death in which both sides discover their identity in their ability to annihilate the other. At times, one or other of the protagonists may have a flash of insight, perhaps simply out of weariness. The confrontation then takes on a cyclical nature.[61] The fascination with self-destruction and the destruction of the Other takes the form of an increasingly tragic crescendo, with each side accusing the other of having broken its word or the moral contract to restrict the violence. It is not only the restricted groups who are always killing each other that are attracted to death. Each side tries to neutralise the other so as to exorcise its own demons. For Jews, the tragedy of the Genocide is played out on a minor scale whenever a Jew is killed. On the Palestinian side, it is the tragedy of *nakba*, spoliation, exile and Israel's expropriation of ancestral lands – either in 1948, 1967 or on so many other occasions – that reactivates the trauma.

For Israelis, the Occupied Territories have a sacred value, and death has been promoted as a sacred value for Palestinians. In symbolic terms, the two are equivalent and they therefore reinforce one another. In both cases active minorities are involved. But both minorities (Jewish settlers and their supporters, Palestinian martyrs and the organisations that support them) share a symbolic vision that takes the whole of society hostage. Society, or at least part of society, empathises with them, shares their prejudices and is powerless to confront them face to face.

The problem is not simply that both parties must drop some of their demands if a lasting peace is to be achieved. They must also give up part of their respective identities. The spectacle of a past in which they were treated unjustly (in the case of the Jews, the Holocaust, in the case of the Palestinians, their expropriation since the foundation of the State of Israel) haunts the present and gives rise to anxiety: they are afraid of the future, but they also fear that a world at peace might heal their wounds. Both the Palestinian martyrs who take their own lives and take with them Israeli civilian victims who are not directly involved in the violence inflicted on them, and the violence used by the Israeli army against Palestinian civilians and the collective punishment it inflicts (the bulldozing of houses, the torture and beating of young men denounced by the Palestinian spies the Israelis recruit and coerce into collaborating with them) create a situation of day-to-day violence that nothing can stop.

The symbolic equivalent of Palestinian martyrdom is neither the Israeli army's formidable ability to repress Palestinians nor the Palestinian spies who give it information about the Palestinian Authority's decisions, but the religious vision of colonisation that leads radical Jews to attempt to create a situation that can never be reversed: they bring into existence Jewish settlements in the very heart of the Palestinian territories. This makes two things impossible.

Palestinians find it impossible to live in peace. Some young people respond to the repressive logic that denies them the right to an autonomous existence by seeking refuge in a beatified death. In Israel, Palestinian terrorism, both in the period leading up to the first Intifada and then in the second Intifada and its suicide bombings, incites the most radical fringes, which are supported by the Jewish state, to build yet more settlements in the Palestinian territories, and even to inscribe their presence on the bodies of their Palestinian enemies by building fortified villages. These are a physical, spatial and symbolic reminder of Israeli superiority. The settlers say that their occupation of the land is inspired by their desire to populate the Holy Land; Palestinians say that Israel wants to take away their ancestral lands. There is a disturbing symmetry about this twofold deadly logic which is, for one side, a defiantly symbolic expression of martyrdom – both psychical and physical – and, for the other, a wish to appropriate and symbolically denegate the other by inscribing a Jewish presence on land inhabited by Palestinians. Both attitudes are sustained by the sacred. The Jewish settlements are founded in the name of a sacred vision of Jewish land, in which Judea and Samaria take pride of place and are an integral part of Israel, as defined in Biblical and hieratic terms. The Palestinian martyr finds his legitimacy in a *jihad* to save the religion of Allah from those who want to dispossess Muslims of their roots in one of the holy lands of Islam. The two logics echo one another. Each amplifies the impact of the other. They reinforce a deadly siege mentality that feeds on the very spectacle of the movements of the other.

Palestinian subjectivity also takes offence at something else, which is partly the fault of Palestinian society and partly the result of Israel's hegemony: the fact that power is in the hands of a Palestinian Authority that has confiscated the embryonic state apparatus and refuses to let the real society have any part in it. Given its current structure, the Palestinian government is made up of elite groups who shared out sinecures between themselves. Their justification for doing so derives from the history of the government's own struggle rather than the legitimacy of the groups that represent it when it comes to the actual management of Palestinian society's day-to-day problems. The corruption of this state and the despotic and patrimonial way in which power is shared within it frustrate the ambitions of young people who are interested in becoming involved in politics, their standard of education and knowledge of the outside world being much better than the previous generation. The continued existence of a government which enjoys little legitimacy and whose only justification lies in the glorious past of a senescent leader and the permanent crisis with Israel makes life even more difficult for the younger generations. Those who have the opportunity to do so leave the Territories and go to live in the West or other Arab countries. Those who cannot, try their luck by retreating into an imaginary that recreates the situation of the exile in Palestinian territory itself. To make ends meet, they become involved in drug-dealing or smuggling or agree, under Israeli pressure, to work for Israel's intelligence services. Whatever the outcome, this is scarcely a glorious project for young people who are trying to assert themselves. Martyrdom is one way of avoiding the dilemma. The case of Khader Gheimat, who worked as a dishwasher in Israel before becoming a suicide bomber to put an end to the rumour that he was working for Israeli intelligence, is symptomatic.[62]

The building of new settlements, the emergence of new martyrs and their commemoration are constant reminders that relations with Israel are characterised by an insurmountable antagonism. On the other hand, it is impossible for the young to assert themselves by becoming involved in the management of social problems because the only way they can play an institutional role is by working for the Palestinian police or intelligence services, or by joining mafia-like networks that are dominated by the acolytes of the Palestinian leadership. Palestinian factionalism is a further source of discontent. Both the groups of young men who join Hamas or Islamic Jihad and family or individual interests create, thanks to the allegiances they involve, tensions that are difficult to resolve. Different political allegiances which, in a democratic society, become an expression of different interests are, in the case of Palestine, a source of opposition that heightens the tension on the ground. The scarcely veiled antagonism between the different Palestinian intelligence services that are fighting for a hegemonic position within the embryonic state apparatus does even more to discredit a government whose main concern is to exploit security imperatives to make sure the money keeps coming in, and to form small closed groups to prevent the incursion of society.[63]

Prior to the second Intifada, the Palestinian Authority often jailed young men belonging to organisations other than Fatah. This caused great frustration to men who, having spent part of their lives in Israeli jails, were now being mistreated by a government that was supposed to be protecting them. Islamist groups like Hamas try, however, to avoid having serious clashes with Fatah, and justify their attitude by referring to the Islamic notion of *fitna* (discord that harms the Islamic community).[64]

The ambiguity of the Oslo Accords now takes on its full importance. In the Israeli view, they should have made it possible to neutralise radical movements preaching violence against the Jewish state so as to arrive at a form of coexistence that would not compromise the status of the Jewish settlements on the West Bank. In the Palestinian view, the Palestinian Authority's recognition of Israel should have made it possible to put an end to the presence of Jewish settlers in the Territories, and to create a viable state and a society that were not dominated by Israel. In their attempt to create such a state, they joined Islamist movements because the PLO was, in their view, too closely associated with Israel and because the corruption of Yasser Arafat and his group, and the way they monopolised power, made it impossible for their demands to find any institutional expression.

Given the various factors that make normal life extremely difficult, if not impossible, the constant double-crossing and the difficult compromises that have to be made by anyone who wants to lead a decent life, give rise to forms of behaviour that can only be described as unstable. This has repercussions on relationships with others, but also on the individual's relationship with himself. An individual may be optimistic one day, and pessimistic the next. Individuals are often totally incapable of taking decisions, and are, in a schizoid way, at once pessimistic and optimistic. Being simultaneously pessimistic and optimistic, they become 'peptimists', to borrow the ironic jargon developed by a Palestinian novelist.[65] The tragedy becomes so absurd that it can become a macabre comedy. Awareness of suffering can lead both some Palestinians and some Israelis to adopt a 'devil may care' attitude. They come to feel that there is no way out of a situation in which every death radicalises both sides and in which vengeance appears to be the inexorable law governing relations on both sides.

After 11 September 2001 and the extension of the activities of al-Qaeda to the heart of the United States things have even worsened. Politically, the conservative government of Sharon has been able to convince the conservative government of the United States that the Palestinian fight against occupation is nothing but mere terrorism, to be fought on a par with other kinds of terrorism that endanger world peace. This has shifted the military balance even more towards Israel and against the Palestinians. But the heart of the problem has not changed and the new threat is that once groups like Hamas or Islamic Jihad have been decapitated, new small activist groups emerge, with which no centralised dialogue will be possible anymore. As a result, there will be a situation of no peace with repressive pre-emptive actions taken by the Israeli army against Palestinian civil society, for the sake of liquidating few members of these 'terrorist' groups. The 'pre-emptive strikes' serve an ideology which encourages radical groups and buys them legitimacy in the eyes of the Palestinian people, in the face of a situation where dialogue is no longer possible.

## Fear and overcoming fear

The first Palestinian generation's relationship with the newly created state of Israel was based upon fear. Its concrete communities turned the avoidance of Israelis into a principle of solidarity. Their more or less traditional mentality described Israelis as formidable beings whose superiority was proportional to their capacity for repression. It was possible for Palestinians to save their dignity by identifying with their Arab brothers and with the pan-Arabism preached by Nasser. That form of Arab solidarity was usually expressed in violent discursive and verbal denunciations of Israel and the West, and it no longer has any credibility in Palestinian society or even the Arab world. When they were able to do so, Arab governments repressed and weakened the Palestinian movement rather than welcoming Palestinians into their countries. Whilst the appeal to an Arab nation may have meant something in the 1960s, it has now lost much of its content. That is why Islam has become the point of reference for the struggle against Israeli hegemony, even though there is no denying that the term 'Islam' contains an element of nationalism. Be that as it may, fear of the Hebrew state and its army was once combined with a feeling of dignity predicated upon a symbolic reference to the Arab world. That world has now had its day, and it can no longer be a source of dignity. As communitarian feelings weaken and as the Arab referent disappears, so too does the Palestinian *shebab*'s feeling of fear. It once feared the Israeli army because adults regarded it as a colonial power that was both of European origin and symbolically invincible. The fact that so many diasporic immigrants had become part of this 'European' civilisation destroyed its 'awe-inspiring' prestige. At the same time, the weakening of communitarian ties within Palestinian society and the modernisation of the mentality of the young made the Israeli military look less formidable. Paradoxically, the fear lessened at the very time when Israel's military might was growing.

For young people who had their baptism of fire as adolescents and who could be neither controlled nor disciplined by their parents, it was as though a veil had been torn away. They learned not to be afraid in the dusty streets as they clashed with heavily armed soldiers who often fired live rounds at them. They provoked the soldiers by throwing stones at them in the hope of drawing them to within machine-gun range. For Palestinians, life did not have the meaning that it had for Israelis and Westerners. Their life-projects were not defined in the same way. The constant fall in their living standards over the previous ten years meant that any hope of improving their lot was illusory, unless they were able to leave the country, as a minority managed to do.[66] The absence of any projects for the future, the inadequate communitarian framework, the loss of parental influence over young boys, the lack of any positive vision of the future exacerbated their intolerable feeling of being humiliated by an Israel that is present throughout the Territories.[67]

Once the *shebab* ceased to fear the Israeli army, they began to defy one another. Israeli soldiers accepted the challenge by pursuing the young men into the Palestinian camps or towns. The *shebab* were not only trying to overcome their own fear, but to achieve a symbolic inversion of the situation by making their more powerful enemy afraid. The most determined of them can take this game of David and Goliath to the point of martyrdom. These young men's response to the sophisticated weaponry of one of the best-equipped armies in the world was to use cheap explosives made with triatomic triperoxide. They are easily made but extremely volatile. Dozens of young members of Hamas have lost their lives making them. The total cost of a belt of explosives is estimated at between $1500 and $4300, depending on the quality of the materials used.[68] That is a derisory sum compared with the cost of deploying the Tsahal in the Occupied Territories.

Having overcome their fear that they might die in clashes over issues grounded in their day-to-day lives, young Palestinians often stress that 'the Jews', or in other words Israeli soldiers, are 'cowards'. This is an act of defiance that attempts to invert the symbolism of a situation in which the military might is on the Israeli side, and the weakness on the Palestinian side. The absence of fear makes those who believe they have God on their side feel heroic, and they are all the more willing to challenge the enemy in that they have so little to lose: they have no worldly goods, no access to the benefits of modernity, and no feeling of pride and dignity.

Palestinians are haunted by the fear of being named as Israel's spies. Being a spy is a source of shame, and the mere suspicion of spying can lead to murder. Becoming an informant for the Israeli intelligence services is a fate that awaits many people who have few other options, but it also allows them to increase their income in an economic situation that is becoming more and more desperate. If word gets out, the individual concerned loses his honour. The 'spy' will be killed or ostracised. He therefore has to avoid being identified. His fear of being found out can lead him to die a martyr's death as he tries, *a contrario*, to prove his patriotism.

This schizoid logic can also take different forms in different sectors of society. There are those who, in the name of a logic of abnegation, join organisations such as Hamas and Islamic Jihad in the hope of dying a martyr's death. They are venerated by those close to them and the vast majority of Palestinian society because they are seen as heroes. Before the Berlin Wall came down, the existence of a bipolar world meant that Palestinians could, at least in theory, enjoy the sympathy of the Eastern bloc, and that even America did not give Israel its unconditional support. Since the Wall came down, the changing international situation has worked to Israel's advantage, and Palestinians see this as another sign of the injustice and partiality of the West, which is spearheaded by America. When they honour their martyrs, they are therefore honouring the whole of their society by proxy, partly to show their opposition to the West and more generally, the world order, dominated by the West. The society is unified, symbolically, in its denunciation of the world through the martyr's choice of breaking off ties with it, the mourners signifying at the same time their approval of his choice and their own refusal to follow him en masse.

This logic of abnegation and devotion to the Palestinian cause can be contrasted with the very different logic of egotism and frantic atomisation. Everyone acts in their own interests and in the interests of their family. The various networks of the informal economy are controlled by official members of the Palestinian regime, its police, its intelligence services, and its intermediary or upper hierarchies. Everyone is, willingly or otherwise, involved in this logic of organised corruption, which brings individuals into conflict with one another at the economic level. The immoral competition makes the poorest even more vulnerable than they were in the past. Organisations like Hamas owe much of their respectability and the esteem they enjoy to the way they provide aid and welfare for the poor. On the one hand, there is a logic of devotion that culminates in death; on the other, there is an insatiable appetite for money that exploits everything that comes to hand, and uses the very mechanisms of Israeli domination and of the corruption of the autonomous Authority to ensure its own survival by sharing the profits of its egotism with family and friends.

During the period between the first and second Intifadas, the situation of the *shebab* became even more tragic for one specific reason. From the Israeli point of view, the Palestinian Authority was not doing enough to control the terrorists and their organisations.

From the Palestinian point of view, the Authority had become the auxiliary that repressed civil society on Israel's behalf from the signing of the Oslo Accords in 1993 to the irruption of the second Intifada. The dominant feeling was that Palestinian forces were doing Israel's dirty work for it by making arrests, beating people and constantly intervening in people's day-to-day lives.[69]

On the Israeli side, the overwhelming impression was that the Palestinian Authority was not doing enough, that it was allowing terrorism to flourish under its protection and that it was colluding in it. The new state was supposed to be an expression of society, but the nepotistic structure of its government made it just as repressive as Israel, and allowed the 'old man' (Yasser Arafat) to establish his personal power and to ignore civil society. The disenchantment was complete. The economic decline of Palestinian society, and the constantly worsening living conditions of the masses left a bitter taste in the mouth. The second Intifada was not merely a challenge to Israeli hegemony; it was also an indirect expression of the Palestinian youth's protest against Palestinian Authority's inability to build a real society by allowing the new generations into politics. This forced the Palestinian Authority to loosen its grip on society and to let the Israelis take care of the repression. For a while, that clarified relations within Palestinian society itself. It also isolated the Palestinian Authority (particularly Yasser Arafat) from the rest of the society, putting the Israeli army and the Palestinian youth face to face, in a situation where the denial of daily life to many Palestinians by Israel increased the prestige of the radical groups and people seeking martyrdom as the sole appropriate answer to repression. Will the death of Arafat bring about radical changes? A lot remains to be done in order to overcome resentment and suspicion on both sides.

### The martyr and his lived experience

The vast majority of 'human bombs' are from Hamas, and a minority from Islamic Jihad. Some of them belong to various branches of the PLO. Hamas is an Islamist group and most of its activities are of an educational, cultural and social nature.[70] It also has a military wing known as the Ezzedine Al-Qassam Brigade. Hamas was originally founded with the encouragement of Israel, which liked the idea of a Muslim faction opposed to the activist PLO. Hamas was once part of the Muslim Brothers movement, but gradually drifted away.

Between April 1993 and the end of October 1998, 22 attacks on Israel were reported.[71] Three-quarters of those responsible lived in refugee camps and had parents or grandparents who left their homes in 1948. They came from large families, with an average of ten or so members. The many unmarried men amongst them lived with their parents, irrespective of whether they had jobs or were unemployed. Four were married and had children. They too lived with their parents.[72]

Not all human bombs are poor. A good number of them are not refugees. There is often a marked difference between their level of education and their professional activities. The Palestinian economy's dependency on Israel makes them fragile: they are turned down for jobs commensurate with their qualifications because these are reserved for Israelis or for other nationalities that are not suspected of terrorism. In the period leading up to the second Intifada, only two attacks were carried out by married men.[73] One of them, Khader Gheimat, worked in Israel. Anwar Sukar was a member of Islamic Jihad, lived in Gaza, and had spent eleven months in Israeli prisons, and one in the prisons of the Palestinian Authority. The other suicide bombers were unmarried, young – between 18 and 27 – and had no family responsibilities.

According to Israeli security sources, Palestinians carried out 42 suicide bombings between 1993 and 2000. Between January 2001 and 5 April 2002 there were 64.[74] The increase can be explained in terms of the repressive policies of the Sharon government, and the growing feeling that the PLO could no longer be regarded as a partner by the Hebrew state. The vogue for martyrdom, which is cyclical, was a further factor, and dead martyrs became models for new martyrs. What was new was the involvement of a few women – more than three to date. The suicide bombers acted as representatives of Palestinian society but without the approval of the Palestinian Authority, whose only justification was that it was the sole Palestinian institutional bulwark against Israeli repression, not popular support for the PLO.[75]

There can be no identikit portrait of the suicide bombers of the second Intifada. The Palestinians involved came from all kinds of social backgrounds, all classes and all age groups. According to Nasra Hassan, none of the 150 or so people involved in suicide bombings had a suicidal profile.[76] None of the martyrs was illiterate, wretchedly poor or even depressed by his surroundings. Many of them belonged to the middle classes and those who were not on the run were in paid employment. Several had jobs, even in the Gaza Strip, where the rate of unemployment is extremely high. They were religious, and most wore beards. A great variety of people were involved, rather as though anger with the Israeli government outweighed middle-class concerns with personal security.

The human bombs belonged, for the most part, to Hamas or Islamic Jihad. They knew that these organisations would, with help from Saudi Arabia, take care of their families when they died. Their families would receive between three and five thousand dollars. Most of the activist organisations' income comes from the Palestinian diaspora and from the Gulf states. It has been estimated that Iran contributes between 20 and 30 million dollars a year. Some charitable Islamic associations also seem to make contributions. In November 2001, the Bush administration added Hamas to its list of terrorist organisations. In December 2001, the United States confiscated the assets of the Holy Land Foundation, which was the largest Islamic charitable foundation in the United States after it was accused of financing Hamas.[77]

Not all the suicide bombers were supported by activist groups. Some, like Daoud Ali, appear not to have belonged to any organisation. He was a quiet 46-year-old family man who, according to his brother, attended the mosque regularly but had not previously had any political involvement.[78] The fact remains that the overwhelming majority are affiliated to some organisation. As he prepares for his martyrdom, the young man is under the supervision of an experienced member of the group. The Koran, and especially those *surahs* that evoke *jihad*, is read assiduously in the week before the bombing takes place. As the fateful date draws closer, the supervision becomes stricter. A written testament and a video in which the future martyr explains his actions are part of the ritual.

How do organisations like Hamas and Islamic Jihad create these bonds of solidarity between young Palestinians? Do they rely upon communitarian ties or are they creating new ones? Forms of local or regional solidarity or membership of a clan or faction undeniably have a role to play in the different groups that make up the *shebab*. But the living conditions forced upon it by the rigours of the Israeli occupation, and the authoritarianism and nepotism of the Palestine Authority provide, as we have seen, the breeding grounds for this new form of solidarity. It is primarily an effect of living in a society that has been in a state of semi-war (the first Intifada), a state of non-peace (in the period following the Oslo Accords of 1993) and then a state of open war (since the beginning of the second Intifada in 1993) with an Israeli army which is incomparably more powerful in military terms and is internationally backed by the only Western superpower, the United States, that makes the solidarity even more tragic and more intense, as much in the Palestinian society as in most of its Western diasporas.

## A personal decision

Whilst Hamas and Islamic Jihad do recruit future martyrs, the fact remains that the demand comes from below. These organisations do not bring any prior pressure to bear and when the blood was being shed – especially in the second Intifada – the supply of martyrs far exceeded the demand for them. That there is an organisational dimension to the 'human bomb' phenomenon is undeniable, but the anthropological dimension, which is bound up with a personal and eminently individual decision, is just as important. The martyrs themselves constantly say so. In their testaments, video cassettes and writing, they often evoke the personal nature of their decisions. Anouar Sukar said: 'It is my decision in this world to be a martyr because God loves us to be martyrs. I hope that He will give me that good fortune.'[79]

It is this feature that makes modern martyrdom so different to that of the sacrificial victim. Modern martyrdom involves an ego. The modern martyr is not, as in the Aztec tradition of Mexico, a sacrificial victim whose 'consent' is obtained thanks to the administration of drugs or highly ritualised techniques of suggestion and manipulation.[80] Although we cannot ignore the fact that organisations like Hamas and Islamic Jihad do manipulate their candidates, they only do so once their decision has been made. This point is essential if we wish to understand the modernity of Palestinian society. In almost all cases, the future martyr is not encouraged to embrace a holy death by his family or community. He usually does so against their wishes, without their knowledge, and as a result of an individual decision. This individuation is inseparable from the aspiration towards nationhood. The candidate for martyrdom seeks death because he lives in a world where the wish to be an individual within a sovereign collectivity cannot be fulfilled in this life.

The religious dimension serves to justify this state of affairs. It is because it acts in the name of Islam that the Intifada can find the resources required to risk lives. The martyr's coveted reward is the bliss of being with Allah. The gates of Paradise are open to those who die 'on the way of God'. By giving their struggle an absolute meaning and making it central to religion, the fighters overcome their anxiety about dying and are, in affective terms, already with the Chosen Ones. They then seek to die at all costs to serve their holy cause.

Places like cafés and discothèques are prime targets because surveillance there is not as tight as it is in the settlements, but also because they are places where young Israelis go to enjoy themselves and have a good time. In the eyes of the martyrs, they are colluding with their parents by joining in festivities from which they themselves are excluded. Their puritanical vision of Islam is reinforced by the bitterness that comes from seeing the very people who refuse them access to the benefits of modernity having a good time. The absence of despair noted by foreign journalists has to be seen in context: the martyr's commitment helps him to overcome the despair he once felt. As his commitment to death becomes more intense, the subject feels self-contained. It is the combination of hatred and despair that allows him to take the final step. Psychiatrists are more alert to the despairing dimension than to the hatred and the social ability to act.[81] And yet, the decision to die a holy death does as much to transcend the feeling of distress as it does to hide it.

One of the major features of this wish to die and to kill the enemy is the feeling of endless animosity, the feeling that the war will never end. There is no future. A collective memory is reproduced by imaginings in which the future is worse than the present, which is itself worse than the past. That is why those who took part in the first Intifada now see it as a golden age, as compared with a present that is in every respect gloomier than the past. They believed that the situation would improve, that they would acquire a new dignity that the long war of attrition with Israel had made highly improbable. Martyrdom promised a more radiant future. It is no longer the portent of a better future. It is a response to the humiliation imposed by an Israeli society that is more highly developed, stronger and richer and which controls every aspect of a confrontation that is at once symbolic and real. Death is the only element that escapes Israeli domination. One of the leitmotifs of the Palestinian martyrs is the claim that their superiority lies in their willingness to die, whereas their Israeli enemies cling to life at all costs and therefore demonstrate that they are inferior to the Palestinians, at least in that respect. They risk their lives in the full knowledge that there is no way out, but they overcome their despair by imagining an apocalyptic situation: being killed and killing as many enemies as possible in a confrontation in which they have no fear of people who live in constant fear of their attacks. They can thus prove that their honour and pride remain intact despite the constant presence of the Israeli army. Because they feel themselves to be powerless in their everyday lives, they become very powerful in death because they can sanctify death by invoking an Islam that has been reworked and reinterpreted to meet the needs of the cause.[82] Islamic organisations do train candidates for martyrdom, but they are not its protagonists. They obviously do manipulate these young people, but they are volunteers.

Martyrdom also serves another function in Palestinian society. Day-to-day life is characterised by 'fiddles' that make people feel dirty. The black market, smuggling, precarious jobs, and petty crime, or a shameful collaboration with the enemy's intelligence services, make them feel like Algeria's *trabendistas* (smugglers) or the 'disinherited' young Iranians (*mostadafine*) whose lives are degrading in economic terms and humiliating in social terms. A religious logic transforms this internalised loss of dignity into a sense of sin and a possibility, through death as martyrs, of redemption. They feel guilty at having been forced into a situation with no way out at a time when, at least for the moment, members of the Palestinian diaspora in Israel or Lebanon with whom they share bonds of friendship or kinship are leading an incomparably happier and more opulent life. Members of the diaspora are not tormented by the shortage of basic commodities that is all the more bitterly resented inside Palestine because it does not affect those who have emigrated to the West. Death allows martyrs to recover their spiritual virginity, to wash away their sins thanks to an enchanted martyrdom that opens the gates of Paradise, even though it does not grant them access to the outside world. A beatifying death releases them from their everyday humiliation. Individual desires for upward social mobility, access to a consumerist modernity and self-assertion are translated into an ambition to be at one with the commandments of Allah. Their one intention is to transcend their own desires so as to espouse the noble cause of God. Dying in the service of Allah makes it possible to transcend the self, to neutralise the pain of an individuality that cannot even begin to socially assert itself, and to attenuate the agony of day-to-day injustice. The arrogant presence of the Israelis and the shameless corruption of the Palestinian Authority's agents combine to make the *shebab*'s life one of desperation. Death allows them to espouse a modernity that cannot be realised in this life but which may perhaps be realised in the next if the candidate martyr succeeds in acting with the purity of intention his action requires. Neo-asceticism also comes into play. Religion helps to justify the renunciation of a world which the *shebab* has, in subjective terms, already renounced in everyday life, covered by the political and economic situation. Martyrs renounce a modernity from which they have always been excluded in material terms but in which they are psychologically involved.

Simplistic claims to the contrary notwithstanding, it is not the presence of *houris* (the transparent and voluptuous virgins of Paradise) that determines the martyrs' desire to go to Paradise. The traditional Muslim imaginary delighted in the magical presence of these sensual women, whose virginity was always renewed and whose role was to satisfy sexual needs that were no longer restricted by the believers' economic position in this world. The modernisation of Muslim societies has given rise to a puritanism that requires the rejection of a Western hedonism which, in the eyes of the believer, is designed to seduce and pervert Muslims. The renunciation of the depraved sexuality of the West is a way of neutralising its ability to tempt and deprave the followers of Allah. The other purpose of this neo-asceticism is to give a united identity to Muslims who want to be on an equal footing with Westerners and cannot be because they are poor and live in those parts of the world where there is no access to modernity in positive terms. Their ostentatious rejection of Western sexuality allows them to control their own desires and to restrict their material and libidinal aspirations. The followers of Allah can turn their rejection of sexuality and consumerism to their own advantage to the extent that their internalised discipline and explicit refusal of hedonism allow them to acquire a strictly religious identity that can be idealised because it resists the unhealthy and satanic attractions offered by the Western tempter. These 'attractions' are all the more unhealthy as they are mostly inaccessible to them in real life.

Once he has formulated his vows and begins his apprenticeship with his organisation, the candidate for martyrdom is in a sense already dead and lives his situation post mortem. He has reached the point of departure, he spends the time that remains to him on earth as though he were awaiting deliverance. If he has doubts, specialists (the Bassidj's mullahs in Iran, two members of Hamas) attempt to strengthen his wavering faith, which might lead him to abandon his task. He then becomes a 'living martyr' (*shahid al hay*).[83] He fasts, says special prayers, immerses himself in the Koran and begs those he has offended for their forgiveness.[84]

During this crucial period when he might revert to a normal way of life or renege on his decision to die, the organisation must keep him cut off from the state of mind associated with everyday life.

Everything is done to make him 'rise above' the petty cares of a life that clings to the perishable goods of this world. He has the feeling that he is about to embrace eternity. The organisation is careful to keep him in this subliminal state. Its members describe his illustrious predecessors: the Prophet's companions or, coming closer to home, the young men who have already achieved martyrdom and who are waiting to welcome him in the empyrean before they enter Paradise.

The type of death the martyr chooses indicates that his decision to die is heavily influenced by contemporary considerations. Laden with explosives, he will be blown into thousands of pieces and will thus reproduce the image of a Palestinian land that has been shattered by the settlements into fragments, each with a different status. Although his body will be shattered into thousands of pieces, his martyrdom will make it intact as is the idealised Palestine in his mind. By ridding himself of a body that has been cut to pieces, he acquires a higher unity that washes away his sins and gives him what he was refused in this world: status, a life, a sublime meaning and, in a word, an individuation that could not be made flesh in a real life in a sovereign nation without a unified territory. When he blows himself up, he takes Israelis with him and reduces them to the situation they have imposed upon his country. Every Jewish settlement is a thorn in his side. Because of the daily searches and raids, he has already experienced fragmentation, mutilation and dismemberment. By blowing his body to pieces, he 'spiritualises' himself, renounces all his ties with life on earth, where it was impossible to understand what it meant to have a fatherland or a country of his own as a metaphorical extension of his body.

In societies that have long been united under the aegis of a nation-state, we often forget that a country is almost an extension of the body and that, as he moves around his country, the individual has a feeling of being at home that is experienced inside the body. We are at one with our bodies in the same way that we experience our identity as something permanent, despite our changing moods and states of mind. A real country means an autonomous administration, a state of one's own, an autonomous mode of organisation that is a reminder of a national identity, or in other words a body of phenomena constructed with reference to a homogeneous geography that is reminiscent of the unity of our own bodies.

For Israelis, the horror of such an inhuman death dehumanises Palestinians still further. For orthodox Jews, the horror is still worse, as their traditions state that a corpse must be completely intact when it is delivered up to God. Explosions in public places that tear apart the bodies of innocents who were, like girls and old people, usually not involved in the repression of Palestinians, make it impossible to bury them intact as it is often difficult, if not impossible, to find all the scattered body-parts. This inability to respect tradition creates problems for practising orthodox Jews, who suffer the additional pain of seeing their loved ones die a profoundly unjust death, that wound even their religiosity. What the human bombs experience as an act of deliverance through death is seen by Israelis as an additional casus belli. The martyrs' inhumanity proves that they do not deserve decent treatment, that the beatings they receive when they are being interrogated are justified, that they cannot be trusted and that the only effective remedy is to expel them from the Occupied Territories.[85]

Martyrdom becomes the emblem of a tainted relationship with the Other, as the death of the Other becomes more important than life itself. The Israeli response to these deaths by martyrdom is an attempt to repopulate the Occupied Territories by both building settlements and using armed repression. This further fuels Palestinian hatred and the feeling of being dispossessed and expropriated. The category that founds the polis is no longer the political, but almost blind hatred. Both parties are caught up in an inexorable vicious circle of violence and counter-violence. Ultimately the protagonists are unable to escape it because they have, like the Greek hero, been blinded by the gods for hubris. No coexistence can be negotiated and so the spiral of violence continues.

### Relations with the family and others

Martyrdom provides believers with an opportunity to make their peace with their families. Palestinian families experience great tensions as a result of their failed modernisation. All these problems come to focus on the family, which becomes a source of friction between young and old, between fathers and sons, and between the various members of what can often be an extended family. Martyrdom provides an opportunity to put an end to these tensions. In their testaments, believers beg everyone to forgive them for their lack of respect. Martyrdom also allows families to profit in this world from the aid they are given by Islamist organisations and Saudi Arabia. The sacrifice ensures that family members will sit at the side of Allah. They will be treated with all the respect due to those whose sons die for the holy cause. In this world, they lead insignificant lives without dignity, but the situation will be reversed in the next world. It is not only the martyr who benefits, but all those who are linked to him by bonds of kinship.

The martyr's act is therefore not addressed to Israel alone. It is also addressed to all Palestinians. While he was still alive, the martyr was an insignificant individual who had no right to a life of dignity. Like the thousands of young Palestinians dumped in the camps or in Gaza, which has one of the highest population densities in the world, they were homunculi and no one cared whether they lived or died. Alive, they were of no importance either to Israelis, who would prefer, at best, to know nothing of their existence, or to the Palestinian government, which saw them as potential troublemakers because they were such zealous followers of the Islamists in Hamas or Islamic Jihad.

A glorious death is the royal road that allows them to escape the mediocrity to which they have been condemned. Their neighbourhood and their society will celebrate their deaths as a major symbolic victory over the enemy. Posters showing photos of them in combat dress and surrounded by comrades singing their praises will make them exceptional beings once they have died. They will be talked about in Israel and, on a broader scale, all over the world. The more Israeli people and military men are killed as a consequence of their martyrdom the more famous they will become. Life becomes stale when it comes into closer contact with the tense situations that are coming to be the norm and that test everyone's mental stability. The example of the Gaza Strip is eloquent. It is 45 kilometres long and 10 kilometres wide, and has a population of 18,000 people per square kilometre. More than 80 per cent of the population are unable to leave it, as access to the West Bank and Israel is restricted by the Israelis. The rate of unemployment is more than 70 per cent. For these young men, death is a glorious escape from a spatial and economic confinement that is literally suffocating them. In Gaza, it is not simply the daily spectacle of deliberate humiliation that is intolerable, but also the feeling of being strangled in an enclave where life is impossible because there are too many people living in a tiny territory, without any occupation or prospects.

### The apocalyptic vision of martyrdom

The logic of martyrdom can give rise to an apocalyptic vision. The martyr leaves this world behind by embracing a holy death because the end of the world is nigh. The basis for the coming Apocalypse will, according to some Palestinians, be laid when martyrdom has been extended to take in the whole of society. The equivalent vision is shared by some groups of Jews and Christian Zionists. They believe that they must hasten the coming of the Messiah by preparing the ground in accordance with the biblical prophecies.

For some 'Zionist Protestants' in America, certain facts have a biblical legitimacy and are portents of the End of Time. The establishment of the state of Israel was a sign foretelling the Second Coming of Christ. The Israeli–Palestinian peace process is an obstacle to the divinely promised coming of the Messiah: the whole of Jerusalem must be under the aegis of Israel for the theological reasons spelled out in the Bible. Blessed be Israel: blessed be they who bless it, and accursed be those who curse it. Palestinians in particular and Arabs in general are pagans, and they represent the party of Gog and Magog. The reign of the millennium is at hand, but the necessary precondition for its coming is that the pagans must perish in the battle of Armageddon.[86]

For some Christian Zionists, several conditions must be met if the Antichrist is to appear before the coming of Christ. This version is close to that of certain Muslims who believe that the reign of Dajjal (the Muslim Antichrist) is at hand and that it will bring us closer to the end of the world and the Resurrection.[87]

According to the biblical predictions, and especially the prophecies of Daniel, Zachariah, and Ezekiel, as reinterpreted by the Christian Zionists, the Third Temple of Solomon must be built. The problem is that the Al-Aqsa mosque stands on the site where it must be built. The mosque must be demolished, as the Bible demands, to prepare the world for the coming of the Messiah.

Some of this vision has been adopted by certain Palestinians, who have made it the touchstone of their experience of the end of the world by replacing the Jewish or Christian Messiah with his Islamic equivalent. In his *The Day of Wrath*, Safar Ibn Abd al-Rahman provides a detailed description of Jewish and Christian Zionisms and their apocalyptic vision, and then makes a contribution of his own.[88] The second Intifada was the beginning of the end of the world, which will be completed by the Apocalypse. The destruction of Israel over the coming decade will be a portent of the Apocalypse to come. Like the Jewish and Christian Zionists, al-Rahman believes that the Holy Scriptures, including the Bible, contain clues left by God that allow us to predict the future, provided that we read them correctly and equip ourselves with the appropriate hermeneutical tools. An appropriate understanding of the Koran and the Hadith (the tradition of the Prophet, as exemplified by his collected sayings) will allow us to see the meaning of the future. To the extent that Christians and Jews reject the light of Islamic prophecies, they are blind and therefore interpret the future in terms of a distorted conception of the Apocalypse. When read in the light of Islam, the biblical texts reveal a content that is identical to that of the religion of Allah. On the basis of *hadiths* borrowed from Al-Bukhari (whose compilation is highly regarded in Sunni Islam), the author of *The Day of Wrath* proves that the beginning of the new era will be signalled not by the coming of the state of Israel, but by Muslim holy war or *jihad*. The second Intifada is a sign that it is at hand. Whilst it may not be the last *jihad*, it is undoubtedly paving the way for it. The Palestinians have been designated its precursors because they have undergone 'the fire of monopoly capitalism, Jewish usury, despotism and an American boycott'. Their very weakness designates them as the actors of the End of Time, as the messages delivered by Joel and Isaiah foretold. There remains the question of when the Day of the Wrath of God will come. When will Allah destroy the 'abomination of desolation', to use the biblical phrase? When will the chains of Jerusalem be burst asunder and when will its legitimate rights be restored? The answer lies, according to al-Rahman, in the prophecies of Daniel. When Daniel referred to the period between despair and consolation, he identified, according to our author, 1967 as the year of abomination and desolation. It therefore coincided with the Arab defeat and Israel's victory in the Six Days War. The end (or the beginning of the end) will, according to the prophecies, occur 45 years later, or in other words 2012 or the year 1433 of the Hegira. There can be no guarantee that this is the right year, but there is every reason to believe that it is. The Apocalypse will, according to this author, occur within a decade.

From the viewpoint of Christian, Jewish and Muslim millenarianists, the Israel–Palestinian conflicts extend far beyond the framework of those two societies. The presence of Jerusalem, which is a holy city for all three Abrahamic religions, new media that allow the instantaneous transmission of data to the entire world, and the various forms of fundamentalism associated with a land that has a holy status for almost half of humanity, all mean that the apocalyptic vision is fuelled by war. It also fuels war to the extent that war is a portent that a new humanity is at last ready to embrace the End of Time. Although it has until now been no more than a marginal phenomenon, the same conception inspires some Palestinian martyrs too. The human bombs would be quite happy to see their deaths hastening the end of time and helping to inaugurate a new era, as well as fighting the Israeli enemy. That would give them an even more glorious position in the pantheon of the chosen that they are seeking to enter.

## Mastery of death and the fascination of death

Martyrs who risk their lives for the sake of a sacred cause have a complex relationship with the Absolute. They are, in the first place, servants of the Absolute, and submit themselves to it. In the Palestinian case, a holy death is an act of witness designed to destroy the Israeli enemy by killing him at the moment of one's own death. The martyr's intentionality is determined by a nation that is both sanctified by Palestinians and denied by the Israeli enemy. But the peculiar thing about his movement towards death is that it can lead to an inversion of means and ends and give rise to an attitude that sees killing and being killed as an end in itself. The movement towards death can be metamorphosed into a denial of life in the Absolute, as it becomes divorced from the goals he originally set himself. This phenomenon, which can be observed in both Iranian and Palestinian martyrdom, can also be found in the decisionist proclivities of both the early Christians and contemporary followers of Allah. A particular effervescence can arise in a society where the intoxication with death becomes divorced from the martyr's original goal of realising the sacred. What was once a means of achieving a holy purpose becomes self-sufficient. In this death-obsessed vision, the joy of dying gives the survivors an even greater desire to follow the martyr's example. Their desire to emulate his holy death can rise into a crescendo, like an itch that grows as it is scratched and contradicts the logic of satiety that should characterise any 'rational' desire. Martyrdom implies an abnegation and a desire for sacrifice that can take on a life of their own. Candidates begin, so to speak, to enter a joust, as each of them wants to accede to death before the others, and in preference to others. Abnegation gradually gives way to an intentionality that is fascinated by death. This is particularly likely to occur in closed groups or in particularly tragic circumstances that induce this internalised feeling of hatred, and in which everyone begins to want to have done with life and to take with him as many as possible of those who collude with an order he holds in contempt. This is not really a conscious process. The effervescence of martyrdom works in a vacuum and unthinkingly follows the meanderings of a subjectivity that is gradually becoming divorced from reality and its original goal of killing in the name of a sacred ideal. The killings sometimes occur when the concrete situation worsens, and when all the exits have been blocked or look blocked to believers. In the Palestinian case, the transition from the first to the second Intifada gave rise to a radicalisation that encouraged a fascination with the death of self and others (for Palestinians) and to an obsession with repression (for Israelis). That dimension has played only a marginal role until now, but it may become more important if the conviction that peace is impossible replaced a confused desire to make it impossible.

### LEBANON: BETWEEN MARTYRDOM AND ABSURDITY

In Iran, the utopia of a harmonic Islamic society was belied by reality. In Palestine, the desire to build a nation has been frustrated. In Lebanon, things were much more ambivalent. This is partly because it was a society in which a mosaic of different Christian and Muslim communities had shared power even since the foundation of the Lebanese state. The crisis affecting the multiconfessional model and Israel's invasion of the country created a new situation in which martyrdom flourished. In the cases of Iran and Palestine, there was a broad consensus as to who the enemy was, but in Lebanon there was no unanimity in that respect. Many Christians believed that the Israeli army's intervention in Lebanon had saved the country from the threat of disintegration posed by the Palestinians and the Iranian- and Syrian-backed Shi'ites. For Lebanese Muslims, this army of occupation, which established and directly subsidised a militia, was public enemy number one.

The civil war in Lebanon was the result of a serious crisis within the state. Between 1975 and the late 1980s, the country was in a state of internal chaos. The Israeli army had occupied the southern part of the country, and had established a Lebanese militia under its control, whilst Beirut was divided into two zones. Communities withdrew into themselves and the antagonism between the different groups and factions caused deaths that can only be described as absurd.[89] When other countries active in the region – Syria, Saudi Arabia, Iran, Israel, Libya, the United States and the Soviet Union – intervened in the Lebanese conflict, the civil war was transformed into a protracted struggle in which various regional powers intervened by using militias and private armies as their proxies. Power was increasingly in the hands of factions that had no ideals.

Massacres and the appearance of gangs that rapidly formed and then broke alliances led to the emergence of communitarian ghettoes that had not previously existed. For twelve years, the Muslim majority in west Beirut was separated from the Christian majority in east Beirut by a line of demarcation known as the 'Green Line'. Snipers killed anyone who attempted to cross it.

During this period, shifting alliances and the growing insecurity gave Beirutis the feeling that no aspect of their day-to-day lives – going for a walk, shopping, or even walking down the street – was safe from danger. The enemy was everywhere, and everything could suddenly change without any warning. Between 1975 and 1983, some 16,780 explosions were recorded in Lebanon and some 4000 people were killed. The charges ranged from one kilo to one and a half tonnes. Although the distribution of newspapers was sometimes disrupted, various radio stations broadcast news about the fighting and the places that should be avoided. They included the Voice of Lebanon (Phalangist), the Voice of Free Lebanon (the Christian militias), the Voice of the Fatherland (Sunni, west Beirut) and the Voice of the Mountain (Druze Communists on Mount Lebanon).

Large numbers of Palestinians began to come to Beirut in 1948. The shanty towns they built in the east, the southeast and the southern suburbs of the city formed a ring of poverty around Beirut. Palestinians were in the majority (63.5 per cent) in the shanty towns, but they were also home to a population of Lebanese Shi'ites from the south (16.5 per cent), Syrians (13.2 per cent) and Kurds (6.8 per cent).[90] Some of the shanty-town dwellers became involved in factional rivalries, vengeance and counter-vengeance. The slums provided a population that could be mobilised by the highest bidder.

Three types of actor intervened in the day-to-day tragedy that was being played out in Beirut: the sniper, the militiaman and the martyr.

### The sniper

The sniper was every Beiruti's nightmare. The city developed a psychosis about snipers because there was no escape for anyone who came into their sights. They waited in ambush for their prey, perched on chairs, and equipped with a rifle with telescopic sights and a box of ammunition. Seventy-five per cent of their targets were fatally wounded by the first bullet. Each sniper killed an average of ten people a day. Their effective range was between 250 and 500 metres, and there was very little chance of escaping them. The snipers were not independent, and worked for gang leaders. Most of them were disciplined. Their commanders knew exactly where they were and what they were doing. The snipers had no ideology and sold themselves to the highest bidder.[91] They killed anything that moved, including animals. Their role was to hermetically divide the east and west of the city and to trace a line of demarcation between the Muslim and Christian communities that no one could cross.

### The militiaman

The other killer who was at work during this period was the militiaman. The militias kidnapped and executed people after checking their 'identity cards', which mentioned their confessional obedience. It was the Phalangists who turned this into a systematic practice. On 6 September 1975, which became known as 'black Saturday', almost 200 Muslims were killed in cold blood. The militias went in for kidnapping and murder. They kidnapped, passed sentence and killed on a confessional basis, regardless of whether their captives were believers or not. After September 1982, after the Sabra and Chatila massacres and the Israeli withdrawal from Lebanon, the Lebanese army lost control of west Beirut. After February 1984, it was driven out by Amal. The security services, the Forces libanaises and other factions then began to make large-scale arrests.

People now died in one of two ways. Some deaths were theatrical, solemn and orchestrated for the media; others were clandestine, and no one knew precisely where or when the executions took place. In the first case, the captives were paraded through the streets, sometimes in chains, mistreated and sometimes tied to vehicles. Onlookers applauded, insulted them, screamed at them and even hit the condemned men. The bodies were sometimes burned and left by the roadside. In many cases, killing was not enough. The killers enjoyed their victims' deaths, humiliating and torturing them before executing them. Destruction of the Other became a form of self-assertion. The process of killing was divided into multiple sequences, as this made it possible to savour the victim's death even more. The punishments inflicted reached a new peak of horror as the tortured body of the victim became the personal property of the militiaman. Destroying a victim was equivalent to destroying the enemy's social and moral values, as well as his religion, which was reified and transformed into a principle of absolute evil.

The kidnapper's control over his prisoner gave him self-confidence and a euphoric feeling of boundless power, the power of life and death, over his victim. Killing gave him an unquenchable thirst for more deaths.[92]

Some did escape the round of hostage-taking, summary condemnation, torture, murder and, in some cases, massacre. For unpredictable reasons, some did escape death, either because they knew an influential member of the militia, because they were able to get someone to pay a ransom, or simply because they broke free from their prison. They were left with the feeling that life was insignificant or even absurd, and above all a feeling of guilt; others died and the fact that they had escaped death meant that they had been selfish enough to abandon them to their miserable fate.

Killing and being killed became particularly widespread as the Lebanese state disintegrated. Every political party, every camp and every faction laid down its own law. The impersonal, normalised violence of the state was replaced by the personalised, arbitrary and subjective violence of individuals, all pursuing their own goals and picking out guilty victims for their groups. In the absence of institutions such as prisons to confine the 'guilty', execution was the easiest and cheapest way of carrying out the punishment. The existence of the camps did not make it possible to hold prisoners long enough to punish them, as they might be stormed at any moment. Death also ensured that the sentence was irreversible.

Once arrested, the hostage was almost certain to be executed at one moment or another, and that terrible ordeal was probably the most terrible punishment. At that level, the subjectivity of the hostage was diametrically opposed to that of the martyr. Both knew that they would die. The martyr knew that he would, in theory, die at a pre-established time; hostages knew that they would die in some indeterminate future. The major difference between them was, however, that the martyrs were volunteers whereas the hostages were unwilling victims.

The militiamen often wore hoods. But a hood could have two meanings, depending on whether one was on the side of the victims or the executioners. The latter wore hoods with eyeholes that were intended to create an atmosphere of terror and to prevent the victims from seeing their faces. The hood could also be a bag that was pulled over the head of a victim to heighten the feeling of danger by preventing him from seeing the outside world and plunging him into suffocating darkness. The hood took away the executioner's responsibility and denied his victim the right to see him.

When the militia killed their victims, the atmosphere was often that of a party or even an orgy. Wounded prisoners and corpses were dragged through the streets by men who were singing, screaming, playing lutes and stamping their feet. The militia men sometimes took drugs or even made love before the ceremony to give the collective feast an even more jubilatory meaning. Taboos were broken in these orgies of blood as a combination of alcohol, dancing and drugs heightened the pleasures of cruelty. The blood of the victims united the members of the clan, family or confession; as in scapegoat ceremonies, the collective killing of its prisoners gave the group a renewed sense of its own strength. In these ceremonies, the killers believed themselves to be heroes because they were breaking the taboo on killing. The lack of respect shown to the corpses and the obscene jokes told about them helped to dehumanise them and to give the group a feeling of absolute legitimacy. In some cases, graves were violated when victims were buried alive in them. Corpses were rigged with explosives and blown to pieces. Women and girls were not spared the horror. Both girls of twelve or thirteen and old women were raped, often in the presence of their husbands or parents. Forcing them to perform the sexual act before they were executed was commonplace. The purpose of rape was sexual pleasure, but also the symbolic destruction of the body of the Other through the destruction of both a family and a female line. The bodies of the women who were raped were injured, but they also suffered the shame of having dishonoured their families and clans, and the fear that their rapists would talk about them afterwards. The combination of sex and death took place in a climate in which anyone could administer his own justice and in which the strongest could exercise the right of life and death over the weakest under the gaze of the gangs of militiamen who both protected them and did their dirty work for them.

In society as a whole, the arbitrary arrests and killings encouraged the relaxation of taboos and social constraints. The children were the first victims. They became egocentric, indifferent to others, and were fascinated by the brutality and the atrocities, and especially by the murders.

The newspapers were full of events indirectly related to the war. 'Man dies as revolver goes off as he cleans it.' 'Children playing in street find severed head in bag.' The style was cold and impersonal. The journalists gave no explanations. They simply reported the individual horrors that made death a banal part of life in wartime. In its turn, the civil war stimulated a need for more horrors. Everyone wanted their daily dose of disasters. This became a source of reassurance. The fact that others had died became a reassuring sign that the reader had not joined their numbers. For the newspaper reader, their deaths 'bore witness' to life and served a perversely proxy function: they died in our place. That was an unexpected stroke of luck for us and a piece of bad luck for them. But it did nothing to ensure the cohesion of society, as a freely consenting sacrifice might have done. The deaths of atomised individuals reminded their neighbours of how lucky they were, and of the how unlucky those who died by pure chance had been.

## Martyrdom in Lebanon

A third archetypal figure coexisted alongside the sniper and the militiaman, and he too played a major role in the war in Lebanon. Martyrs first appeared in suicide operations against the occupying Israeli army.

Lebanese martyrs died for politico-religious reasons bound up with Hezbollah's interpretation of Shi'ite Islam. Their initial motivation was exclusively political and stemmed from their devotion to the national struggle. Martyrs from both the nationalist parties and the Lebanese Communist Party were also motivated by a desire for national liberation. Two types of martyrs were involved in the suicide operations.[93] The professionals planned their operations in advance, visited the places where they were to be carried out and postponed them if conditions were not right. There were also those who were primed like time bombs, and they could not be turned back once they had set out.

The suicide operations were carried out against American and French targets. The destruction of the US Embassy in east Beirut claimed 23 dead and 69 wounded on 18 April 1983. On 23 October 1983, truck bombs were driven into a building where American Marines and French forces were based, killing 262 Americans and 80 other victims. The two men who carried out these operations were known by the names Abu Mazen and Abu Saj'an, and were 26 and 24 respectively. One of the first suicide attacks on the Israeli army took place on 11 November 1982. The target was a building housing the Israeli contingent in Tyre. Forty-seven were killed and 27 reported missing. The bomber was Abu Kassir, who was born in southern Lebanon in 1967. In 1985, a 17-year-old girl called Sana Mhaydli launched a suicide attack on Israeli patrols. Born into a

Shi'ite family from southern Lebanon in 1968, she belonged to the Syrian Social National Party, a non-confessional party calling for the establishment of a Greater Syria which would unite Lebanon, Iraq, Syria, Jordan, Palestine and Cyprus. Its martyrs claimed to be fighting to free Palestine and southern Lebanon from the Israeli yoke. Women played a far from negligible role in it, whereas Shi'ite women played no role in this type of action. The secular Lebanese Communist Party also sent out martyrs to attack the Israeli army. In his testament, Jamal as-Sati, who was a party member, addresses 'the poor of the whole world'. He came from a modest family from the Bekaa valley. The young Lola Abboud, who was also a communist, was another martyr. She was nicknamed 'The Flower of the Bekaa'.

Most of the martyrs came from modest or even underprivileged families from southern Lebanon. The Bassidji martyrs in Iran often left written testaments and audio cassettes and, more rarely, video cassettes. It was the Lebanese martyrs who popularised the use of video cassettes. Sana Mhaydli worked in a video shop in east Beirut. She left a video of herself saying goodbye to her family. It expresses all martyrs' favourite themes. The first is the transformation of sadness into joy. She then explains the reasons for her actions: the struggle against the oppressor. The third theme is the identification of the martyr's death with marriage, which calls for festivities, a rejection of sadness and the need for collective joy. A martyr does not die, and continues to live amongst his or her family. A holy death is neither a duty nor a chore. It is the fulfilment of her most burning desire. The theme of the blood of martyrs is just as important. When it is spilled on the ground, it gives new life to the sacred cause of those who are fighting the forces of Evil. Its thaumaturgical virtues can be seen when it spurts from the body: this releases the fighters' energy and guarantees a future victory over their oppressors. The tape ends with an invocation of the martyr's family, and especially his or her mother, who is asked to bless her son or daughter. This is intended to promote the sacred ideals for which he or she has been beatified. Sana, for instance, declared: 'I am the martyr Sana Youssel Mhaydli; I am 17; I am from the South. Southern Lebanon. The occupied, oppressed South, the South of resistance and revolution ... I am from the South of the martyrs, the South of Sheikh Raghab Harb ... the South of the hero Wajdi al-Sayegh ... May your joy burst forth on the day I die, as though it was my wedding day ... I hope that my soul will join those of the other martyrs and will rebound like thunder on the heads of the enemy soldiers ... I am not dead; I am still living amongst you; I am singing, dancing and fulfilling all my ambitions, I am filled with joy at being the embodiment of heroism and martyrdom ... do not weep for me ... be happy and laugh, because there are still living people to give you hope for liberation ... I am putting down roots in the land of the South, and making it stronger with my blood and my love. I am going towards death so as not to have to wait for it ... My last wish is that you call me "the bride of the South".'

No matter whether it is secular or Shi'ite, the discourse of the martyr is a product of the sacred. The themes developed by Sunnis are no different to those of Shi'ite martyrs in Iran or Sunni martyrs in Palestine. They all want to fight the enemy, and they beatify their desire thanks to a discourse in which the desire for immortality is combined with the wish to die. Shi'ites will meet Allah in their fight with the ungodly enemy. Communists and nationalists will achieve immortality thanks to their identification with the national collectivity and, beyond it, the community of the whole world's poor.

# 3

# The Transnational Neo-*Umma*: al-Qaeda's Martyrs

## DIASPORIC *UMMAS*

Whilst some martyrs mobilise the forces of religion in order to build an Islamic nation, the ambition of others is to build a transnational *umma* rather than a nation. This type of martyrdom is the product of globalisation, the vicissitudes of the Islamic diaspora in the West and the crisis in the Muslim societies of the Middle East and the former Soviet Empire.

The establishment of Islamic diasporas in the West has transformed what was once the possibility of building an Islamic nation into the possibility of building an *umma* on a world scale. Now that there are sizeable Islamic diasporas in the West, some minority groups of Muslims (like Al Muhajiroun, which wants to turn Britain into an Islamic country) dream of establishing an *umma* that will encompass the world, and especially the West. Being a universal religion, Islam, like Christianity, has always had worldwide ambitions. Those ambitions were, however, frustrated by the existence of other religions. The West has been largely secularised and has now lost its religious militancy. Like other identitarian constructs, religion is now seen as a plurality of faiths competing in a market. Like any other market, it is controlled by the law of supply and demand. The meaning of proselytism has changed radically. It once meant establishing the legitimacy of the struggle between Good and Evil in a world in which the state and its military might were directly involved. Proselytism now means competing to win a bigger 'share' in the market for religious goods. This makes it much easier for Islam to expand in the West than was previously the case. Successive crises in Muslim societies undergoing what is often an authoritarian modernisation have made religions increasingly strict and intolerant of other confessions. That is why the Christian and Jewish minorities in these countries are shrinking. The Islamic dynamic is then displaced towards the West, where Muslim minorities have become established in almost all countries:

the United States, France, Germany, Britain, Italy and Spain, but also in Sweden and the Netherlands.

Diasporic Muslims do not simply reproduce the communities of their countries of origin. They undergo two influences. The first generation is very strongly influenced by its society of origin, which has less influence on the second. Muslims are also influenced by their host societies. This is especially true of the new generation of children who have been educated in the West and exposed to the influence of the media, and television in particular. A new dynamic is now at work especially with respect to Islamisation or re-Islamisation within these societies. The vast majority of immigrants espouse the cultural orientations of their host society. Schools and television play an essential role in their acculturation. A minority espouse new forms of radicalism, partly because they feel they are being economically marginalised by exclusion, and culturally stigmatised because of their religion or their ethnic origin. Identitarian reactions can be identified amongst a minority of those who do integrate. These include the need to stand out, the need to inscribe themselves symbolically in an origin that can give a meaning to life in increasingly anomic societies, and the longing to have a restricted group reference that allows them to feel some human warmth in societies that are becoming colder and colder.

Disaporic Islam is often a source of cultural enrichment for both believers and advanced societies where cultural diversification leads to increased creativity. As a general rule, multiculturalism, defined as the appearance of a plurality of interrelated subcultures, gives a new dynamism to social and cultural relations. The downside of this state of affairs is a form of radicalism and sectarianism that rejects and demonises others in the name of authenticity and sincerity. New forms of radicalism appear, together with an identitarian closure and introspection. This radicalism can take one of two major forms. It can lead to introspection and to the formation of a peaceful but introverted neo-*umma* or, in contrast, to a rejection of society and the formation of an aggressive neo-*umma*. An introverted neo-*umma* establishes a cordon sanitaire and relegates others to the periphery. Believers attempt to live their faith in a closed environment so as to protect themselves from the intrusion of the society that surrounds them. In Western societies, the Tabligh provides the prototype for this attitude on the part of Muslims.[1] Its members live in mental and sometimes physical isolation, but they are not at war with the world outside. An aggressive neo-*umma*, in contrast, preaches rejection of an ungodly society. Its goal is to preserve its own purity in a world that has been largely defiled, or simply to defend itself against the widespread impurity that is lying in wait for it.

Groups like al-Qaeda are based upon financial networks and recruitment networks that cannot be understood in terms of a national logic. Their networks are based upon the loyalty of individuals, many of them motivated by this aggressive neo-*umma*. It is a by-product of a plural modernity that no longer has any centre of gravity, and its cultural orientations are a perversion of those of multiculturalism: the radicalisation of individualism within a plurality of modes of being which, as a general rule, respect one another whilst at the same time becoming hybridised to some degree. Such modes of being can, however, just as easily reject one another when they begin to seek authenticity. The quest for authenticity can rule out peaceful coexistence within a society whose dominant culture no longer commands the loyalty of its minorities.

The schema governing the forms of martyrdom characteristic of these neo-*ummas* is very different to that governing the behaviour of the desperate young men of Muslim societies. It is the community and not the individual that is the unattainable object of desire. In diasporas, a minority fringe begins to dream of an *umma* it can bring into being only by cutting itself off from the outside world. Western societies in which individuals often feel that they have been left to their own devices are the breeding ground for such neo-*ummas*. That is why they can only come into being in a sectarian vacuum that sets them apart from others or, failing that, in death. For that to happen, there must be grievances – part real and part imaginary – against society, and an organisation that can make death possible. In the case of al-Qaeda, the grievance is the West's invasion of the Muslim world and especially the fact that the Islamic holy land of Saudi Arabia was occupied by American troops after the Gulf War of 1991, American attitudes towards Palestine and the way the West behaves towards countries where Islam is repressed, as in Algeria. This kind of grievance can also be seen in cults opposed to what they see as a hostile global society. Examples include the Aum cult which released poison gas into the Tokyo metro to take its revenge on an ungodly society on 20 March 1995, or the Seventh Day Adventist cult led by David Korish in Waco. Its members died on 28 February 1993, when FBI agents stormed its headquarters. The Solar Temple, which programmed collective suicide and murder in October 1994 is a further example.[2] The frontier between life and death becomes blurred in all these cases. The taboo on life and the religious and social commandment not to take life – one's own or that of others – disappears. What is new about al-Qaeda are the motives of its members, the way they construct both self and other, or both their community and the enemy group, and the meaning death acquires for those who take their own lives or the lives of others.

The religion preached by al-Qaeda and other associations of the same type is often directly inspired by hatred of the West in a situation where the organisation in question, which is part affective and part cultural, is largely dependent upon its Western enemy. Our analysis will focus on this hatred. That makes it possible to understand the new type of martyrs who were involved in the attacks of 11 September 2001 and the train bombings that took place in Madrid in March 2004, and the identitarian mechanisms they mobilise.

## FORMS OF HUMILIATION

If we are to understand the mental universe of al-Qaeda's new martyrs, two major ideas have to be taken into consideration. The first is that of their feeling of humiliation, and the second is that of Western arrogance. Several kinds of humiliation are involved, and three are of particular significance to this type of martyr. First, there is the humiliation they experience in everyday life because they feel that they have been economically marginalised and made to feel socially inferior, as is the case with the excluded Maghrebin youth in France, or young West Indians and Pakistanis in Great Britain. Second, thanks to the media, they experience the humiliation of the Muslim world in Bosnia, Afghanistan, Iraq or Palestine. Mechanisms of identification then lead to the internalisation of that feeling. Finally, there is sometimes a feeling that their immersion in the Western world has defiled them. For immigrants or their sons, the fact that they left their country of origin, either as children or at some later date, makes them feel that they have unfairly been spared the sufferings of their coreligionists in Muslim societies. They feel strongly that the West dominates (in either real or imaginary terms) Muslim countries as well as their homelands, and believe that they must act in order to save them from the utter depravity that will result from Western influence. Taking part in the operations of a group that is fighting Western hegemony and arrogance inside the West gives the individual a new sense of pride and restores his lost dignity. The first type of humiliation affects young men living in the poor suburbs of France or England and, more generally the poor inner cities of the West. They avenge themselves for the snubs they have received by becoming very aggressive towards the society that has excluded them. A tiny minority may become involved in terrorism, like Khaled Kelkal in France in 1995. Members of diasporas belonging to the middle classes are, as a general rule, unlikely to be victims of exclusion, even though discrimination and insidious forms of ostracism still affect them. Their feeling of humiliation is to a large extent one of humiliation by proxy, and it is exacerbated and sustained by the media, which show the tribulations of Muslims in the face of Western complicity with the despotic or nepotistic regimes which, like Saudi Arabia or Tunisia, defend Western interests, or in the face of non-Muslim societies that are, like Israel, at war with Muslims.

## A NEW SELF-CONSCIOUSNESS

The interviews I carried out from April 2001 onwards with some 15 inmates of French prisons who were accused of association with wrongdoers in order to commit terrorist acts reveal a disturbing portrait of some of al-Qaeda's members.[3] On the one hand, they have neither an archaic mentality nor the mentality of modernisation's victims. Irrespective of whether they are French because they were born on French soil or because they were naturalised, they are perfectly familiar with, not to say steeped in, what might be termed Western culture. One speaks six languages, and two others speak five. A fourth speaks three languages, and the others have some English and Arabic as well as French. Most of them studied at universities in France, the Middle East or elsewhere. One studied theology in Turkey, and then business management in Malaysia. Two others studied science, and specialised in information technology. Another worked in commercial management in Canada. One of the least qualified worked in France, having left Algeria in 1992 because of the military coup. Their wives were French, Japanese, Italian and Bosnian. One man had, to my knowledge, two wives, both converted to Islam by him. He had, he said, quite honestly told them that he wanted to live with them both. Some of them had lived in Europe since they were children. One had spent ten years in Italy, and five in Canada. Another had lived in France since he was five. All but one spoke very good French.

Although the sample is small, it completely contradicts the archaism or submodernisation thesis. Although I cannot claim to have an intimate knowledge of all of them, the length of the interviews – an hour or up to two hours with each of them – does allow me to paint the most realistic portrait possible. I was not dealing with individuals who were disoriented because they had difficulty in adapting to the West or because of their lack of cultural baggage. They were not incapable of understanding the mechanisms of our modern and overcomplex societies. Most of them were at least as well integrated as so-called 'normal' citizens and were better educated than the average European. They spoke several languages, had lived in several Western countries and had mastered different cultural codes. They could move from one cultural code to another without any major difficulty.

We therefore have to look elsewhere to find an explanation for their radicalisation. On the one hand, they are 'multicultural' and well-versed in 'code-switching'. On the other, all firmly reject what they called Western civilisation, or simply the West. One of the most educated evoked 'Western hubris', and another spoke of the hypocrisy of dominating the rest of the world in the name of democracy. They were all convinced that Islam was being oppressed and mistreated. In Bosnia, Iraq, Afghanistan, Palestine, Algeria and Western countries, an alliance between Christians and Jews was putting Islam in a position that could only lead to *jihad*. Some of them were from families that attended mosques fairly regularly, but several of their own brothers and sisters were non-observant. Others were from families who rarely went to the mosque, and it was they who had become the most devout. It was, finally, their search for Islam that led them to improve their knowledge of religion and, in some cases, to learn Arabic, and not the other way around.

Islam crystallises their rejection of the West. This phenomenon is not specific to al-Qaeda's new martyrs and can be observed in others, and especially Western converts. Islam lends itself well to being a religion of the dominated, or of those who are being crushed by 'Western arrogance' – the phrase is one of the interviewees'. The fact that most of them come from families with religious roots does not prevent the one or two converts from having a conception of the West that is identical in every respect. Some, who had lived in France since childhood, had had a brutal awakening. Until they were adolescents, they believed they were French. Forms of ordinary racism suddenly made them aware of the unfathomable gap that existed between them and the evil West, as represented by France. They had, in other words, cherished the feeling that they were completely integrated into what they thought was their society. Apparently minor incidents occurred: one man's sister was called a 'dirty Arab' because she refused to go out with boys like the other girls at her lycée. He himself had had to put up with wounding remarks about his swarthy skin from other children. Political events in Islamic countries, and especially the questions of Algeria, Bosnia, Afghanistan, Chechnya and Palestine made them aware of their solidarity with Muslim peoples, and that they were living in a country that had never given Muslims any serious aid. Their feeling that they had been betrayed by those closest to them, which they experienced existentially, either in everyday life or out of solidarity with the Muslim world, then became the element that determined the break with the West.

These two features are often combined, and they are corroborated by other phenomena such as the modern discontent with anonymity and exaggerated individualism. For most people, such phenomena give rise to a feeling of disorientation and a form of mental confusion that exacerbates narcissism and encourages introversion. In their case, it led them to reject the West and to demonise it by making it an absolute principle of Evil. For most people living in the West, there is no principle of adversity. We do not know precisely whom to blame for our discontents in our very complex societies. We come to terms with our situation by living on several different registers at once and by oscillating between the various fragments of a manic-depressive ego.[4] The identification of the 'enemy' has the effect of removing the individual from this situation of chronic indecisiveness and from a plurality of registers that are often incoherent. Such people also live in between several cultures. They live in the culture of their parents and that of French society – but also the culture they acquire by living in a Western society, be it German, British or American. At some point, they experience an existential rupture that would be insignificant for other people in their situation. In their case, it triggers a sudden rejection of the West, which they come to see as the incarnation of absolute Evil. This triggers a process in which the discontents of modernity (mental fragmentation, oscillation, instability and scepticism) are suddenly dissipated by an absolute transparency. Transparency is the source of unshakeable convictions, an action-logic and a unified ego predicated upon a clear distinction between the sacred and the profane, and the licit and the illicit. This identitarian construct allows the believer to scapegoat a satanic pole, and he mobilises all his energy as the fight against Evil becomes his existential project. The Manichaeism of this religiosity overcomes the discontent of our late modernity, which offers us no more than quasi-convictions and imperfect motives, a mental landscape painted in half-tones, and a vision of self and other that oscillates between narcissism and rejection.[5]

This type of identification is related to contemporary cultist mechanisms, and thus displays an undeniable modernity. Islam itself espouses new forms of polarity which restructure its old features (such as *jihad*, martyrdom, exodus and eschatological expectations). This new religiosity is crossed with a modernity whose features are inverted as they become radicalised. Whereas the modern individual's sins are an excessive 'softness' and mental incoherence, the future martyr displays a unity that turns into inflexibility or even complete intransigence. Whereas modern individualism finds expression in a rejection of unconditional identification with any community, the believer strives to create a monolithic neo-*umma* that has never existed at any point in history, but which opens up the possibility of a belief that knows no doubts. Western religiosity is subject to the relativism of faith, but the new believer's apprehension of the sacred is exclusive and monopolistic. And whereas the concern with death, and especially with salvation after death, is considerably weakened in a modernity centred upon life and consumerism, many adepts are obsessed with death and purity. How can they ensure that they are pure at the moment when they leave this world, and how can they have a happy death (*hosn ol khetâm*, as one believer put it)? How can they avoid heresy and impiety (*shirk*), and how can they maintain their faith to the bitter end? The answer to these existential questions lies in commitment to a militant faith. Struggle is the best way to purify their faith and to protect the believer from the temptations of a corrupting modernity that serves the purposes of a perfidious West. The more Westerners themselves come to see the West as a loosely knit structure that has no unified and homogeneous 'civilisation', the more the neo-*umma*'s believers unify it by giving it a deeply satanic character. This inversion says a lot about their involvement in the world of Evil that they are fighting. The domineering, egotistical and imperialist nature of some Western tendencies is extended to the Western world as such. Believers turn the unity of the domineering and arrogant West into an essential feature of this 'civilisation', whereas the vast majority of Westerners believe, on the basis of their actual lived experience, that the world in which they live is disjointed and characterised by the loss of any overall meaning. There are two stages to the Islamists' argument. First, they select certain features of their imaginary West, such as sexual depravity, intolerance, arrogance and the desire to dominate the world, and Islam in particular. They then combine them in such a way as to construct a West that is trying to undermine and destroy Islam. This is an inversion and radicalisation of the lived experience of the many Westerners who are ill at ease precisely because they can find no unitary principle and because they see the infinite multiplicity of their ways of life as an indication that their world has no unified meaning.

The feeling of being humiliated by proxy is, as we have seen, a further feature of this subjectivity. The sufferings of the Palestinians, the Chechens, the Bosnians and the Iraqis, who have all hit the headlines over the last two decades, have convinced Islam's new followers that there is an absolute antagonism between the West and their religion. News broadcasts play an essential role here, and the media become a spokesman for the downtrodden Muslims whose sufferings are shown on television day in, day out. Both the conflict in the Middle East and the breakup of the Soviet Empire have rekindled conflicts and tensions related to the Islamic nation and religion and have given rise to a feeling of deep injustice on the part of the many Muslims (who are not necessarily observant) for whom Islam has become the religion of the oppressed.

Abnegation for the sake of this repressed Islam can lead believers to abandon what should have been a promising future. One of the interviewees, who had proved himself to be a brilliant student of information technology, dropped out of university. He said that this was a deliberate choice: he was willing to commit 'hara kiri' for the sake of his faith. The more he devoted himself to his religion, the more alive he felt. He felt less oppressed by the West, whose perfidiousness was so great that it could even integrate Muslims, provided that they abandoned the true faith. The idea that Islam is in danger and that it must be saved, even if it meant spilling his own blood, so as to preserve the *umma* has deep roots in these groups. The cultural diversity to which they have been exposed in the West, and the fact that they can speak different languages and have lived in societies with different modes of life proves to them that the truth lies elsewhere, in something that transcends them all. If Islam is to be saved, war must be waged on the domineering and oppressive West. The West is perverting Islam both from within and from without with the spectacle of its power and thanks to its ability to cast a spell on

Muslims. The consumption of goods and commodities is replacing the worship of Allah. This is *shirk*, which is the ultimate heresy. When asked if their religiosity was 'anti-modern', one interviewee replied that it was the very quintessence of modernity, as the Koran begins with the imperative: 'Read'.[6] It is this authentic modernity that is being threatened by the perverse modernity of a depraved West which is destroying Muslims, subjugating them and reducing them to mental slavery (by seducing and integrating them) at the same time that it is repressing and excluding them. No matter whether it mistreats them or seduces them, the West is to be condemned, either because it is bewitching Muslims or because it is perverting them. The feeling that the West has to be completely rejected is similar to the feeling that motivated the hardest left factions in the struggle against imperialism: all reconciliation is impossible because the enemy is absolute Evil incarnate. As it is the one thing that is meaningful and that can give their lives a meaning, their metacultural Islam cannot survive unless they sacrifice themselves to it, and unless their commitment to the cause is total.

## THE WORLD METROPOLIS

The great metropolitan cities are places that have seen the development of a multitude of economic, political and social activities, but also and above all cultural creativity. They are the birthplace of modern culture and its stupefying diversity. They are the places where it is transformed and from which it spreads. New forms of conviviality, cultural hybridity and new forms of art and thought are being created. It is in the big cities that foreigners mix with the natives. Eventually there will be as many 'nationals' as there are people in the world. But the modern metropolis is also a place where things lose their meaning. It fosters the multiculturalism that provokes mutual respect for differences amongst society's subcultures, but it also makes us feel dizzy, and gives us the feeling that we do not belong anywhere. Because they are no longer governed by central and exclusive norms, modern cities are places where hybridity promotes cultural diversity, but they are also lonely and insular places, especially for people from the Islamic world, where the quest for a community or *umma* is part of their imaginary. In their own way, they therefore try to become part of a globalised neo-*umma* that is often a counterpart to the myth of the global village promoted by the affluent classes of the West.

Modern cities are like a *Janus bifrons*. Living in them gives one both the impression of being part of modernity, and a feeling of absolute exile. Many immigrants living in Western cities come to feel profoundly foreign. It is not simply that they do not belong in the countries where they are living: the question is simply meaningless. Living in different countries and different cities heightens the feeling that they do not belong rather than the feeling that they have at last found somewhere hospitable. The whole world feels like a place of exile. That is why they join a neo-*umma* whose main characteristic is that it lies beyond all geographical determinations and all fatherlands. It is stateless. It is no more than an outline of a network whose nodal points create an abstract configuration where the names are purely formal: London, Paris, Leicester, Hamburg, Madrid, Rome... It is not that these stateless people who are 'European or American on paper' (naturalised citizens) or immigrants believe that these places are all the same. The point is that they have no concrete content in the eyes of individuals whose feeling of 'not belonging' dominates everything else. This is one of the unexpected dimensions of these great cities. They are global cities where different cultures mingle, but they are also places where new forms of rejection and exclusion are concocted.[7] They are places where some people develop a new imaginary based upon a 'siege mentality': they become deeply antagonistic to a globalised whole, and metaphorically describe it as 'the West'. It is mainly in the Western megalopolis that the feeling of absolute antagonism to the West prevails amongst people who feel that they are being mistreated – either in person or by proxy – by this dominant power. Islam becomes the name for a new principle of opposition that contrasts an imaginary past of conquests and triumph with a pitiful situation in which it is dominated by the West or its extensions, such as Israel or autocratic countries which, like Russia, lay claim to 'Westernness'.

Overflowing with wealth and temptations, the great cities of the West exacerbate migrants' consumerist desires. In many cases, and especially if they come from Arab countries, their imaginary has already been stimulated by the magic of oil. Immigrant workers from Egypt, Pakistan, Algeria, Morocco, Syria and Tunisia caught the bug when they came to the Arabian peninsula to make a living in the 1970s and 1980s and fell under the spell of an oil-based magical consumerism and of what were wrongly believed to be infinite resources.

Western cities reproduce the wealth they dream of, and which is often out of reach, on a vast scale. Those who come to work there as labourers or who take unskilled jobs are exploited and live like the working poor, no matter whether they are in Paris, London, New York or Rome. Many Muslims who find themselves in this situation overcome the feeling that they have lost their dignity, thanks to the harsh necessities of material life and their obligation to provide for the needs of their families. Loss of dignity, which is often experienced by proxy, is the fate of the minority who are better off and therefore have the time and the leisure to take offence and to brood about their loss of dignity all day long, either in solitude if they live alone, or in the company of compatriots or coreligionists who are suffering in the same way. The vast majority do, however, try to take a 'positive' approach to their situation and to establish cross-border relations with compatriots who may live in the same city or on the other side of the world. They create diasporic communities where cross-border trade, the exchange of goods and services and the transfer of money can develop and flourish. These 'transnational' communities quickly developed in Europe's border towns (Marseille, Strasbourg) and they now constitute a diaspora where everyone tries to get rich and to share their new-found wealth with their family and friends on both sides of the border.[8]

A minority, however, find this situation unacceptable and resent it because it is both intolerable and shameful. They feel ill at ease, humiliated and stigmatised. And they feel that all the more deeply because they are Muslims. The myth of a neo-*umma* that will rise from its ashes to establish a new caliphate in this world[9] is born of the fragmentation experienced by Muslims in cities that mock them with their wealth, marginalise them and make them feel a shameful loss of dignity by arrogantly displaying their affluence and offering them no way to share it. The big city engulfs everyone, encourages consumerism and 'depravity' and gives them neither moral comfort nor the feeling that they are living in the same world. To be more accurate, the feeling of being part of the same world is reduced to the quest for money, which is the one standard by which everyone is judged in this society. For a tiny minority of diasporic Muslims, there is something aggressively disconcerting about the multiple and heterogeneous phenomena of overwhelming technological efficiency, 'shameless' sexuality and both male and female homosexuality, the absence of spiritual leadership and the scepticism that are all part of modern citizenship. They cannot understand how it is possible to both watch the repression of the Muslim world on television, and live peacefully in a world of arrogant wealth and immoral complicity with the oppressors without raising their voice in protest or without taking action.

For these minorities, the obscenity of living quietly in a world of affluence that, at best, ignores Muslims, that despises them and usually excludes them in either cultural or economic terms (or even both) is literally intolerable. Their Islamism is a combination of Westernisation, hatred for the West, the mythologisation of the early Muslim community, a utopian desire to restore Islam to the splendour of the past, and a desire to die as martyrs in a *jihad* against a West that is afraid because, unlike them, it does not want to die. This readiness for martyrdom is in part a defiance of Western superiority at the technological, economic and military levels. Sacrificing one's life challenges this material superiority, which has as its corollary a fear of death. Westerners want to go on living at all costs, and candidates for a holy death see that as weakness in the face of Muslims who are prepared to sacrifice their lives.

## ORGANISATIONAL FORMS

In Iran and Palestine, the feeling that there has been a basic failure means that martyrdom arises in a national framework: the undermining and collapse of the Islamic utopia in Iran, and the impossibility of building a Palestinian nation on Palestinian soil. This does not apply to transnational martyrdom, which has a very different meaning. The differences are apparent at the level of the body, relations with the other, the enemy, the self and Islam and, at a still more general level, with culture and politics. The origins of the first type of martyrdom lie in the crisis or failure of a political project, whilst martyrdom of the second kind has no state basis and no explicit political project. Iranian and Palestinian martyrdom had a more or less clearly defined enemy; the enemy of the transnational martyr is much more global and vague. One is based primarily on a nation; the other is based on a community that has yet to be built, but which already exists at a world level. Signs of its existence can be seen in a number of Muslim societies, but also in Western countries with Muslim minorities. The methods are also different. Martyrdom of the first type has the support of organisations that are part of a state or that can be a state's auxiliaries. Significantly, this kind of martyrdom can be divorced from religion and can lead to the beatification of the nation. Witness the many suicide bombings carried out by the Tamil Tigers, a minority demanding independence in Sri Lanka.[10]

The destruction of the twin towers of Manhattan's World Trade Center on 11 September 2001 marked the political beginning of a new era and the end of the post-Cold War era. In the period that followed the demolition of the Berlin Wall in 1989, there was complete confusion on the international scene. The communist enemy was dead. The bipolar world that had shaped international relations for half a century no longer existed. In global terms, there were no longer two superpowers. There was only one: the United States. The euphoria did not last long, and the 1990s were punctuated by various ethnic wars, like those linked to the breakup of the former Yugoslavia and those in Chechnya.

On 26 February 1993, three basements in the World Trade Center were demolished by explosives planted by the al-Qaeda group. Six people were killed, and over 1000 wounded. Even before that, the attacks on the American air base in Dharan on 22 June 1996, in Dar Es-Salaam and on the US Embassy in Nairobi on 8 August 1998 announced the emergence of a new type of 'terrorism' which was fundamentally different to the terrorism the world had experienced in previous decades.[11]

This type of activism, which some call hyperterrorism,[12] differs from classical terrorism. It has no overriding political purpose. It does not attack political entities and is not intended to challenge a politically defined order. It is directed against the world as a whole, as symbolised by the United States, although countries such as France, England, Spain or Saudi Arabia may be its actual targets. The almost exclusive presence of non-state actors is also a characteristic feature. Classic terrorism, which was usually state-dominated, took into account the capacity to retaliate of the societies or states it attacked, and that made it accountable for its actions. The new terrorism does not. Sovereign states play only a minor role, though some may provide financial or military support by supplying arms. Of the 330 terrorist incidents recorded by the US State Department between 1992 and 1996, only six were the work of agents directly linked to a state. States were, in other words, involved in less than 2 per cent of these incidents.[13] This demonstrates the scale of the new terrorism. For the authorities, the distinction between 'state-sponsored terrorism', 'state-relevant terrorism' and 'state-irrelevant terrorism' is now crucial.[14] We have moved from ideologically motivated terrorism to a new type of terrorism. Rogue states may encourage it, but they do not control it. The essential feature of this new terrorism is its privatisation. It is financed through charitable foundations, or by wealthy individuals such as Arab businessmen in the Gulf (in the case of al-Qaeda), by the drugs trade (opium in al-Qaeda's case), the extortion of funds from shopkeepers and businessmen, the illegal sale of cigarettes or other goods in Western countries (as in the United States) or by taking Westerners hostage (the Abu Sayaf group in the Philippines specialises in taking tourists hostage).

Classic terrorism restricted the loss of life by confining its actions to the strategic area that concerned it so as to send a message to the political authorities. The demands of ETA in the Basque country, the IRA in Northern Ireland and the FLNC in Corsica are territorial. Similarly, the far left ideological demands that inspired Action Directe in France, the Red Army Faction in Germany, the Red Brigades in Italy and the Red Army in Japan had an explicit content and a more or less coherent ideology based upon a concept of imperialism.[15] The new terrorism does not have that conceptual armature, or at least has not constructed it so explicitly. Having no specific territorial demands and no ideology that can give rise to actions on a restricted scale, it operates indiscriminately and can inflict heavy losses on civilians who have no direct involvement in the conflict. This gives rise to the phenomenon of so-called 'grey areas': low-intensity warfare that is neither state-sponsored nor led by groups making demands of a state, but which is still a growing security threat. Terrorism's operational zones have also changed: until recently, Africa and most of the United States were spared. Numerous acts of terrorism are now taking place in those zones and, strictly speaking, there are no neutral zones. Witness the attacks on American interests in Dar Es-Salaam and Nairobi in June 1996 and August 1998.

This new form of terrorism came into being after the breakup of the Soviet Union. The predictability of classic terrorism, with its more or less clearly defined political goals, disappeared along with the Eastern bloc. The field was open for a new form of activism that is no longer guided by the existence of a bipolar world. Indifferent to the number of deaths it causes and with no interest in respecting a code of good conduct guaranteed by states, it is destroying the distinction between terrorism and war, and this leads politicians to speak of a new kind of 'future war' characterised mainly by its unpredictability. There was no declaration of war before the Clinton administration launched missile attacks on al-Qaeda's bases in Afghanistan in reprisal for its acts of terrorism.

The best-known example of an activist network in the Islamic world is without doubt al-Qaeda. But although this is the most important group in financial and logistical terms and because of its ability to operate anywhere in the world, it is not the only one. There are other more or less autonomous networks, and one of their characteristics is that they form a 'nebula' but still retain their specificity, their specialisation and their 'preferences' when it comes to 'choosing' their targets. The Harakat al Jahad-al-Islami is one example.[16] The group has close links with Pakistan, and Kashmir is one of its main operational zones. But it is also active in Bangladesh, Chechnya, in Xinjiang in China, in Uzbekistan and in Tajikistan. Its activities in Indian Kashmir are carried out under the semi-autonomous leadership of Mohammad Ilyas Kashmir, who is fighting for a 'Free Kashmir'. The group has produced more martyrs than any other. It is made up of graduates from Islamic seminaries and is in competition with other Islamic groups such as Jaish-e Muhammad. Harakat's leader in Uzbekistan is Sheikh Muhammad Tahir al Farooq, who has so far lost some 30 of his men in the conflict with Uzbekistan President Islam Karimov. Operations against the Russians in Chechnya are carried out under the leadership of Commandant Hidayatullah. Military training is being given to Chechen fighters. The struggle in Burma is led by Abdul Quddus. Many other examples could be cited. Like al-Qaeda, the Harakat is loosely structured and every cell is autonomous to some extent. In a world governed by modern means of communication, this kind of structure can be established by using instruments like the internet and mobile phones. The notoriety of al-Qaeda, finally, encourages other groups to make a name for themselves by adopting much the same model and trying to adapt it to local conditions. Modern means of communication, and especially television, act as resonance chambers, and demonstrate how to strike a blow against the arrogant powers that are humiliating Muslims, and how marginal, insignificant groups can become 'central' and leave their mark on history. The way in which the attack on the twin towers of the World Trade Center was shown ad nauseam by television stations all over the world gave al-Qaeda a particular pre-eminence. Its combination of political and economic importance and worldwide notoriety made networks carrying out local operations feel powerful, even though the international media hardly mentioned them. Centrality is now essential, and not only in the struggle against Western powers and the United States in particular. It is also a prime symbolic issue in the rivalry between the various activist groups. The attack on the World

Trade Center was an attack on America's symbolic space as well as its economic heart. For several weeks, that space was saturated by an event that became a paradigmatic act whose importance was further enhanced by the fact that it was endlessly replayed on television sets all around the world.

In the case of al-Qaeda, we know that internet communications and the use of new communication resources (cryptography, data compression) played a far from negligible role in its formidable strategic effectiveness. Indeed, the new activism will succeed only if it can exploit the mechanisms of economic globalisation to its own advantage and succeed in ensuring its financial autonomy by using tax havens and offshore investment banks.

One of al-Qaeda's major characteristics signals the emergence of an ultra-modern mode of action: the disappearance of the rigidly hierarchical structure that typified classic terrorism. Its networks are governed by a much suppler logic, and by more decentralised forms of action. Members of the group are highly mobile, come together for specific actions but do not know one another, and then vanish into thin air once the operation is over. The way certain computer programmes evolve provides a model for the establishment of groups in which there is no one centre but a plurality of centres, no rigidly stratified and hierarchical levels of command, but the same suppleness that we find in the new approaches to modern governance and their emphasis on autonomy. This network structure is not specific to al-Qaeda. It can be seen in extremist groups in the United States, where the Patriots and the Militias have no unified ideology or hierarchical organisation but are made up of hundreds of autonomous nuclei held together by their complicity and a worldview dominated by a rejection of both the American federal state and international organisations.[17]

In order to combat these networks, which are more or less invisible and have no basis in a state that would allow the use of classic punitive measures, the United States is trying to develop 'rapid decisive operations' to hunt them down in a sophisticated electronic war by attacking their computer networks and by using special reconnaissance operations and selective bombing.[18]

Al-Qaeda's networks have several distinctive features.[19] First, they are structured like a decentralised transnational mafia rather than a centralised terrorist structure with a real organisation. Second, they are not dependent upon one backer and have a financial autonomy that prevents them from coming under the control of any one state, such as Saudi Arabia or Libya. Third, they are in contact with a host of groups, which are themselves controlled by a charismatic leader or leaders. Over the previous decade, al-Qaeda was in constant touch with the Egyptian Al-Gamaa al-Islamiya group led by Shiekh Omar Abdul Rahmane, with Ayman al-Zawahiri from Egypt's Islamic Jihad, with the International Islamic Front Bin Laden established with Pakistanis from the Harakat al-Ansar movement by sending Pakistanis to Kashmir, and Arabs to Chechnya and Bosnia.

Anti-Americanism and anti-Westernism is a further characteristic of al-Qaeda. The enemy is of course the United States, but it is also the West in a more general sense. Bin Laden appears to have had a hand in the violent actions perpetrated on French soil by the Algerian Armed Islamic Group (GIA) between 11 July and 17 October 1995. They killed nine and injured 198, the most murderous attack being that on the Saint-Michel metro station on 25 July, which left seven dead and 84 wounded.[20]

It is usually difficult to recruit both the excluded and people from the middle classes. In the case of al-Qaeda, the former do not seem to be particularly hard to recruit. The group's vanguard comes from categories close to the upper or middle classes. During its Afghan period, however, the group did recruit members from Islamic countries, including young men from the lower classes of Algeria, Egypt, Pakistan and Yemen. It was able to integrate heterogeneous groups and get them to work together because they shared the same vision of the enemy and the need to fight for Islam. The immense advantage of these simple themes was that they had a wide appeal in an Islamic world that had been wounded by assaults on several Muslim countries: Bosnia, Afghanistan, Iraq, Pakistan (Kashmir), Chechnya and Algeria.

The other specific feature of al-Qaeda is that it was able to train its members in autonomous camps in Afghanistan under the reign of the Taliban, and in Bosnia during the first half of the 1990s. The Afghan and Bosnian recruitment and training networks gave it a lot of room for manoeuvre and considerable autonomy at the operational level. America's invasion or Iraq in 2003 and the ability of al-Qaeda members to survive on the frontiers between Pakistan (Waziristan), Afghanistan and Iran (the Sunni Baluchistan) after the downfall of the Taliban regime have given the group a new impetus and it has chosen Iraq as its new laboratory.

The network has no concrete project other than fighting the West, and no specific political platform. Its goal is not to form a government in any specific state, even though Bin Laden does denounce Saudi Arabia for being under America's thumb, and Arab regimes for their inability to challenge the West. Unlike the Islamic Revolution in Iran which did at the beginning cherish the project of an Islamic justice that would benefit the *mostadafine* (the oppressed), al-Qaeda has no coherent economic project. It is made up of preachers who express in terms of pathos their rejection of an arrogant West and an ungodly world characterised by injustice and moral and sexual depravity. They are not military leaders, but imams who preach a rigid and 'salafist' version of Islam without playing any role in a military command structure, and activists from all walks of life. In the West, the modern sector of the economy is a major source of recruits.

In financial terms, the movement's great strength lies in its ability to guarantee its own autonomy and to carry out autonomous operations. It has been able to become self-financing when its operations are planned in the long term (a fishing boat was purchased to subsidise its crew by selling the fish).[21] Just as there is no centralisation in its political organisation, there is no centralisation in its financial operations.

The network has several types of members, and this makes it fearfully effective. The many different types of action in which it is involved are unrelated in terms of motivations or ideals, but the network contrives to carry them out simultaneously without bothering too much about their specific nature. In a traditional pyramid structure, it is difficult to bring together very different individuals because they are supposed to obey a hierarchy but do not necessarily share its aims. In a network structure, it is much easier to deal with the presence of actors with very different intentionalities and aims. The only thing that matters is that members belonging to the same cell do not have too many differences. As the cells act autonomously, rather as though they were the network's satellites, their coexistence does not pose any major problem. The bond between their members is based upon friendship and cultural closeness, as well as the shared feeling of 'humiliation'. That is the source of the strength of networks like al-Qaeda, Aum in Japan and the Patriots and Militias in the United States.

Al-Qaeda displays many of the essential characteristics of modern cults, but there are two important differences between it and them. The first is that cults shut themselves off from the world, either by isolating themselves from it or by fighting it, but the fact that they often have few members means that there cannot, by definition, be many 'chosen ones'. The existence of over 1 billion Muslims, in contrast, means that the various Islamist groups are constantly tempted to recruit 'inauthentic' Muslims by transforming them into 'authentic Muslims'. They have to be awakened by the call to *jihad*, and they must be shown the real threat facing Islam. There is a further difference between groups like al-Qaeda and cults. It leads an underground existence, not only because it is clandestine but because of its network nature. Every network is autonomous, and has its own local charismatic figures, forms of financing that make it self-sufficient and an ability to adapt to local conditions that make it a subsect in its own right, even though it has links with the centre. Al-Qaeda is like a federal organisation made up of a multitude of sects, or a 'hypersect'. Until 11 September 2001, Bin Laden was not very well-known and lacked charisma, when compared with Khomeini in Iran, Kishk in Egypt or Musa Sadr in Lebanon. Every subnetwork in England, France, the United States or elsewhere has a cultist structure in the true sense of the word. Each network is largely autonomous from the others, and operates in ways that combine the benefits of modern technology (especially computer networks and the internet) with forms of religiosity which look, in the West, like an inverted multiculturalism. This feature can also be found in many other transnational Islamic organisations. Although its various European centres are more interdependent and more visible, Tabligh leaders from various countries meet a least once a year in Dewsbury in England. The group enjoys great autonomy in France, Germany and England.

The second way in which al-Qaeda differs from modern cults derives from its military origins. The organisation took shape during the war in Afghanistan and that has had a lasting influence on its organisation, management and ideology. It was a secret organisation from the outset. It has not undergone any major changes, unlike groups like Al-Fatah, which had to emerge from its clandestinity and turn itself into a political organisation. We are talking about a group which, ever since it came into existence, has always been clandestine and military, and it has retained those characteristics throughout its existence although it underwent major transformations after the fall of the Taliban and as Western countries began to hunt down its members.

These new forms of activism and terrorism have not, however, made a complete break with classic terrorism. The new and the old often mingle to such a degree that one specialist in international terrorism speaks of the 'final stage of classic terrorism' rather than of the emergence of new forms.[22] In Chaliand's view it has made a 'quantitative leap' but not a 'qualitative leap'. There is, he remarks, nothing new about suicide attacks. As for the vague and inarticulate project of a new Islamic *umma*, it is as utopian as the pan-Arabism and the pan-Africanism of the past.

As we shall see, there is something very new about the subjectivity of these activists, and that makes them very different to the terrorists of old. The new terrorist actor has a representation of himself, the other, the sacred and the world that makes him different to the protagonists of the 1970s or the 1980s. This phenomenon is not specific to al-Qaeda alone, and its equivalent can be seen in violent cults and loosely structured activist groups The American Militias and Patriots of the early twenty-first century have many features in common with al-Qaeda.

Al-Qaeda's members are not the only Muslim activists to have adopted a cultist form. The diversification of religious forms in the West has been accompanied by a great increase in the number of Muslim groups and sects, and some of them have adopted a militant or even aggressive attitude towards the West. These new associations exploit modern forms of communication and management – information technology, decentralised management and multinational finance – that escape traditional forms of authority. They are sometimes led by Western converts to Islam, some of whom demand a position within an Islamic hierarchy and thus challenge the exclusive right of Arabs or Muslims from non-Western countries to take decisions in the religious domain (the distinction between the licit and the illicit, between what is permitted and what is forbidden, between duties and their limits). The Murabitun movement is one example. It was founded by Sheikh Abdalqadir As-sufi, alias Ian Dallas, and its political leader Umar Ibrahim Vadilla has attempted to establish a gold-based Islamic monetary system to challenge the dollar-based system. The group's economic project is to re-establish Islamic networks of caravans to challenge the West's monopoly on distribution, and to re-establish a so-called Islamic economy. The movement asked its members to give aid to the Taliban during the war waged on them by America in 2001–02. Its aim is to convert skinheads and members of the British far right. Its ideological leitmotifs are anti-Americanism, anti-Judaism, the rejection of usurious economics and the fight against freemasonry.

Like many others of its kind, the movement subscribes to the ideology of the decline of the West and the 'death of democracy'.[23]

In his *Islam and the Death of Democracy*, the founder of the Murabitun takes as his starting point the observation that Islam has always flourished in decadent societies, and argues that faith in Allah will allow the world to flourish anew. He makes a distinction between *dine* (Islamic religion) and *kufr* (heresy and impiety; the Western system in general). The West is in a state of complete decline. If it is to recover from this state, it must turn to the worship of Allah (*Iqama as Salat*) and to the religion of the truth (*dine al haqq*). The decadent West is in the same situation as the pre-Islamic societies of ignorance and depravity (*jahiliyya*). If it is to halt is own decline, it must turn to Islam. What is the basis for the moral depravity of the West? Its failure to recognise that we are finite and limited beings, and that our physical, biological and psychological reality is without hope unless we can have recourse to a transcendental reality. Authentic reality means a form of awareness. There is a similarity here with the key motifs of contemporary Muslim thinkers such as Shariati, who speaks of *agahi* ('consciousness- raising') and Qutb, with his reference to doctrine (*maktab*). According to the founder of the Murabitun, 'awareness' refers to our mortal condition and fragility, as compared with the condition of Allah. He then makes an acerbic critique of modern society, which he describes as a neurotic or 'insane' society that tries to ignore death and conceals the finite nature of human beings by giving man and women purely worldly ideals. He is a harsh critic of the women's liberation movement: the emancipation of women makes them slaves to a modern industrial system that cannot function efficiently if it does not enrol them in its service. Similarly, American society is undergoing a slow death as it breaks up under the impact of the contradictory pressures of Zionism, freemasonry and their affiliates. America is dominated by media that manipulate its population. They are the servants of the Zionism that rules America and Palestine. The phenomena of world dominance are possible only because the religion of the true, or Islam, is not recognised because it is a religion that takes account of our mortality.

Islam provides an overall answer to the problems of a lunatic world in which the concealment of death, the political and economic dominance of depraved elites and the sense that life has no meaning have reached epidemic proportions. The author notes that Islam has no clergy, no rituals, no magic, and no mystical figures. It is a rational religion that concentrates on the worship of the Creator to the exclusion of everything else. We must reject the way America dominates the world and return to Islam. Islam will create a unified and organic society that will eventually replace the chaos of Western civilisation, in which murder, mental breakdowns, immorality and rising criminality are typical features of everyday life. The neo-*umma* the leader of the Murabitun is calling for is vaguely inspired by the original Islamic community, which was both simple and ethical. There were no class differences. Everyone could find fulfilment in their own lives. The religion of Allah provides the answer to the problems of modern life: fear of death, the feeling of abandonment and the idea that crime makes the great urban centres unsafe.

This Islamic religiosity was concocted mostly in the West. It combines modern subjective considerations – the concealment of the fear of death, unbridled consumerism, a society without norms or systems of spiritual values – and an activist ideology drawing on the themes of both the far left and the far right. Its enemies are Zionism, world freemasonry and the corrupt elite of a depraved America which is manipulating individuals by mystifying them with alienating ideologies. This type of network, which is purely Western in origin, complements those which, like al-Qaeda, originated from the Middle East at large and which still have strong links with their countries of origin, despite their worldwide expansion.

The organic community the author is calling for has fascistic tendencies reminiscent of the ideas of Ahmad Thomson, who is another convert. The author of *Dajjal the Antichrist* makes a distinction between two systems: the system of heretics, or the *kafir* system, and 'the path of Mahomet'.[24] The system of Dajjal (the Muslim equivalent to the Antichrist) is dominated by the world freemasonry that Hitler and Ezra Pound tried in vain to fight. They were defeated because they did not know the real nature of existence: nothing exists outside Allah. Anything but Him has only a semblance of existence. We must go back to Allah and turn away from heresy (*kufr*) if we are to fight effectively against the ungodly West's world dominion. We can do so all the more easily in that the system is in a state of advanced decay. The idea that the West is undergoing a serious decline and that Islam will regenerate the world is basic to Murabitun ideology, and it is borrowed from Spengler's pessimistic writings on the 'decline of the West'. The remedy is an organic religion that can give birth to a neo-*umma* capable of putting an end to the discontent with anomie, mental disorientation and the loss of meaning by identifying the enemy who must be destroyed and the sacred values we must embrace.

The central project of certain other associations is to re-establish the caliphate, which was abolished in the Islamic world by Kemal Ataturk in 1924. The new caliphate will begin to be built in the West. In the Sunni world – but not the Shi'ite world[25] – the caliphate meant the unification of Muslims under the aegis of a single government. Even though the actual caliphate was, after the fall of the Abbasids, a very limited form of government dominated by leaders from the four corners of the Islamic world, it is still remembered as a government that unified Islam within a single political institution, just as the Holy Roman Empire was believed to be the incarnation of the symbolic unity of Christianity in the West long after its actual eclipse. The idea of the caliphate still gives meaning to the political and religious unity of Islam. For its supporters, it means that the community and politics can come together in a single institution that mirrors the unicity of Allah. This myth has taken on a new meaning in modern times, thanks especially to the establishment of sizeable Muslim minorities in Western countries from the 1970s onwards. Hizb al-Tahrir in Britain and Kaplan in Germany are typical examples.

The Syrian Omar Bakri, who plays a leading role in Hizb al-Tahrir, belongs to that generation of Islamists that wants to establish the caliphate in Muslim countries, and then the whole world. Its construction will begin in the West and not in Muslim countries living in *jahiliyya*.[26] Like Hizb al-Tahrir, Cemaleddin Kaplan's community in Germany calls for the establishment of the caliphate, first in Turkey and then on a world scale, beginning with Germany, to which Kaplan emigrated in the 1980s. The community was established in Germany after a split with Milli Görüs. Most of its original members were Turkish workers.[27] They were later joined by young Turks of the second generation, who had a much higher standard of education and often belonged to the middle classes. Kaplan declared a holy war in 1991, then demanded the establishment of a government in exile in 1992 and finally declared himself Caliph in 1994. Before his death is 1995, he named his son Metin as his successor. There was then a split within the movement when Metin's opponents nominated Dr Ibrahim Sofu as Caliph. Metin Kaplan was arrested by the German police in 1999 for inciting criminal acts. The 1990s saw both the radicalisation of the movement and a change in the social structure of its members. The second generation who joined it in Germany had, as we have noted, a much higher standard of education than their elders. Many had studied at German universities and were easily seduced when they were offered a leading role in the establishment of a new Islamic community that would spread around the world thanks to the rebirth of the caliphate.

In England the role played in Germany by the second-generation Turkish diaspora, which is deeply imbued with German culture, is played by young second-generation Pakistanis, many of whom are highly educated and who are fascinated by the important role the association gives them: they are the vanguard of the new Islamic world that is about to come into being. They therefore feel that they have a prophetic role to play in their parents' country of origin. That allows them to recover much of the dignity they have lost in Western societies, where they feel themselves to be the object of scorn and an almost palpable racism. Although they are not excluded from society, these young men are deeply discontented because of the discrimination they suffer. They have no access to the jobs and opportunities for which their level of education and their abilities qualify them. They have been insidiously marginalised by stigmatisation and racism, and their imaginary amplifies the effects of both. Because they feel themselves to be victims, they explain their failures in terms of their stigma, but they lose sight of their own inability to adapt to the new constraints of modern society. They also feel a vague but crushing sense of guilt about their parents' societies, especially when, like Pakistan, most Arab countries or even Afghanistan (which is Pashtu-speaking; the language is similar to Urdu) are hit by crises. Thanks to these associations, they become Islam's world actors, and they can therefore feel that they are re-establishing their links with the Islamic societies from which they have been cut off. They also have the impression that, as actors, they are more important than the Western societies that stigmatise them believe them to be. In symbolic terms, this allows them to feel superior to the West that despises them.

There is a further reason why members of Hizb al-Tahrir resent the United Kingdom so much. Unlike the majority of British subjects, who supported the Americans against the Taliban, part of the Pashtu-speaking Pakistani community in Britain defended the Taliban, most of whom were Pahstu-speakers.[28] According to its leader Bakri, Hizb al-Tahrir has offshoots in 21 countries, including the United States,[29] whereas Kaplan has restricted his activities to Germany, despite having some support in Turkey. The primary concern of Turkish Islamist associations in Germany is with Turkey, where they are trying to combat secularism, and they have until now retained their Turkish-German character. Although they are closely linked to

Pakistanis living in Britain, associations like Hizb al-Tahrir are, in contrast, capable of extending their ramifications to other Western countries with a Pakistani diaspora. They are able to exploit anxieties about both the Kashmir problem and Pakistan's close involvement with the Taliban in Afghanistan.

## DIFFERENT TYPES OF ACTOR

Five types of actors can be found in networks like al-Qaeda.[30] The first are the great Qadis of radical Islamism who surround bin Laden. They originate from Egypt, the Arabian peninsular and Palestine and some have links with Algerian, Afghan and even Philippine networks. A second circle is made up of fighters of Arab origin who fought in the Afghan war and then returned home to launch a *jihad* in the name of a radicalised Islam. Some subsequently became involved in violent activities in the West. A third group is made up of Arabs who left their home countries to live in the West and then turned to Islamic radicalism. The distinctive thing about them is that the vast majority of them were actually indoctrinated in the West. A fourth group is made up of young Europeans – and, more rarely, Americans – from immigrant families who have been educated in Europe and who joined al-Qaeda after having been indoctrinated there or after coming into contact with the network in Pakistan or Afghanistan. The fifth group consists of European (and a few American) converts to Islam. In terms of their motivations, these various groups are in agreement over certain points, but they still have their differences.

The extensive literature on the first group provides fairly precise information about bin Laden's immediate entourage.[31]

It is the other four groups that concern us here, as they are representative of a radicalised and inverted modernity. Studies of members of these groups reveal that they are by no means traditional, that they have been exposed to modernisation to a greater or lesser extent, that many of them have had access to schools and universities, that the majority speak several languages and that many have lived in the West, often for long periods. That is why, where the first three groups are concerned, the subjective reasons and objective circumstances that led them to join groups lies in their experience of modernisation. The explanation for the radicalisation of the Europeans of immigrant origin and of the converts who make up the fourth and fifth groups is to be found in their way of life in the West. The groups of young men who rallied to al-Qaeda during the anti-Soviet war in Afghanistan have elective affinities with Palestinian youth. They have been denied access to modernity and are faced with the impossibility of building an autonomous nation.

## THE NEW MIDDLE-CLASS DIASPORA

Many French and British-born young men from immigrant backgrounds say that they espoused an activist Islam because there was no room for them in society. They suffered racism and stigmatisation. They attempted to remedy this by going into exile in other European countries or elsewhere, sometimes in the United States. They eventually joined the Taliban in Afghanistan. Those who live in the West but who come from the Middle East, in contrast, form a diaspora with specific features of its own.

Of the 19 people involved in the 9/11 hijackings, 15 were from Saudi Arabia and had no financial worries. They had a modern education and the vast majority of them had lived in the West for a long time, either in Germany, Britain or the United States. They were not motivated by the same discontents as the young men of the European diaspora, many of whom live in a situation of economic exclusion and racial stigmatisation. Their espousal of the *jihadist* version of Islam therefore cannot be explained in terms of their feeling of being pariahs. How, then, are we to understand why they went down that path, when most of them could have been integrated into the West and could have enjoyed a middle-class, and in some cases upper-class, standard of living? Why did they choose to join al-Qaeda?

As we have seen, al-Qaeda brings together a wide variety of militants. We can identify three groups on the basis of how they joined it and how they lived in the West. There are those who fought the communist regime in Afghanistan at the time of the honeymoon between al-Qaeda and the United States, and who then dispersed and went home after the regime had been overthrown. Some spread the good news about *jihad*. This was particularly true of Algeria where the 'Afghans' – Algerians who fought against the communist regime in Afghanistan – swelled the ranks of the FIS, and then those of the GIA after the military coup d'état. One group of militants settled in the West after leaving Afghanistan but remained part of the network. In the decade that followed the end of the war in Afghanistan, a third group joined the organisation after having lived in the West. This group had no previous links with al-Qaeda.

The first group came into being mainly as a result of the struggle against the communist regime in Kabul in the 1980s. In 1981, Reagan's America, Pakistan and Saudi Arabia formed an alliance to arm and train the *mujahedeen*. The al-Qaeda group – the word means 'base' in Arabic – owes its name to the volunteers who had travelled through Pakistan or other countries to join the Afghan *mujahedeen*, and whose families had lost track of them. A computerised database was established to identify them in 1988, and subsequently gave its name to bin Laden's network.[32] Its goal was to mobilise Muslims to fight the communists in Afghanistan. Between 1980 and 1990, Muslim volunteers trained in Pakistan by Western instructors helped to fight a guerrilla war against the Russians. They became known as 'Arab Afghans' or simply 'Afghans'.[33] It was at this point that bin Laden raised his Islamic Legion. It was made up of several tens of thousands of 'Afghans'. After the Soviet invasion, the Pakistani consulate in Algiers issued some 2800 visas to young Algerians who wanted to fight the communist regime in Afghanistan. Many departures went unrecorded, and the volunteers travelled via Iran or Jordan. The British defence journal *Jane's* estimates their numbers at 14,000, including 5000 Saudis, 300 Yemenis, 2000 Egyptians, 2800 Algerians, 400 Tunisians, 370 Iraqis, 200 Libyans and a few dozen Jordanians.[34] Many of these young men came from the working classes of their countries of origin. In Afghanistan, they met others from similar backgrounds, learned Pashtu and Dari (Afghan Persian) dialects and above all got to know one another. This created ties of friendship and affective relations that were consolidated by their common experience of war. Those from North African countries had previously known each other only because of the French connection, whilst those from Middle Eastern countries met through American or British connections. Two hundred years ago, people from these regions were in close contact with each other thanks to Islam. As a result of colonial domination and post-independence modernisation by Western-style secular states, Muslim societies became more focussed on the West and relations between the various Muslim countries were to a greater or lesser extent marginalised. The war in Afghanistan made it possible to revive in modern terms a type of experience that had become forgotten.

The Afghanistan and Pakistan of the 1980s and 1990s thus acted as a melting pot where Muslims from various parts of the world could meet without Westerners being present. They all wanted the same thing: to fight Evil. In the Sunni world, Afghanistan and Pakistan played much the same role that Iran had played in the 1980s in Lebanon and elsewhere. At that time, Iran's Shi'ite message did not get the favourable reception its protagonists expected because of Shi'ism's minority position within Islam. So long as the communist regime remained in power in Afghanistan, the connection was made with the blessing of the West, and of America in particular. The Americans did not realise that, as well as fighting the communist enemy, its allies were beginning to unite around an Islam that objected to a modernity most of them regarded as sinful and anti-Islamic. Those who migrated to Pakistan favoured the Deobandi version of Islam (it takes its name from a village in Pakistan), which is itself modelled on the Wahhabism advocated by Saudi Arabia. It protected them from a modernity that had been tainted by the corrupting presence of the West. The *mujahedeens'* rejection of it was masked by their hatred of the atheist communist regime in Kabul.

In the 1980s al-Qaeda mobilised and trained young men from modest backgrounds, most of them from the Arab countries or Pakistan. In the 1990s, the network began to attract different recruits. There were fewer of them, but they were better educated. The Gulf War can be seen as the turning point. By allowing American troops to be based on its soil, Saudi Arabia gave the West what the Salafists saw as an opportunity to profane the country responsible for protecting Islam's holiest place, namely Mecca. There had been a similar reaction when 40 thousand American troops were based in Iran in the 1970s. Khomeini exploited the situation as a further sign of the Shah's regime's subservience to America, and denounced the infidel's so-called desire to profane Islam. It was the explicit hostility to the United States and to the West in general that was attractive to this new group.

### Disaporas in America

Most of those who operated in America and took part in the attacks on the World Trade Center were Arabs from the Arabian peninsula. They came from the Middle East, Europe and a few of them had lived in the United States. The Saudi-born Hani Hanjur, for example, spent much of the 1990s there.[35] Their self-image and worldview were broadly similar to those of young Europeans of immigrant origin.

When interviewed in prison, some of these men revealed a feature that is not so pronounced in al-Qaeda's European supporters. It seems obvious to them that the West is pernicious in terms of its culture, or at least in terms of the way it dominates the rest of the world.

They cannot tolerate its unbridled sexuality, unnatural promiscuity, the totally deregulated relations between men and women, male and female homosexuality, family instability and the loss of male authority, or in short its immorality and depravity. There is also the further trauma of the hegemony the West exercises over Muslims, either indirectly and through the intermediary of corrupt Muslim regimes, or directly by having recourse to arms. That the West actively colludes in Israel's dominance over the Palestinians shows its perverse nature. They have countless grievances against the West, and they are long-standing. They have developed a siege mentality and a collective memory centred on events specific to each Muslim country. In Iran, the key moments are America's coup d'état against Mossadegh in 1953, its unfailing support for the Shah's regime, and the support it lent the Iraqi regime in its war against Iran (1980–88). In the Arab countries, the trauma of the formation of Israel and the unfailing military, economic and political support lent it by America are the main themes of the anti-American memory. The successive defeats of Arab armies, and especially that of 1967, fuel their hostility towards the United States still further. In its turn, the Palestinian question fuels an anti-Americanism that is increasingly becoming a permanent feature of Arab and Muslim countries because television stations all over the world broadcast pictures of the humiliation of the Palestinians day in, day out. The influence of television is gradually replacing that of the concrete communities that once gave their members a homogeneous worldview. As those communities are now in advanced state of decay, it is the media and especially television that provide their worldview. A 'televisual community' is replacing the decaying communities of old, and it is increasingly that community that is shaping societies' memory, and especially the memory of the rootless groups that have recently become involved in it. Over the last few years, it has been television that has provoked the Judaeophobic reactions of some Muslim prisoners in French jails, where Muslims sometimes make up 80 per cent of the prison population.[36]

What is particularly disturbing for those who came to the West to continue their studies or to escape the crisis in their countries of origin is that they were looking for a breath of fresh air and wanted to espouse the modernity from which they felt themselves so unfairly excluded. Many of these young people do integrate into these societies but some of them do not find an answer to their questions and anxieties. Now that they are living in the West, the modernity they wanted so badly looks to them like the emperor's new clothes.

It gradually loses the prestige it had when they imagined it in their countries of origin. It means nothing but access to consumerism, and has no 'noble' meaning that might insert them into a 'warm' social fabric with a meaning commensurate with their cherished ideals. Their day-to-day experience of the West they dreamed of so much teaches them that living there means nothing more than making minor compromises with a life that simply has no higher meaning. There is no sense of the sacred. When the rhythm of life is dictated by a consumerism and a mediocrity that do not seem to offer any future, life cannot be meaningful. The lack of meaning and the deep feeling that Muslims are being repressed and humiliated by the West fuel Islamic radicalism.

Whilst many of these young men do eventually become involved in sexual relationships with women, they often conclude that they are doomed to failure. It is impossible for women to remain faithful in a West where different social categories no longer exist, and where the difference between men and women no longer means anything to them. Men have become effeminate and there is no longer any room for male virility. Life goes on in a closed world where communication is often impossible. Many of these young men live in urban isolation, and that leads them to search for meaning outside the usual circuits of Western sociability. The promiscuity of this part of the world and the fierce individualism that prevails within it finally convince these marginal figures of the basic immorality of a civilisation that claims to rule the world but which makes it impossible for anyone to live a 'healthy' life. This grievance combines with the others and deepens the hatred of the West.

On the one hand, living in the Western world undermines that world's prestige to a dangerous extent; on the other, there is an acute sense that the West's unfairness to the Muslim world is intolerable. Thirdly, even those who are not excluded in the economic sense still experience a more or less covert racism and find it profoundly humiliating. For a minority of young men, these three factors make it impossible to reconcile themselves to a world where arrogance, deception and immorality go hand in hand. They reject Western society as a whole. They want to fight it. They refuse to see the West as a non-monolithic and autonomous set of countries and cultures, and identify it with a mythical unity that legitimises the use of blind violence against it. Members of al-Qaeda feel no guilt about the innocent victims of their attacks because there are no real innocents in this part of the world. They are 'guilty' because they are part of an organic totality whose members are not individuals but closely related particles. Al-Qaeda's response to Western individuals is to deny the individuality of the societies they are fighting. There are no individuals. The only thing that exists is an inhuman order that oppresses Muslims, and it deserves to be treated as a single totality in which no one is anything more than a stitch in a tightly woven fabric that is all of a piece. The Westerner's individual reality disappears, and a gulf opens up between reality as it is lived by the Westerner and the unifying and totalising vision the Islamist superimposes on it.

The experience of an almost virtual and opaque world in which everything can be interpreted in antagonistic terms encourages al-Qaeda's members to see the West as a mythical and satanic totality. This was not the experience of the young Iranians of the 1980s, and it is not that of the young Palestinians of the second Intifada. Their experience was that of the concrete destruction of a utopia (the Islamic nation and the Palestinian nation respectively) and the identification of a real enemy (even if the demonisation of the enemy was largely the result of a mythical construct). The experience of those young men living in the West who become involved in terrorist activity is not so much that of direct domination – they have been away from home for quite a long time and live like the majority of the Western middle or lower-middle classes – as a hatred for an ignominious West that is so difficult to grasp. In complex societies where modes of inscription in social reality are becoming increasingly difficult and demand constant revision and adjustment, reality does often look like an opaque whole that can be difficult to read. For those who come from a different world, it is not just incomprehensible, but satanic. Its opacity is interpreted as a deliberate attempt to deny Muslims who are looking for human warmth and hospitality access to any transparency. The anonymity and coldness of this strangely unfriendly world is exacerbated by the indecipherable attitudes and 'reflexivity'[37] of Westerners who distrust others. Their refusal to open up is interpreted as arrogance, and as a sign that they despise others. For Westerners, distrust is a way of protecting oneself from strangers whose intentions are not immediately obvious. Keeping one's distance is a form of self-defence, a way of erecting a barrier between self and other so as to neutralise the other's potentially aggressive or malevolent intentions. Keeping one's distance has become a widespread habit in the West, and especially in the great urban centres, where everyone is exposed on a daily basis to a multitude of people belonging to other cultures. Muslims interpret this reflexivity as a further sign that they are despised. The welcome they are given does not meet their expectations. They are kept at arm's length and no one establishes a social bond with them. The fear and distrust inspired by Islam is of course proportional to the crimes attributed to Islamism by the Western media.

Immigrants react to the coldness of modern societies in much the same way as the many Westerners who chose to join cults in an attempt to establish 'warm' groups where physical closeness can provide the basis for a new morality. But Muslims also have the poignant feeling that they share the sufferings of the societies from which they come. As we have already said, their sufferings in the symbolic dimension are even greater thanks to the media, to which they have much easier access than they did in their societies of origin. Their feeling that they need to shut themselves away is exacerbated by their growing realisation that the 'West' is vacuous, immoral and emotionally unstable. Ultimately they find it impossible to arrive at any modus vivendi with a world that is ruled by the forces of evil.

This inverted multiculturalism in which access to other cultures leads to a combination of radicalisation, closure and rejection of the Other has a further important feature. Muslims feel that this is a chaotic world in which the family is disintegrating, where men have become slaves to women, where an unnatural and detestable homosexuality has ousted normal and divinely sanctioned forms of sexuality, and where everything is unstable and precarious. In the West, where sexual liberation was the historical product of a critique of Christian puritanism, homosexuality has become normal because the central norms, and especially those of the patriarchal family, have disappeared. Women's movements have destroyed the dissymmetrical family model dominated by the all-powerful figure of the husband and father. In the Islamic part of the world, male sexuality has never been accompanied by the sense of guilt instilled by Christianity. Normal male sexuality took the form of polygamy, which, in theory, allowed men to satisfy their needs by contracting legal marriages with four women, and 'temporary marriages' with others. Polygamy has of course always been the privilege of the very tiny minority of men who could afford it, but it still plays an important role in the Muslim male imaginary and makes sense of the great dissymmetry in relations between men and women, as men can have several wives whilst women cannot have several husbands. The veiling of women is also an expression of a culture that 'covers up' the female body so as not to provoke men's sexuality, which is sovereign in social relationships. Some Muslim men who come into contact with Western promiscuity convince themselves that Islam is superior in matters of sexuality.

Whereas the majority do adapt, their experience of life in the West proves to a minority of immigrants that this insane world is satanic. In the nineteenth century, some of the colonised internalised their colonisation and believed in the intrinsic superiority of the white man, but now that they live amongst those who once colonised them, their sons and grandsons reject the idea of their superiority. Indeed, they find themselves living in a shapeless world that is too diverse to be the embodiment of any superiority, and sufficiently diabolic to conceal its evil nature behind a mask of unbridled complexity. To the neo-Muslims who live there, this diversity hides an underlying unity that is designed to deceive them, and that makes the West's anti-Islamic prejudices, which they both see on television and experience in their everyday lives, still more humiliating and still more abominable. The humiliation is, in other words, even greater when they see the chaos and sexual and moral depravity that surround them. It is not simply that they do not integrate. They have every reason to reject the West, and they now do so on the basis of their actual lived experience. As they said in the interviews, Islam gives them simplicity and transparency. In a world where nothing is clear and in which everything is the subject of exhausting debates and negotiations, the verdicts of Islam have the virtues of an undeniable univocity, and their transparency is in stark contrast to the impenetrability of the norms whereby life is lived in this ungodly region of the world.

The West is ungodly, incomprehensible, arrogant and depraved. It is incomprehensible because it has made progress despite is moral corruption, whilst Muslims remain in a pitiful state. Many radical Muslims thinkers have an explanation for this. Muslims live in a state of dependency and underdevelopment because they have strayed from the straight path (*sarat mosqtaqim*) prescribed by Allah. They are living in the state of idolatry and ignorance (*jahiliyya*) that characterised Arab societies before they were converted to Islam by the Prophet. These ideas circulate widely amongst Muslims who have become radicalised in the West. Whilst their deviation from true Islam explains why Muslims have become decadent, the material progress made by the perverted West still remains enigmatic to these diasporic Muslims, who are convinced that it is evil. One explanation finds favour with activists who are trying to rationalise this. The West makes progress because it enslaves Muslims and others and because of its imperialism. This is described in Arabic as *istikbar* (from *mostakbar*, meaning arrogant and oppressive; the term derives from the root *kbr*, meaning pride and presumptuousness). In its modernised form, the term is applied both to Muslims who are eager for individual comfort and to the West's accomplices both inside and outside the Islamic world.

These Muslims' concrete experience of the West provides them with a further interpretation. The Western world is perverted but fascinating. Its wealth and its women fascinate them, but its transgression of divine norms horrifies them. The West is not only something that has to be proscribed. It has to be banished from the believer's interiority, which has been infected by the virus of 'Westernness'. Some Iranian intellectuals who have had contact with the American world have theorised this by coining the term 'the Western disease' (*qarb zadegui*) or 'Westoxication'.[38] The Western cancer must be fought by driving it out of the soul. This is the key to the 'inner *jihad*' (*jihad akbar*, or 'greater Jihad', as the Sufis call it). The term is borrowed from Islamic mysticism. This explains their undying hatred for the West, whose anonymous population can be put to death in acts of violence because every Westerner has a role, no matter how small, to play in the fascination the West exercises over the new supporters of radical Islam. One effective way to root out the evil within is to eradicate its physical supports, namely the thousands of Western men and women who, wittingly or unwittingly, are exposing the souls of Muslims to the 'Westoxication' virus by contaminating them from within. This inner struggle can no longer be restricted, as it was in the past, to waging war on those who are directly responsible for it. It has to be extended by declaring open war on the whole world.

Justifications are sought – and found – in the work of Islamic thinkers such as Ibn Taymiya, who was a seventeenth-century theologian. He lived at a time when the conflict between the Mameluks and the Mongols made classic warfare between Muslims and non-Muslims a thing of the past. There were Muslims and non-Muslims in both armies. The traditional prohibition on killing other Muslims – even in a war against other Muslims – made this type of mixed warfare difficult. Taymiyah refuted the argument that Muslims must not be killed by their coreligionists and found a theological justification for mixed warfare. He was, however, referring to those who were directly involved in the war and not the civilian population.[39] His verdict has now been extended to include that population. If it is permissible to kill Muslims in battle, it is, a fortiori, also permissible to kill non-Muslims. And if those who are not directly involved in the hostilities are killed in the higher interests of Islam, that is also permissible. In the West, the same argument is put forward in technical and non-religious terms. Hence the use of the expression 'collateral damage'. The Islamists I interviewed in prison inevitably pointed out that Westerners hypocritically killed innocent people in their confrontations with Islam.[40]

Several registers are combined in this picture of the satanic West. In order to paint a unified picture, its complexity is transformed into a satanic transparency that is hidden by Western cunning. Some diasporic Muslims who live in the West and who have the same everyday worries as anyone else living there conclude, finally, that Muslim countries are being mistreated by a West that has lost the old prestige it once enjoyed.

Radicalisation also allows these militants to differentiate themselves from the vast majority of Muslims living in the West. Unlike the vast majority, who do adapt to Western habits and customs, they advocate a strategy of rupture. That is why they must fight both the West and lukewarm Muslims who refuse to accept their Manichean version of events. The demonisation of the West thus helps diasporic groups that are in a small minority to adopt a hostile stance towards both the Western enemy and the Muslim majorities who live peacefully there.

There are Muslims and converts to Islam in the United States. The former come from Arab, Indian (Pakistan, India, Bangladesh) or other Muslim countries. Aside from the minority group of 'White' and 'Spanish' whites who have espoused Islam, the vast majority of converts are blacks who have constructed their religiosity by using models that often deviate from what is described as orthodox Islam (this is true of many Black Muslims and followers of the Nation of Islam). Relations between the two groups are not close, and they appear to distrust one another. The groups are autonomous, and have their own mosques and imams. The new activists, terrorist or *jihadists* of recent years are usually recruits from groups from the Arab countries, though there are also a new non-black American converts amongst them. Because the blacks and the others tend not to mix, there are no organic links between the two groups for the moment.

### The young diaspora in France: multiculturalism inverted

The available data, together with the prison interviews I carried out in 2002 and 2003, allows us to identify certain of the characteristic features of these young men. Most of the prisoners have Algerian or Moroccan parents, but chose England as their place of residence. Few of them are French converts. Their primary characteristic feature is a sense that they have failed in France. They have an antagonistic relationship with their parents' adoptive country, even though most of them are French nationals. They have a higher-than-average level of education, and are very familiar with new technologies such as computers, aeronautics and commerce. They belong to the middle classes, which have a real identity problem because of their relative success and partial failure. They are profoundly discontented with France, which has, in their view, dispossessed them of all their roots in their families' country of origin but which has failed to integrate them fully.

The time they spent in England did not open up the path to integration there. They did, however, find a 'Muslim community' that gave them a feeling of belonging to a much wider *umma* that existed outside the United Kingdom. The fact that they left France and then lived in England – for several years in some cases – heightened their feeling of being stateless. They could identify all the more easily with an extended neo-*umma* in that they had distanced themselves from any feeling of belonging to any particular nation. Their new identity allowed them to become, in their own way, citizens of Islam. That made it even easier to reject a French world which was, in their view, opposed to their integration into the wider community of believers. Living in Britain, they experienced their 'non-belonging' in a twofold sense: they belonged to neither France nor the United Kingdom. As Britain was tolerant enough to accept the preaching of *jihad* and took little notice of deviant groups so long as they did not pose a direct threat to its security, they had a heightened sense of their own marginality and therefore rejected Europe and the West in general.

Their experience of the United States, where some spent several months, confirmed this impression. The fact that they had spent time in many different Western countries heightened their feeling of being different. They now had no strong ties with any one country precisely because they had lived in so many. Having lived in Britain, they had an identity that had nothing to do with belonging to a particular nation. Islam now became the basis of their identity. They originally left France because they had doubts about their identity, and those doubts were exacerbated by one or more failures and by their decision to learn English so as to have easier access to better-paid work. Before they went abroad, the harassment began with their exclusion from certain jobs, and especially better-paid jobs in public relations. A racism that was sometimes covert and sometimes much more explicit denied them access to the jobs that 'native' candidates with the same qualifications could obtain.[41] Then came one of those incidents that can happen to any young person, especially if they are 'Arab', for reasons that are often specific to the individual and his or her sensibility. The general context is one in which they feel rejected or stigmatised. Khaled Kelkal was one such example. Unable to pursue his studies normally at school because he was an Arab and unpopular, he became involved in terrorism in 1995.[42] There was also the fact that working 'for the French' revived memories of how their parents had been exploited. The colonial relations older generations of Maghrebins had suffered under French colonialism were transposed to the present. All these factors mean that they were in a fragile financial and mental state even before they crossed the Channel.

Although they may have encountered a strict Islam in France, it was, in most cases, in England that they forged their new identity. Its purpose was not to make them Europeans or to use the language of Shakespeare to gain access to a wider world, but to Islamise them within networks that allowed them to live modest lives in financial terms but also gave them a holy vocation to serve the religion of Allah.

The many faces of the West discovered by this generation of rootless young men – who were neither French nor North African – had the effect of producing an inverted multiculturalism. Their exposure to other cultures did not produce a feeling of euphoria or hybridity. They distanced themselves from all cultures as though they were an artificial whole, and strongly identified with the message of Allah because it transcended them all and provided them with a strict code of human behaviour that was beyond all human contingency. Whereas human rights promoted a vision of a humanity that had inalienable rights that were not tied to any specific culture, they went one step further by preaching a transcultural Islam that did not recognise specific cultures because it spread the message of Allah and knew nothing of societies, countries, nations or peoples. Their experience of the many cultures of the West gave them a heightened awareness of their artificiality and imperfection. Those cultures were powerless to resist the message of Allah, which is essentially transcultural. They could thus rise above all cultural particularisms by identifying with a metacultural and purely scriptural Islam in which the words of the Prophet were not subject to any historical or cultural determination.[43]

Their familiarity with various Western cultures also made them hostile to a West that left them no space in which they could assert themselves. This is true of both the excluded and, in a way, those who have been able to integrate in social and economic terms. The slightest reference to their different and stigmatising origins causes them real pain and takes on a symbolic dimension that is out of all proportion to the anodyne attitudes that usually inspire this 'ordinary' racism. The paranoid way in which they often reacted to their degradation was disproportionate to the 'minor racism' that teases and mocks 'Arabs'. The vast majority of immigrants from the Maghreb are not especially scandalised by the mocking and ironic form of racism that rarely goes very far, and tell themselves that it is worth putting up with a few wounding remarks that are of little consequence if that is the price they have to pay for their social integration. Others swell the ranks of the excluded, who have many objective reasons for resenting a society that has marginalised them because of their origins. The die is cast, and they are on the sidelines. Their identification with a particularly strict neo-*umma* then inverts the terms of the problem: the reason why there is no place for them in this inhospitable society is that it is corrupt. Whereas they once saw themselves as members of a tragically marginal group to which others were indifferent, they now see others as enemies who are denying them access to the true Islam. They now turn against this promiscuity, this confused state of affairs and the absence of norms that makes it impossible to tell the difference between men and women, between big and the little, between adults and minors, between the righteous and the depraved, or between the virtuous and the licentious. Before their conversion, the West was a place of indecision and confusion that made it opaque; now that they have discovered the true faith, they can see that it is insidiously satanic.

Information technology, which is a sector where many of them find precarious jobs, provides further confirmation of the abstract nature of the world they are living in. In the circumstances, the expression 'computerised abstraction' is not inappropriate, particularly as some of them are addicted to it and know how software can be used to manipulate things. Modern techniques such as the practice of so-called 'defleshing' give us some idea of how they see things. An image is gradually impoverished so that its essential characteristics can be stored on a hard disk. It is so compressed that it takes up only a fraction of the space the complete image would take up.[44] At this point, matter becomes non-existent in any real sense of the term. To be more accurate, matter is nothing more than the various ways in which forms can be moulded. Like reality, matter is no more than an abstraction. Just as we have an almost complete freedom to mould forms, the real can, in its turn, be shaped at will. All that we have to do is reduce it to the status of an image. The imaginary now has complete control over the real. An abstract society has become a spectacle that unfolds in an almost virtual world that 'normal' people master as best they can. There is, however, a danger that those who feel themselves to be excluded or unloved will take it literally and then try to make it 'virtual' thanks to the magic of the imaginary's control over reality.

These young men who are diasporic two or three times over no longer had any feeling of belonging to any nation or country until they acquired the reassuring certainty that they were members of an *umma*. Their case is symptomatic. Because there was no authentic European community to adopt them when France failed to integrate them, the United Kingdom provided them with an opportunity to establish a neo-*umma* that was at war with the West. In the United Kingdom, they discovered a community that existed within an extended Islam that recognised no frontiers. Because it was also the religion of Pakistanis and Indians, this religion was seen by young Franco-Maghrebins living in England as the incarnation of a truth that transcended all cultures. They refuse to be integrated into a nation; they deny the European dimension; they espouse Islam. That is an adequate description of the state of mind of these diasporic exiles. Their discontent has been heightened by Europe's refusal to insert them into a modernity that is still out of their reach. In their eyes, Europe is no more than a hoax that reproduces on the grand scale the rejection they suffered at a national level. It is the incomprehension they feel they have encountered that cements together their neo-*umma*, which cuts itself off from the host country.

The treatment they receive in the United Kingdom is less hostile, but this is a matter of cold calculation rather than of any particular affection for them. Unlike France, Britain leaves them alone, which is why they do not commit acts of violence in that country.[45] Following the advice of the radicalised imams of mosques like the one in Finsbury Park in north London, where Abu Hamza al-Amazei used to preach, or the Piety mosque in Leicester, they obey the principle of *maslaha* ('public interest'). *Maslaha* allows Islam and their community

.to flourish under Her Majesty's protection. For the moment, a sort of ceasefire is necessary but when the right moment comes they will break it in order to advance the cause of their religion in an ungodly country. Abu Qatada, the Islamist cleric suspected of being Bin Laden's ambassador to Europe, lived in Bolton. Omar al-Bayumi, who is accused by the American intelligence services of having been involved in the partial destruction of the Pentagon on 11 September 2001, lived in Birmingham, and studied for his doctorate at Aston University. Anas al-Liby, who is suspected of having taken part in the attacks on the US Embassy in Nairobi in 1998, lived in Manchester. Lofti Raissi, who has been accused by the CIA of having been involved in the 11 September attacks, although there does not seem to be any convincing proof of that, lived in Slough, near London. These British cities were the birthplace of networks and the Islamist *umma* rather than the cradles of future citizens of Europe. Even though the accusations made against them are far from proven and even though the suspicion that hangs over them is in part the result of the fear of more attacks in Europe, the fact remains that the neo-*umma* is the pole of identification for an activist minority of European Muslims who have not succeeded in putting down strong roots in either the nation or Europe.

Most of these young men had gone over to the other side and espoused the cause of a merciless *jihad* before they went to live in the United States. Some, however, joined radical Islamist groups after experiencing life in America, and not before. The Lebanese Wadih al-Hage is one notable example. The fact remains that the diversification of their multicultural experiences in Western societies had had the effect of shutting out these minority groups, often from a world that should, in theory, have been theirs, if we ignore the fact that their parents came from south of the Mediterranean.

A pernicious dialectic is at work here. Whereas humanists like Erasmus and Montaigne favoured a rich diversity of habits and customs, and whereas some forms of hybridity and multiculturalism break down the barriers of societies by making them receptive to other conceptions, we have here a cultural closure, or even a denial of the right to culture as a legitimate form of human experience. If it is to be authentic, religion must be transcultural and indeed transcend all cultures. It must be subject to the strict code of a deculturalised Islam. This religious feeling has no concrete referent and no tangible roots in human experience. Its only basis is a holy book: the Koran and the *hadiths*.

This deliberately disembodied religiosity, which is inscribed in the imaginary of young emigrants who have become spiritually stateless derives further legitimacy from its hostility to a chaotic world that requires the imposition of a new order. That new order could not be brought into being by the passion of Iran's Bassidji martyrs, or by Palestine's human bombs, who were tormented souls compared with these cold new followers of Allah. The new Islamic order has no roots in any one nation, but will be born under the cold gaze of the computer expert and the webmaster who works by cutting and pasting, compressing and decompressing and by operating in an almost surgical way on the disembodied images that are their only experience of a directionless world that has no existential meaning. The anthropological content of the deaths imagined by these young exiles in England, Germany or America is not that of the deaths contemplated by human bombs in Palestine or the Iranian martyrs who seek a violent end. For all but the most radicalised of them, the enemy has a particular face. For the Iranian, he is an Iraqi. For the Palestinian he is an Israeli, and for the Chechen, he is a Russian. For the exiles, in contrast, the dead are a sign in an abstract semiology, and have no particular face. Their sole identifiable characteristic is that they are 'Westerners' simply because they live in the West. The attack on the World Trade Center took place in New York, and was directed against America, but al-Qaeda has organised other attacks in Europe. And given that New York is a cosmopolitan city, many of those who died there were foreigners. The twin towers were a symbol of an arrogant and 'globalised' America.

In the world of France's *banlieues*, some young people who are not of Maghrebin origin occasionally adopt the lifestyle, accent, clothes and the body language of young 'Arabs', who actually have French nationality even though they are of Maghrebin origin. Because they live in the same conditions, they come to identify with them to such a degree that imitating these 'Arabs' becomes a legitimate way of being. They then begin to adopt the same attitude towards girls as the *'beurs'* (French-born 'Arabs'), use the same terms to describe them, and exclude them from their small circles of friends. In these neighbourhoods, Islam becomes attractive for the same reasons: it is the religion of those they live with. It is the religion of those they mix with, and they all share the same fate, tastes and lifestyles. For the marginal young delinquents who live by petty theft and drug-dealing, Islam is not a religion like any other. It is the only religion they might possibly espouse because it is uncontaminated and has never been the religion of the dominant.[46] Some French youngsters from a Catholic background eventually turn to Islam because a Muslim is the only thing to be in this selectively multicultural world. The same phenomenon can be observed in England, where Islam is seen by the underdogs as the religion of choice.

This created the necessary reasons for joining radical groups, but not the sufficient reasons. The fact of belonging to a gang or association that explicitly rejects what is sees as an exclusive society is a source of comfort to those who join it because it offers its members an anti-French or anti-English identity. If a network is established and escapes the vigilance of the police, membership can lead to activism or even terrorism.

### Disaffected British-Asian youth

Whereas France has young people of Magrhebin descent, Britain has young people with parents of Muslim Pakistani, Bangladeshi and Indian descent. In theory, communitarian structures, which are much more widely recognised in Britain, make it possible to deaden the shock experienced by these fragile populations who live there. As the existence of communities is recognised and as they are helped with special subsidies, they can, as a general rule, promote integration during an intermediary period by ensuring that recent immigrants do not get out of their depth and are supported by their compatriots until the second or third generation is emancipated. Although it is much less restrictive than the French integration model, which refuses to recognise the existence of communities, this vision also creates specific problems. Whilst the French reject communitarianism in the name of the citizen's individual membership of the one legitimate community – the nation – the British claim that successful integration requires an intermediate phase. Without that, individuals are in danger of getting out of their depth in an individualistic society in which no place has been prepared for them. According to this view, much of the task of integration falls upon communities. In return, those communities guarantee that their members will obey the law. They agree to exercise at least indirect control over their members, even though they are all individually responsible in the eyes of the law. Neither the controls nor the internalisation of norms work with those who, for one reason or another, find themselves living outside the community, or who refuse to accept communitarian norms. Such individuals are often described as disaffected young Muslims.[47] Their communities cannot integrate them, and society cannot tame them.

The case of Richard Reid is often cited, but others Like Afzal Munir and Aftab Manzoor also joined the Al-Muhajiroun association.

Of the four British citizens who died fighting alongside the Taliban in Afghanistan, at least one is reported to have been a member of Al-Muhajirun. Afzal Munir was 25 and studied information technology at the University of Luton before finding a job in industry.[48] Aftab Manzoor, who was the same age, also lived in Luton, less than two kilometres from the home of Munir's parents. Luton's Muslim community is well-structured. Manzoor had his A-levels. His father emigrated from Pakistan some 20 years ago, and his son divided his time between the two countries.

Al-Muhajirun is a direct expression of some British-Asian students' feeling that they are living between two cultures, but they are also disaffected with Pakistani communities in Britain. They are also disturbed by Britain's close cooperation with the United States in the repression of Muslims in Iraq and particularly Afghanistan. The association was the product of a split within the Hizbul Tahrir Islamist party and is mostly university-based. It exploits the students' feeling of disaffection by exacerbating it and referring to a *jihadist* conception of Islam. Like the marginal young people who feel they have been rejected by their communities, this type of association reveals the limitations of the British model in the same way that the non-integration of young people of Maghrebin origin reveals the limitations of the French model of integration.

For the young people who join this association, the integration of Pakistanis into British society is a trap. They feel rejected, not simply because they are treated as inferiors but also because they have little respect for members of their own communities, who are too corrupt or too compromised with England to represent their true feelings. In the absence of any real community to protect them from marginalisation, many young people of North-African origin from modest backgrounds in France become delinquents and find themselves behind bars.[49] Some see exile (in the United Kingdom, the United States or Canada) as the answer to their problems. British Pakistanis leave for America when they can. Until recently, they also enjoyed the benefits of British tolerance and were able to express their conviction that they were not really part of British society by professing radical Islamist opinions that would have landed their coreligionists in jail if they had expressed them in public on French soil. France was affected by Islamist terrorism in the 1980s, and especially 1995, because the French state approved of the Algerian army's repression of Islamists, but also because it did not try to find a modus vivendi with Islamists in France. The repression frustrated their desire to assert themselves on the French public stage. Britain took a different line and, because there are few Arabs in the country, was not directly affected by the fallout from Algerian Islamism, except insofar as a minority of the Islamists who could find nowhere to go in Paris chose London as their place of exile. The fact remains that the greater freedom of expression available to them in England has allowed young Pakistanis who feel alienated because Britain's foreign policy is too subservient to America and therefore hostile to the Muslim cause in Afghanistan and the Middle East, to express their discontents verbally and by joining associations that would not be tolerated in France.

The feeling of outrage was just as strong in the minority groups that came together in associations like Al-Muharijun. For them, Islam is an identity principle that is much more powerful than their British nationality, which they symbolically revile by calling on Muslims to join the holy war against Anglo-American troops in Afghanistan. The same feelings of rejection, inferiority, non-belonging to the nation, and stigmatisation in Britain or France can be found amongst a minority of young people of immigrant origin who feel that their dignity has been slighted and who see Islam as a sign of greater dignity that can restore their lost honour by symbolically cutting them off from a nationality that has never really existed except on paper. The religion of Allah functions as a symbolic rejection of a 'Britishness' that is equivalent to the feeling of *citoyenneté* (citizenship) in France. No matter whether they choose real exile, like French Islamists, or choose to be symbolic foreigners in England by adopting a militant Islam like British Asians, the outcome is the same: they make a symbolic break with a society that never gave them the impression that it was welcoming them with open arms. There is, however, one striking difference between radicalised French Islamists of Maghrebin origin and British-Pakistani Islamists. The former group began to turn to activism in the 1990s, and especially with the terrorist attacks of 1995. In the case of England, we find a radicalisation of language rather than action, at least until 2001. Until then, there had been a few incidents, but nothing to compare with what happened in France, where young people of Maghrebin origin and a few converts did become involved in networks that had links with radical Islamist groups affiliated to the GIA. The fact that Algeria is so near, France's political position and opposition to the Algerian Islamists, and the relatively higher number of Muslim immigrants (some four million in France, compared with one and a half million in Britain) go some way to explaining this. The fact that France and Britain have different conceptions of rights is a further factor. The French concept of democratic rights is influenced by the Jacobin model, whereas Britain's concept of rights gives much greater freedom in terms of political affiliation and radicalism, provided that they do not pose a direct threat to basic freedoms.

## The United States

The situation in America differs from that in the main countries of Europe in three respects. On the one hand, there is the fact that a far from negligible number of Arabs in the United States are not Muslims; second, many American Muslims belong to the middle classes and not the lower classes, as in Europe.[50] Muslims began to settle en masse in France and Britain from the 1950s (Britain) or the 1960s onwards (France[51]), whereas the mass immigration of Muslims to the United States occurred more recently.

All these factors mean that there is something very specific about American Muslims. The proportion of people who have been radicalised in the name of Islam and who have become involved in terrorist activity is much lower than in Europe. It is almost as though more people in Europe than in America had a 'vocation' for martyrdom in the name of Allah, or for fighting the West in organisations like al-Qaeda. This is not simply a matter of methods of policing, although it is true to say that the European police system is very fragmented and does not have the institutional unity of its American equivalent. Every European police force and intelligence service has its own culture and procedures, its own ways of gathering intelligence and its own ways of passing it on to the national agencies. Since the terrorist attacks in Madrid in March 2004, attempts have been made to establish better coordination between the various national forces, but they have not been as effective as those made in the United States, where the various agencies already worked together. And yet the division of responsibilities between the FBI and the CIA, the feeling of invulnerability that prevailed until 11 September 2001, the fact that the attention of Republican leaders (the Republican presidency of Georges Bush Jr) and the fact that the intelligence services rely heavily on a cutting-edge technology that does not take sufficient account of the human factor did play a role in the system's failure on 11 September. Even so, the various agencies do work better together than those in European countries, where every police force has its own characteristics, its own national tongue and a history bound up with the history of the country in which it operates. These phenomena do not, however, fully explain why so many Europeans and so many people living in Europe have become involved in so-called terrorist activity.

## THE CASE OF BRITAIN

It should be noted that many al-Qaeda-type terrorists come from Europe's former colonies, and especially from the former colonies of France and Britain. Although 15 members of the group responsible for the 11 September attacks were Saudis, some of its members studied technology at European universities (mainly in Germany). A whole generation of terrorists with at least some links with the al-Qaeda nebula is made up of individuals from the Maghreb or Pakistan (there are exceptions such as Richard Reid, who has a white mother and a black father) or, in some cases, from the Middle East, where they were either directly or indirectly involved in activism (Abu Hanza, for instance, is Syrian in origin, and was the spiritual teacher of some of the activists). Leaving aside exceptions like Abu Hamza, Abu Qatada and a few others from the Middle East, the vast majority of the terrorists who operate in Europe come from Morocco, Algeria, Palestine and Tunisia (there are also a few from Lebanon). The former colonies of France and Britain are well represented in this nebula. These groups can be divided into two subgroups: those who were educated and socialised in Europe, and those who were educated and socialised in their countries of origin, and who have been living in Europe for a few years at most.

Those who were educated and socialised in Europe often speak the language of their adoptive country and are not grounded in strong Islamic traditions. What is more, they were socialised in the modern sector of the economy: computers, information technology, business studies and so on. They do not support a *jihadist* version of Islam because they had a strictly religious education. The same appears to be true of the vast majority of those from North Africa or Pakistan: in most cases, they were not trained in the traditional religious sciences and do not identify with *jihadism* because they are deeply steeped in traditional Islamic civilisation and culture. Most of them belong to a younger generation that has been both modernised and urbanised. They have been deeply humiliated by politico-religious issues that would not have troubled their parents or grandparents to the same degree, if only because they were not exposed to media such as television or the internet, which make it possible to watch events taking place on the other side of the world in what is effectively real time.

There are other factors that explain the radicalisation of these groups. Some are historical. The creation of the state of Israel and the fact that there is no solution to the Palestinian problem come into play in two distinct ways. For Palestinians, the failure to find a solution fuels the activism of groups like Hamas or Islamic Jihad, but significant numbers of people of Palestinian origin have yet to become involved in al-Qaeda. For other Muslims throughout the world, with the exception of a few countries like Iran (where a government that has lost all legitimacy is identified with the Palestinian hard-liners) or parts of Kuwait (the leading Palestinian groups supported Saddam Hussein's Iraq when it invaded the country in 1990), the Palestinian problem is of the utmost symbolic importance. This is one of the reasons why some Muslims on both sides of the Mediterranean have joined the *jihad* against a West that supports Israel.[52] Palestine has become a mirror that reflects the way the West treats Muslims, and Israel is often seen by Muslims as the United States' lackey rather than as a country in its own right.

The memory of colonialism and the racism experienced by former colonial subjects in Europe are a further factor. In the case of France, we can see how the Maghrebin problem is still symbolically linked to the memory of the Algerian war of independence and the traumas on both the French (over one million French citizens had to leave Algeria) and the Algerian sides. There is the problem of the *harkis* (Algerians who collaborated with the French army), but also that of the Algerian workers who came to France: in some cases, not even the second and third generations have become integrated. Part of this Maghrebin population has a deep sense of humiliation and loss of dignity because they live in poor suburbs that resemble enclaves, and feel that they have been rejected by both France and the French. Some young men of Pakistani origin living in Britain feel as alienated from Pakistani communities in the land of Shakespeare as they do from a British population that regards them as 'non-white' or 'different' and calls them 'pakis' – a pejorative term for dark-skinned people who do not integrate into British society in a 'civilised' British way. Although Britain in much more tolerant of multiculturalism than France, the disturbances that broke out in industrial towns like Bradford in

July 2001 were a forceful demonstration of the problems and crises affecting these young men. The vast majority of those who were sentenced by the courts to several months (or years in a few cases) in prison were young men of 'Asian' origin aged between 20 and 30. Most were of Pakistani origin.

Britain's support for America and active involvement in the war against Iraq in 1990–91, in the war in Afghanistan in 2002 and then in the war in Iraq in 2003 has had a negative effect on some of these young people. British involvement in the war against Afghanistan exacerbated their antagonistic feelings toward Britain because the Pashtu spoken in Afghanistan is similar to the Urdu spoken by most Pakistanis. What is more, the British tradition of liberalism and recognition of the communitarian system meant that the vast majority of the Muslim population and 'Asian' population turned against those minorities who had been radicalised by the call for a *jihad*.

The war against Iraq also provided a significant section of the British Muslim population with an opportunity to show that it sides with the majority by taking part in anti-war demonstrations alongside other British citizens. They thus identified with public opinion in their adoptive country, for the first time in many cases.[53] For many of them, taking part in public demonstrations reinforced the feeling that they were citizens who belonged to Great Britain. For the vast majority of British Muslims, it was not so much the call for vengeance against Britain and the West, as the feeling that they shared a common destiny and they joined in the flux of the demonstrators that made them feel, probably for the first time in their lives, that they were 'British'. Women, for their part, came together to denounce the evils of terrorism and to mobilise young men against radicalisation.[54]

Two mosques – one in Finsbury Park in north London and the other in Brixton – have become notorious for the sermons that led a minority of young men to radicalism. Islamic activism, or even terrorism, has been blamed on the influence of two organisations: Hizb al-Tahrir and Al-Muharijoun. The latter was founded in Great Britain in February 1996 by Omar Bakri Mohammed, whose real name is Al-Fostock. He is a Syrian who was born in Aleppo in 1996. He studied at Cairo's prestigious Al-Azhar university. He lived in Saudi Arabia until 1986, when he was deported because of his activism. He chose Great Britain as his place of residence. Together with his fellow Syrian Farid Kasim, he founded the British branch of Hizb al-Tahrir (whose literal meaning is 'liberation'). Like Al-Muharijoun after it, Hizb al-Tahrir recruited mainly in the universities and in Muslim communities, most of them middle-class. For reasons that are still unclear, Bakri left the party in 1996 to found Al-Muharijoun in 1996, and became its spiritual leader. He is the founder and director of the Al-Khilafah publishing house. Both organisations call for the establishment of a worldwide caliphate and for the Islamisation of Great Britain. They are opposed to existing Islamic regimes and contest their legitimacy. They have anti-Semitic tendencies and denounce Israel's occupation of Palestine. Hizb al-Tahrir, in particular, is anti-Hindu (because of the war in Kashmir), anti-Sikh, homophobic, anti-feminist and resentful of Western culture's influence on Islam. Between them, the two parties have a few hundred members.

Some of these groups' sympathisers were involved in the war in Afghanistan. At least two British citizens were killed by American bombing in Afghanistan.[55] In order to defend itself against terrorism, Britain passed a Terrorism Act in 2000. An amendment added in 2001 allowed foreigners suspected of belonging to terrorist groups to be held for an indefinite period of time. Since then, both groups have adopted a more moderate tone and their public activities now concentrate on the establishment of the caliphate. It should be noted that the Terrorism Act was immediately denounced by human rights activists in Britain: in December 2003, 500 arrests were made. Sixteen people are in prison, and six of them have been there for more than a year.[56] Hundreds of mosques have protested about the way British Muslims are being treated in the 'war on terrorism'.[57]

The leader of Al-Maharijoun is Bakri, the self-styled Ayatollah of Tottenham. Anjem Coudary, the British-Pakistani chair of the Society of Muslim Lawyers, is also a prominent member of the group. Iftikhas Ali, another member of the group, was found guilty of incitement to racial hatred in May 2002.

Hamza al-Masri (Abu Hamza), the Egyptian founder of the Supporters of Shari'a, is another prominent spokesman for militant Islam in Britain. In 1996, he began to give his charismatic sermons at the famous Finsbury Park mosque and continued to preach there until he was evicted. Before finding his vocation as a radical preacher, he worked as a security guard. He continues to preach outside the mosque on Friday mornings to protest against his eviction. He is so prolific that he gave some 200 or more sermons in 1999 alone. He was a major influence on a whole generation of young British Muslims throughout the 1990s. Many of them have now distanced themselves from his radicalism, but his influence persuaded certain of them to join the *jihad* against the West. He has supported Bin Laden and has said that *jihad* is a religious duty in the present circumstances. It was probably in this mosque that Islamist recruiters first met Zacarias Moussaoui (the twentieth member of the 11 September group) and Richard Reid (the shoe-bomber).

A third charismatic spokesman for activist Islam in Great Britain is the Palestinian Abu Qatada (Sheikh Omar ab Omar). He entered Britain in 1993, after having been found guilty in Jordan of being a member of the Jaysh Mohammed (Mohammed's Army). He is known to be 'bin Laden's ambassador to Europe' and has been placed under arrest by the British authorities. The three men held joint meetings under the aegis of Al-Muharijoun.

On 29 April 2002 two British kamikazes carried out a suicide attack in Tel Aviv. Asif Mohammed Hanif was 21 and lived in west London, and Omar Khan Sharif was from Derby. They had contacts in Al-Maharijoun and sympathised with its objectives. They were not excluded from society in the economic sense of the word, and neither of them seems to have had any problems with the police until they chose the path of martyrdom. Their prime motivation appears to have been the Palestinian problem. They passed through Damascus, where other Westerners in search of spirituality have sought refuge. It seems that it is possible to contact Hamas, the Al-Aqsa Martyrs Brigade or even the Lebanese Hezbollah there.

There is, however, one difference between the situation in Britain and that in France. In France, young men from the *banlieues* have fire-bombed synagogues and desecrated Jewish cemeteries in protest at Israeli's Palestinian policies; young British Muslims like Hanif and Sharif became directly involved in martyrdom and became living bombs.

A more or less loosely connected assortment of facts suggest that Al-Maharijoun played an indirect role in the radicalisation of some young British 'Asians' (Pakistanis). The men who acted as catalysts were from Syria (Bakri Mohammed), Egypt (Abu Hamza) or Palestine (Abu Qaada), but the young men who were radicalised and then went to fight in Afghanistan were 'Asian' (several were Pakistani in origin, one was Zambian, two were converts and one was Ugandan in origin). Others went from France (Zaccaria Moussaoui) or the Maghreb. Kamel Daoudi was extradited from France at the end of September 2001 to London to be trained in religious radicalism, as it was by far the biggest Muslim city in Europe, if not the West. It was called 'Londonistan' because its Muslim population was so diverse in terms of both its socio-economic status, its ethnic origins and its religious loyalties (Shi'ite, Sunni, Sufi) and culture (Arabs from all over the world, 'Asians', Africans and so on). North-African networks sometimes operated autonomously in Britain without putting down any roots in radical British Muslim circles, rather like Zaccarias Moussaoui. In January 2003, the police took in six North Africans for questioning about a home-made laboratory where ricin poison gas was being made. Some people suspected of involvement in terrorist activity, including Noureddine Moulef, the 36-year-old Algerian accused of terrorism in 2003, appear to have come from the Algerian community in Britain.

## THE CASE OF AMERICA

There are no American equivalents to the major Moroccan or Algerian networks that exist in Spain, Britain or Canada, where Moroccan *jihadists* (including Adil Charkaoui and Ahmad Ressam) have been identified. There are a few *jihadists* from Saudi Arabia or the Gulf Emirates. What is more, the networks that do exist have not succeeded in establishing organic links with African-American Muslims. Khali Shaikh Mohammed, who was arrested in Pakistan in March 2003, revealed that he did have some al-Qaeda contacts in the United States.[58] He was able to establish contacts in Baltimore, Columbus, Ohio and Peoria through mosques, prisons and universities. One member of the network was the Brooklyn-born José Padilla, a Catholic Hispanic who converted to Islam. Another member identified by Khalid was Adman e. El Skukrijumah, a 27-year-old Saudi who attended school in southern Florida.[59]

Another al-Qaeda member arrested in Pakistan tried unsuccessfully to find political asylum in the United States, after a brief stay there. According to Khalid, he and Khan tried to involve a Pakistani company in the fraudulent import of explosive materials into the United States. A woman known as Aafia Siddiqui, who had an American visa and who had lived in the country for ten years or so, rented a PO box to help Khan forge American papers. She fled to Pakistan, where she was arrested.

Lyman Faris, a naturalised American truck-driver and a practising Muslim living in Columbus, Ohio, was also involved in the network. The Qatari Ali S. Al-Marri, who had studied in the United States, was another member. In September 2001, he returned there to take a diploma in computer systems at Bradley University in Peoria. Adnan

Shukri Juma, a Saudi citizen permanently resident in the United States, was also a member of the network. He had been living in the country for six years and had an associate's degree from a school in Florida.

The Canadian authorities arrested Afil Charkaoui, a Moroccan pizza salesman, and Ahmed Ressam as they tried to enter the US via Canada during the millennium celebrations of the year 2000.

These elements show that al-Qaeda's networks have not been able to put down deep roots in the United States or to exploit fringes of the Afro-American population,[60] far right American groups or the members of anti-establishment cults. As we have already stressed, their failure to do so has to do with the nature of Arab and Muslim immigration to the United States (most immigrants are middle-class) and with the fact that unlike their counterparts in Europe, white Muslim Americans, who are mostly from the middle classes, do have life projects and do not, or did not until 11 September 2001, feel that they were stigmatised, rejected or regarded as inferior by other Americans. Unlike the young men of north-African origin who live in France's *banlieues* or British Asians (who are mostly Pakistani), most American Muslims did not feel rejected until 11 September. The Palestinian problem is, of course, a painful issue for some of them. But until George Bush was elected, the extent of American support for Israel was not as great as it is now and they did not feel too despondent about it. What was more important, some Muslims believed that if they established lobbies in the same way that American Jews have done, they would, in the long term, be able to persuade the United States to adopt more pro-Palestinian policies.

The great difference between American and European Muslims (especially British and French Muslims from immigrant families) is that the Americans did not, unlike Europe's young Muslims, experience any profound humiliation and did not feel rejected (or did not until 11 September 2001). Nor did they feel that their dignity had been taken away from them. In Europe, some Muslim extremists have been able to penetrate the immigrant Muslim population. In the case of France, this happened even before al-Qaeda began to operate. The attack on the Paris metro in 1995 was carried out by a group of young men, the most prominent being the Algerian Khaled Kelkal. He felt that he had been rejected by the French even though he had lived in France since he was a child.[61] The GIA (Armed Islamic Group) came into existence after the radicalisation of the FIS in the

1990s, and was able to operate in France thanks to its contacts with a small number of young men from a north-African background. The French cultural model is another important factor. This model places great emphasis on *laïcité* (secularism) and views any public manifestation of religious orthodoxy with suspicion. The dominant view in France is that all religious fundamentalism probably leads to radicalisation. Any *intégriste* Muslim (the term is equivalent to 'fundamentalist') can became an Islamist or even a *jihadist*. There is little evidence to support this argument. Religious 'fundamentalism' can be an obstacle to radicalisation, and 'strong religion' can be a way of warding off the feelings of loss and dereliction that encourage radicalisation.[62] The 2004 law banning the wearing of 'Islamic headscarves' to school is based on the same argument. It too encourages the radicalisation of small numbers of Muslims who think that they are being treated with suspicion and distrust by public opinion. If the radicals and *jihadists* are to be defeated, what is required is an alliance between the middle classes and Muslim society. But the dominant cultural attitude in France is both based on fear and grounded in the history of the country's difficult relationship with the dominant religion (Catholicism). Ever since the French Revolution, any public display of religious affiliation in public has been frowned upon. For many Muslim men and women, however, beards, headscarves and other religious insignia are part of their Islamic identity. This forces them into what public opinion sees as the 'suspects' camp, and makes it difficult for orthodox Muslims (who are described as *intégristes*) to ally themselves with the rest of society in order to isolate religious extremists.

Groups of young north Africans who left France to settle in Britain have succeeded in establishing networks there. Islamist networks have been established in European countries like Italy and Spain, where Muslim immigration is a more recent phenomenon, but they have no roots in the immigrant communities. The example of Germany is significant. Al-Qaeda-style terrorists have not succeeded in finding a base in the predominantly Turkish immigrant communities there. If we compare the British and French models with the model of America, where few American Muslims have joined terrorist groups, it becomes clear that, in Europe and especially what were once the major colonial countries (Britain and France), it is the alienation of young people who come mainly from the former colonies and who are convinced that they are unloved, or even rejected and humiliated by society that has allowed terrorist groups to find a favourable welcome.[63] The case of France is even more alarming than that of Britain. There are more than twice as many Muslims in France (some four million) as there are in Britain (one and half million), and both the painful memory of the Algerian war and the intense feeling of rejection on the part of young men from Algerian and Moroccan backgrounds in a France that appears to dislike or even hate them prepared the ground for extremist networks. Unlike the Algerians (and some Moroccans) whose communities have been so disrupted that they can do little to help their members, French Turks live in much more solid communities. They can rely upon them to provide material and psychological help and they succeed in finding jobs (as builders, plumbers, or businessmen) that help them feel that they do have a future, and that upward social and economic mobility is possible in their host countries. When they do become radicalised, their radicalism is directed at Turkey and not France. To a large extent, the French model of radicalisation operates in Britain, in spite of the major differences between the two countries (France, unlike Britain, does not recognise the existence of communities as such).

Turks in France and Germany do not, in a word, have the same feeling of humiliation, loss of dignity and rejection as France's Maghrebins or Britain's 'Asians'. That is one of the reasons why there are no major or self-avowed al-Qaeda-type networks in their host communities. In short, there appear to be two major models governing the relationship between Muslim communities in Europe and Islamic radicalism. Some feel humiliated as a group because of the colonial past, social patterns of behaviour or the host countries' policies towards Muslim societies. They hold a grudge against the host country. In the case of France, they are humiliated by the Republican model, which denies that Islam has any legitimacy as a world religion, by the colonial past and by France's relations with contemporary Algeria; in the case of England, they are humiliated by the colonial past and by the government's close cooperation with the US in Afghanistan and Iraq. In one case (that of people of Turkish origin living in France and Germany), there is no place in the community for an al-Qaeda-type organisation. In the other (that of the Moroccan and Algerian 'communities' in France, and that of Pakistanis and north Africans living in Britain), Islamic radicalism does find favourable echoes among some minority groups within those communities.

## *JIHADIST* FAMILIES

It is very unusual for most of the male members of the same family to become *jihadists*. Such families can, however, prove to be very dangerous to the security forces, as family ties make it difficult for the police to infiltrate them. The naturalised Canadian Khadr family is one example. The grandparents of the 21-year-old Abdurhman Khadr, who has Canadian nationality, live in Toronto.[64] His father, Ahmed Saïd Khadr left Egypt in the 1970s and emigrated to Canada. He had six children (four sons and two daughters) and settled in Ontario. In the 1980s and 1990s, he travelled frequently to Pakistan and Afghanistan. In the 1980s, he was working for Human Concern International, an aid organisation working with Afghan refugees who fled the country after the Soviet invasion of 1979. He settled in Pakistan with his family, where he became the NGO's regional director, returning to Canada in the winter to raise funds in North America. In 1995, while he was still living in Pakistan, he was arrested and charged with being involved in the car bomb attack on the Egyptian embassy in Islamabad on 19 November 1995. The Canadian authorities intervened to have him released, but it was probably because he bribed the local police that he was freed. In 1996, the family moved to Kabul in Afghanistan shortly before the Taliban seized power. After the Canadian administration cut off Khadr's organisation's funding, he founded his own Health and Education Project International and continued to raise private funds to aid widows and orphans in Afghanistan. According to the Canadian authorities, his eldest son Abdullah joined the Jihadis and ran a training camp in Afghanistan.[65] His brothers Omar and Abdurahman joined the same movement. Abdurahmam claims to have undergone three months military training at the Khalden camp, which is where some al-Qaeda militants trained. He claims that he was encouraged to do so by his father. In October 2003, the Islamic Observation Centre in London announced that Ahmed Saïd Khadr was dead and identified him as one of al-Qaeda's founding members. This was denied by his family. He was reportedly killed when the Pakistani army attacked a camp on the Afghan border. His youngest son Abdul Karim was seriously wounded in the same attack. Abdurahman was arrested in Kabul in November 2001 and handed over to the Americans, who sent him to Guantánamo. His brother Omar was arrested in Afghanistan and charged with killing an American soldier in a grenade attack in July 2002.

Although Abdurahman denies having any ideological involvement with the al-Qaeda network, the fact remains that the case of the Khadr family is symptomatic of the ideologisation of a generation of Muslims who found their raison d'être in the struggle against Russian and then Western hegemony. Abduraham's grandparents appear to have avoided the same ideologisation. The Khadr sons fought alongside the Taliban as a result of their father's commitment, because they lived in Pakistan and Afghanistan and because practically every man in the family was involved. In this case, it was the whole male side of the family that became involved in *jihadism*.

The case of the Benchellalis, a family from an Algerian background living in Les Minguettes in Vénissieux, near the French city of Lyon, is equally instructive.[66] Imam Chellali, his wife Hafsa and their son Menad are currently in prison in France. Menad has been charged with plotting a chemical attack in France with the 'Chechen networks'. He previously lived in Spain and in Georgia. In December 2001, he left the mountains of Georgia, where he had been waiting in vain to be transferred to Chechnya to take part in the war against the Russians, and went back to France. His father Chellali Benchellali was arrested on 6 January 2004 and issued with a deportation order by the Ministry of the Interior, which thought he should be removed from French soil as a matter of 'extreme urgency'. He appears to have been close to the Algerian Groupe Salafi pour la Prédication et le Combat (GSPC), which is a dissident faction of the GIA.

His other son Mourad is being held in Guantánamo. He and Nizar Sassi travelled to Afghanistan in June 2001. Vénissieux, like some other *banlieues* in the Lyon area, has a history of radicalisation and anti-police militancy that goes back to the 1980s. Nizar Sassi, Khaled Ben Moustafa and Mourad Benchellali are all from Vénissieux. Their radicalisation was bound up with the history of their *banlieue* but also with their networks of friends. In the case of Mourad, family ties were also an influence, as his father was a radical preacher.

We can, broadly speaking, identify two tendencies in Islamist extremism. In most cases, a family member (usually a man) joins the Jihadist movement on an individual basis, often without the rest of the family knowing anything about it. The individual's decision to join the movement is influenced by networks outside the family, such as a group of friends in the same neighbourhood, contacts made at the mosque or through a local NGO (such as an Islamic humanitarian NGO) or religious association. It is still very rare for whole families, or most of their male members, to take part in the *jihad*. During Iran's war with Iraq, whole families did sometimes join the Bassidj, which young volunteers joined to take part in the fight against Islam's enemies with a view to becoming martyrs.[67]

In the case of individual martyrs, the decision to join the *jihad* is an expression of a principle of individuation in what is seen as a profoundly unjust, often irreversible and desperate situation in which humiliation and the exasperation that follows appear to be the dominant affects.[68] In the case of *jihadist* families, it is the establishment of a closed community inside the family and a reconstructed neo-patriarchal family that is the symbolically determinant factor. Individual *jihadis* often leave their families. In the case of *jihadist* families, individuals and their families unite in an attempt to overcome the hatred and the feeling of humiliation by constructing a family that shuts itself off from society. Internal disagreements can be resolved in symbolic terms because the authority of the father is recognised within the reconstructed family. These families are a new type of anthropological construct. The relationship between father and sons may or may not be inverted: the son may persuade the father to become a *jihadist*, as was the case with many Bassidjis in Iran, but the Benchellali family does not appear to follow that model, as the father appears to have played an important role. Such families show how a new form of commitment based upon the family cell can emerge in crisis situations. It is astonishing that this type of attitude has not become more widespread in the case of Palestine, Chechnya or al-Qaeda.

## CONVERTS

The phenomenon of conversion has always existed. Where there is a religion, there are converts. Conversion can be either forced or spontaneous. Cases of more or less forced conversion in Western societies (during the Spanish Reconquista) and Muslim societies (conversion was a way of avoiding taxation or *jiziya* and of ceasing to be part of an oppressed community) have occurred throughout history. The new forms that allow Christians to convert to Islam are, at least in the West, usually based upon an individual's desire to embrace that religion, and there are no institutional constraints. The converts' motives can be very varied, but they do have certain features in common. Conversion can be a way of espousing modernity; by choosing one or another religion, the individual leaves his personal mark on it. His or her faith is now strictly individual, as opposed to the religion bequeathed by his or her parents in accordance with the impersonal mechanisms of inheritance. The new converts resort to the modern 'pick-and-mix' method that allows individuals to reconstruct their relationship with the sacred by choosing their communities and giving them a meaning that is not predetermined.[69]

Converts can be placed in one of two categories. Some convert to put some order into their lives, but their conversion does nothing to change their relationship with the political; other converts begin to redefine themselves, and that does imply a new relationship with the political. It is the second category that concerns us here. Such converts are usually from a Christian background – Catholic in France, and Protestant in northern Europe. In the United States, they tend to be Protestants. Until very recently, only a few Americans seem to have had any direct involvement in *jihad*. Wadih al Hage was from a Christian Arab background, embraced Islam in the United States, and became involved in *jihadist* activity by joining al-Qaeda. John Walker Lindh joined the Taliban and was arrested in Afghanistan.

The few *jihadi* converts I interviewed in French prisons felt very strongly that they were part of a Muslim *umma* that is being unfairly treated by the West. For the young Palestinians of the second Intifada or Iran's Bassidji, the *umma* was an extension of the unease they had already experienced for themselves. For *jihadi* converts, in contrast, the *umma* is a community they joined after their conversion, and onto which they project a suffering they have experienced only by proxy and because of their desire to identify with other Muslims. It is not necessarily underpinned by any concrete experience other than the sympathy they feel for their new brethren in religion. It is a virtual and the abstract totality that allows them to exist collectively, to overcome the feeling of loneliness and of not belonging to a group. There is a coldness about individualism, and especially about the feeling of 'not belonging' that appears to be unbearable to many of the new converts, and embracing Islam helps to overcome it.

In my conversations with the converts, certain recurrent features emerged. To begin with, the decision to embrace Islam was an individual one, but it is also a religion that allows individuals to decentre themselves in a novel way in the West. In a modern world in which everything is down to him or her, the individual is the key to everything that happens to him or her, and individuality can become a crushing burden. Individuality is everywhere and in everything. Everything depends upon it, and nothing sacred can resist it. The old forms of the sacred – the nation, science, progress, or even the class struggle and the various forms of Christian commitment – have been weakened as a result. Islam, in contrast, decentres the individual by handing their responsibility for their own life over to a transcendental agency and relieving them of the crushing burden of having to be at the origin of everything. The same attitude could be observed in some of the Western volunteers who went to Chechnya, Bosnia or Afghanistan in the 1990s and the early years of the twenty-first century. Some left written accounts of their conversion, like the Norwegian convert who went to fight the Russians in Chechnya.[70]

Converting to Islam is a way of escaping a society that is abstract because it is so complex. This is a society characterised by a worrying anonymity, a world in which it is every person for themself and in which the image of the Other gradually becomes blurred as the self becomes more and more introverted, or even narcissistic. By converting to Islam, the individual joins a new humanity that gives him new obligations and new rights. Most important of all for idealists, this is a suffering humanity made up of underdogs and those who are being oppressed and mistreated by the evil West to which they belong. Going to Afghanistan, Bosnia or Chechnya is a concrete act of witness to their commitment to this new humanity, which is not characterised by the sins of consumerism, egotism and excessive materialism. The idealist fringe that turned to communism in the first half of the twentieth century in order to realise the utopia of a new society washed clean of the sins of capitalism, is now embracing Islam in its search for a utopia that will give life a meaning by committing them to a 'noble' cause that transcends the individual but which is still based upon a sovereign individual decision. Converting to Islam can result in the establishment of a restricted community that dwells in the peace of the soul (the Sufi or neo-mystical forms that are proliferating in the West). It can also lead to an active commitment to an extended community of more than a billion men and women who are believed to be under the yoke of imperialism. *Jihad* or martyrdom is a way of contributing to their liberation. It is a way of overcoming the feeling that everything looks the same, as well as the discontent associated with a disturbing hyper-individualism. Being martyred in a *jihad* is seen as the most sincere act of witness. It is a testimony to the martyr's rejection of the insincerity that governs life in the disenchanted, anomic West where there are no 'noble' causes. Unlike the diffuse and lax religiosity of a diluted Christianity, Islam is seen as a transparent and coherent religion. It is altruistic, whereas the West is egotistical. It is spiritual, and rejects the materialism and consumerism that prevail in the West. Within the fraternal neo-*umma*, converts can realise the new values that give a new meaning to life by putting it to the test of death.

Turning to Islam can also reflect a desire to find a clear distinction between the roles of men and women. When they turn to Islam, men (and a minority of women) find a self-definition that escapes egalitarianism and gives a particular relief to a 'male' self and a 'female' self. This is not a return to the past or to the ancestral Islamic tradition, but a religious way of posing the problem of male and female identities that sheds light on the role of both. Muslim women often put forward new feminist demands in terms of their 'complementary' roles and demand greater justice. Western converts are not so much interested in 'dominating' women as in escaping both a world in which roles are indeterminate, and the exhausting need to constantly negotiate their identity, both inside and outside the family. Islam allows them to embrace, in their imaginary, a version of male and female identity that does not give rise to constant arguments and challenges. This confirms the feeling of male converts that they are superior to women because they can join in a *jihad*, whereas women still do not have the right to do so. If they convert to Islam, they can marry Muslim women who are, in their eyes, less demanding and more 'docile' than Western women. The need for women to wear the veil (*hijab*) further underlines the distinction between roles and identities. Converts who wish to join the *jihad* often adopt a strictly puritanical version of Islam that underlines still further the difference between the two identities and gives a new confidence to a masculinity that is at bay in the West because it is felt to be meaningless there. Some converts turn to Islam because it gives distinct roles to men and women within a field marked by men's explicit hegemony over women.

In the interviews, it was also argued that Christianity cannot, by its very nature, provide the basis for a strong community. It is a religion for the weak. It asks believers to turn the other cheek. One prisoner pointed to this Christian weakness: no one could be proud of belonging to such a religion. What is more, its distinctions are too confused. It explains the obscure in terms that are even more obscure, especially when it comes to the notion of the Trinity. No concrete community can be built around such a notion, they contend. Converts embrace Islam because it offers incontrovertible proofs, and because it offers an escape from a world with no sense of direction or meaning. Islam offers a certainty which, because of its very simplicity, has something of the sublime about it. One book – the Koran – states what is true and, by the same criterion, what is false. One Prophet, who is God's servant, indicates the right path (*sarat mostaqim*) and invites Muslims to follow the way of God (*fi sabil ellah*). Unlike Jesus, the Prophet is not the son of God. There is nothing enigmatic about him, and nothing to sow doubts in the mind or to make it difficult to understand faith. The simplicity of Islam goes hand in hand with its rationality. The distinction between what is permitted and what is forbidden, between the licit (*halal*) and the illicit (*haram*) traces a line of demarcation between Good and Evil that does not exist in Christianity, within their own field of existence. In Christianity, the distinction is blurred, often absent, and its vagueness is a source of anxiety. By clearly spelling out what is permitted and what is forbidden, Islam clarifies things in a way that converts find comforting. Islam is transparent whereas Christianity is opaque. It is simple, whereas Christianity is complex. In short, Islam is a religion for 'human nature' to the extent that it provides a remedy for the ills of life. There is nothing new about this vision of Islam. As early as the eighteenth century, certain major Western intellectuals such as Lessing identified it with the 'natural' religion of simplicity, as opposed to those religions that provided overcomplicated versions of faith.[71] The context of a directionless modernity in which there is no shared truth makes this vision of Islam particularly attractive.

The religion of Allah proclaims the unicity of God and the unity of the community based upon it. Clarity and transparency go hand in hand. Righting wrongs by resorting to legitimate violence is a source of pride and virility that cannot be found in other religions. Islam's answer to the feeling of loneliness and abandonment is the indestructible unity of an *umma* based upon the unicity of God. Its answer to the feeling that everything is flattened and that the self no longer exists that is characteristic of everyday life in what some Muslims regard as decaying and disenchanted democracies, is a recourse to force and power that can meet the challenge of war. Islam can make a frontal attack on all the ills to which we usually have only half-solutions that are often characterised by a refusal to take decisions.

*Jihadi* converts often come from modest backgrounds. They are worlds apart from the highbrow intellectuals and upper-class converts, who are mostly *suffis* (Islamic mystics) or have an intellectualised image of Islam. They do not have the same circles of friends and so not share the same worldview. The *jihadi* converts are looking for concrete solutions to their identity problems. Their attitude towards their own society is antagonistic because it does not, they believe, give them equal opportunities for social promotion. In France, they often live on poor suburban estates. They are surrounded by other young people of north-African origin who are hostile to a society that has excluded them and who have a strong feeling that they are being victimised.[72] Islamisation becomes synonymous with the legitimisation of a revolt against the 'included', and sanctifies the feeling of being one of the excluded. Hatred takes on religious attributes and becomes legitimate because it can be defined in absolute terms. This is the starting point for a proselytism that can suck the convert into a spiral of violence. Thanks to an inverted racism, young people of Maghrebin origin often distrust French youngsters who embrace their religion. They often mock their poor understanding of Islam and attempt to humiliate them. Their Arabic is poor and they often speak a dialectal Arabic that is far removed from Islam, whose mode of expression is an Arabic script that most of them cannot decipher. Realising that they are fragile and know little about Islam, young Maghrebins are all the more touchy about French converts to their religion, who seem to want to teach them a moral lesson and to humiliate them on their own ground. When, in other words, their 'French' neighbours convert to Islam, the immediate reaction of young 'Arabs' is to assume that they are attempting to reproduce a colonial relationship and to demonstrate that they can be 'better' Muslims, they become suspicious of them. In order to overcome this tendency, which is inherent in their relations with young Muslims, the converts often feel the need to be overzealous. They must prove to themselves and others that they are true Muslims who are willing to die for their faith. *Jihad* thus comes to be seen as a symbolic confrontation with those who were born Muslims. It is as though the converts' religious honour was at stake. The discontents of the poor suburbs are translated into a religious symbolism that reinforces Islam's radical tendencies, so as to convince those who are sceptical, or even suspicious, about the sincerity of these new warriors of the faith. 'Islam' comes to mean '*jihad*', partly because it can sublimate the discomfort of exclusion and can be transformed into a confrontation with other Muslims. When new 'white' (of non-immigrant origin) converts espouse Islam in the poor suburbs of French cities, their conversion often takes on another meaning. It is a way of expressing their solidarity with the dispossessed, with the underdogs, with young people on estates where the rates of unemployment and delinquency are proportionately much higher than that in 'normal' neighbourhoods. They may react in one of two very different ways. They may come to hate the second-generation immigrants who are giving the neighbourhood a bad reputation and making it look run down. They may join far right groups as a result. Alternatively, they may empathise with them, and perhaps even go so far as to convert to Islam by taking the logic of identification to extremes. In that case, their motives can be altruistic or even self sacrificial.

The negative image of Islam as a religion of violence and bitter struggle that has been spread by the Western media over the last 20 years can also have the effect of giving it even greater prestige in the eyes of those members of the population who are trying to espouse values that run counter to those of society. They are motivated by a feeling of rejection and cherish the hope of being able to take a violent revenge on the institutionalised violence that is insidiously used against them. From that perspective, this version of Islam becomes a virile Islam. Thanks to a symbolic shift of meaning, the violent version of Islam becomes, in its turn, the religion of righteous retribution. The rigidified Islam that prohibits women's freedom turns into a religion that gives men and women roles that are defined by a natural and immutable order, and that reintroduces morality into the home. An Islam that has been rendered archaic thanks to a regressive interpretation becomes the Islam of the Golden Age, of the dawn of a happy humanity that was never affected by either the ravages of time or the distortions of Christianity. An Islam that has been made more puritanical than traditional Islam becomes, finally, a religion that consoles its converts by protecting them from the evils of a sexual depravity that feminises men and perverts women in the modern world by taking away men's honour and women's modesty. For groups that are seeking to be the embodiment of society's countervalues, an ill-famed and discredited Islam is transformed into a religion of offended dignity and wounded virility. Its followers then exacerbate its inflexibility and rigidity.

Their obsessive concern with purity is also exacerbated in modern societies, which are by definition full of temptations. How can anyone resist the attractions of women when relations between the sexes are no longer subject to rigid norms? This is equally true of the women who espouse this version of Islam and reject a sexually licentious society. The French wife of one of the Islamists I interviewed converted long before she met him, and she would not take him as her husband until she was convinced that he too rejected the sexual licentiousness and depravity of the West. The war on corrupting temptations becomes an integral part of a faith that cannot survive in its fundamentalist form unless it promotes a constant struggle against sexual depravity and moral corruption.

Charismatic figures play an important role in conversion. It is the imam of the mosque, or groups of young people from the Tabligh, which is a multinational Islamic association, who make the *da'wa* (call to Islam) and take it upon themselves to convince others of the validity of the religion of the Prophet. So long as the convert is a member of one of these groups, he is unlikely to go off the rails, if only because such associations are trying to establish themselves in Western societies in the long term, and in order to do that they need to look respectable. It is when they leave these religious groups that some converts are likely to take the path of radicalism. In order to do so, they need the help of a network or group and, if they find one, they may embark on an adventure that may cost them their lives. Be that as it may, the convert is often prepared for extreme experiences that are intended to prove, both to himself and others, that his or her faith is true and sincere.

Not all converts are from modest backgrounds. Members of the middle classes sometimes join the followers of Allah, for various reasons. They find, first of all, answers to questions to which they cannot find answers in their day-to-day lives. The 'deinstitutionalisation' of social relations,[73] the fact that the state no longer plays a fundamental role in shaping individuals' lives, and the undermining of values such as citizenship or, in the case of France, *laïcité* (radical secularism), mean that individuals experience a vacuum that makes them dizzy, irrespective of their position in the economic world. Membership of the middle classes exacerbates this discontent. Individuals belonging to the lower or working classes can blame the duplicity of the ruling classes or the corruption of political elites for their failures and problems. For members of the middle classes, however, there is another dimension to their failures and problems. As they are not of an economic nature and do not demand a concrete or tangible solution, they become 'metaphysical'. We are witnessing a globalisation of discontent as the political elites become increasingly unable to make citizenship meaningful and as our leaders are unable to construct a social field in which membership of the nation can have a noble meaning. It is as though *laïcité* had become a spent force after its Pyrrhic victory over the Catholic Church, and as though its triumph was in fact its swan song. A world that has lost its soul, and in which the feeling of belonging to one nation regardless of cultural and economic difference is in decline, gives birth to the idea that religion, unlike politics, can be our salvation. Islam is one of the many possible choices on offer in a vast selection ranging from Buddhism to a multitude of cults, each more exotic than the last. What makes Islam stand out is that it does not avoid the question of legitimate violence. It resorts to violence when justice requires it to do so. It gives a sense of righteousness that knows no ambiguity. The fact that violence is a legitimate way of managing society and that it can be sanctioned by recourse to the sacred is balm to the symbolic wound inflicted by the daily encounter with problems when we instinctively know that the usual political solutions are powerless to resolve them. As society becomes increasingly complex, and as everything conspires to make it look like a more and more enigmatic sphinx – in terms of both its nature and its future – Islam supplies answers that are delightfully clear. Christianity – and especially Catholicism – complicates life to no avail. According to the converted prisoners, it interposes a Son between God and men, and then claims that the Son is represented by the Church. This makes God an even greater stranger to men, and destroys their direct relationship with Him: He is a transcendent being who cannot be known by His creatures but who can disclose His commandments to them. In Islam, in contrast, men's direct relationship with God suffers neither the interposition of a clergy nor the mediation of a Son. It offers simplicity, transparency, univocity, rationality and, above all, a vision of the body and sexuality that restores men's sense of virility and superiority by reintroducing order into gender relationships. Being the religion of human nature, Islam is the answer to the exhausting lives we live in a society where there is no longer any central norm, and where all norms seem to have been reduced to impotence by the tolerance that makes no distinction between true and false, or between justice and injustice. A society in which tolerance is absolute weakens all norms, and when all normative principles are equivalent, truth vanishes from our lives. One of the negative features that late modernity does believe in is the rejection of violence. The reintroduction of a legitimate and divinely sanctioned version of violence is one reason why the religion of Allah looks so reassuring in a world that has lost its soul and which is nostalgic for it.

Then there is the unrivalled prestige of death. Death is the antidote to the sickly sweet modernity that characterised our last *fin de siècle* and the first years of the new century. Death is something of a paradox. It is constantly hidden by the cult of eternal youth that haunts our late modernity. But death also give the subject the demiurgic capacity to control his or her life at the extreme point where life turns into its opposite, or at least becomes an alterity that cannot be transcended. The quest for absolute power and knowledge, if they are taken to their extreme limits, means exultation *in* and *for* death. That is the ultimate fascination where 'becoming master and possessor of nature' can be metamorphosed into 'becoming master of one's death' by testing oneself against it and by exhausting life in the very attempt to overcome it and transform it into its opposite: far from being life's limitation, death becomes a way of transcending life by exulting in its domination.

Jihadist Islam can provide converts who are bored with the cowardly approximations of everyday life with a response to their intoxication with death. The followers of Nietzsche once sought an answer in war or in the decisionism of an individual who had been transformed into a superman who could imprint a final meaning by leaping into the unknown dimension of death. In the absence of a war that is synonymous with a general conflagration, Islam becomes a new kind of Nietzscheanism. Dying for the sacred cause is a stratagem that helps to overcome the feeling of emptiness that haunts the middle classes of Western societies in which there is little possibility of generalised warfare, and in which there is no heroic solution in sight. In the absence of any great struggle that might galvanise minds, there is simply the derisory spectacle of everyday life. The only distractions are minor news items that have no meaning, or the distant wars that we experience by proxy on television. They may well be unreal, but they do distract us from our boredom with a real world that is always the same.[74] *Jihad* is a substitute for an Apocalypse that is slow in coming. The times are, in other words, gradually transformed into a continuous crisis that can have no end. The transcendence of the Apocalypse and the End of Time are transformed into the immanence and continuity of an ending that we constantly approach but can never reach.[75] *Jihad* puts an end to a crisis that goes on and on without ever producing a true apocalypse that is worthy of the name.

For converts, adopting a *jihadist* vision is a way of giving life a meaning by assigning a tangible end to it. It is a form of defiance that allows death to consume the feeling that time is almost immobile and that everything has been reduced to the same level. *Jihadists* begin with a virtual Apocalypse, with a simulacrum of catastrophe.

Joining a *jihadist* group may look like a minor gesture to begin with. The converts seem to be part of a group that is amusing itself by concentrating the energies it might otherwise expend in other ways. The member moves a cursor and transmits data and information. His involvement in the group looks harmless; it is as though he was playing a game. He is, however, becoming caught up in a system. Its meaning usually escapes those who join the group without knowing what the ultimate consequences will be. Once they are in the group, it is difficult, if not impossible, to get out. Once they have taken the first step, the feeling that they are playing a game can be heightened by intermittent escapes from virtual reality. Outside the game, they find a reality that tells them that the coming catastrophe is at hand. From that point onwards, the Apocalypse is no longer just an electronic game. It is a game that is being played in a real space and its implications go far beyond the realm of fiction. But this reality can be experienced as a virtual computer game. What we see here is the uneasy relationship between reality and fiction, between the immanence of an electronic battle where the damage done is purely imaginary, and the kind of discontinuity that occurs in a world that is all too real. The death and destruction do take place on a citywide scale. In abstract terms, this mutation is no more than one more game that is being played inside a generalised simulacrum.[76] But there has been a change of scale, and those involved are not always aware of its implications because they remain trapped within their vision of a never-ending crisis. Their crisis occurs in an immutable virtual dimension. They want to get out of it, but they are also convinced that it is extremely difficult, or even impossible, to transpose it to the reality that lies outside. Converts who become involved in this dangerous game are caught between the unreal on the one hand and, on the other, their desire to transcend it by having recourse to a *jihad* in the name of Allah. They dream of a new world that will rid them of the feeling that they are living through a permanent crisis against a backdrop of virtuality and immanence. They want to experience a transcendental God who can write His name in fire on a world that is unjust to Muslims, which has no consistency and has no sense of the sacred. The advent of the sacred in the guise of a jealous and vengeful God gives meaning to a holy war. That war will be a disaster or an Apocalypse that will completely destroy the ungodly West. The register of the *tremendum* that inspires a fear and trembling that modernity has excluded from the sacred now reappears thanks to a vision that wants to provoke the Apocalypse rather than being a passive witness to its advent, which is constantly postponed. The modernity of this expectation lies in the feverish activity that is designed to bring about the catastrophe. There is no time for quietistic waiting and fear. The fear and trembling are inspired by the spectacle of mass destruction in the name of God. The believer becomes His pitiless lieutenant. The wrath of God may well exist only in purely virtual terms, but its effects are terribly real.

## THE EXCLUSION OF WOMEN

Whilst a few Palestinian women have taken part in suicide bombings in recent years, the same cannot be said of either the Iranian martyrs or the members of al-Qaeda. The exclusion of women is deliberate, and not of their own making. Their exclusion does however often go hand in hand with a more or less tacit acquiescence on their part, and it can take novel forms. Al-Qaeda supporters who have lived for several years in modern Western societies have been able to espouse cutting-edge technology, such as information technology, and have studied modern engineering – usually in Germany or the United States – but they trail behind the West in terms of relations between men and women. At this level, they deliberately keep themselves apart from the West. The family is one of the places where it is possible to construct an Islamic identity that is profoundly different to Western identity. The sexes are complementary, but not equal. A woman's mission is to perpetuate her family, and a man's mission is to provide her with a decent life in material terms and a dignified existence in which she lacks for nothing. A woman's place is in the home, and a man's place is in public space. Women should be chaste and modest. Men should be virile and should protect the family's honour. There is nothing specifically Islamic about this ideology, which is as old as the world itself. What makes it so distinctive is that it survives in a context where, in other respects, modernisation has completely transformed the lifestyles and mental structures of the very people who describe themselves as 'Islamic'.

If this whirlwind has led to the political transformation of Muslim societies, why do relations between men and women remain unchanged? The absence of change is in fact more apparent than real. What we find here is regression, pure and simple, an identitarian reflex, a refusal to change and a new rigidity rather than the preservation of a traditional attitude. Women are the Achilles' heel of Muslim civilisations undergoing profound and critical transformations. Islam's cultural ideal was that of a civilisation in which women covered themselves up and in which men and women were kept apart.[77] The harsh reality is that many Muslim societies have always strayed from that ideal in, for example, tribal regions where the need for women to work made segregation difficult during periods of transhumance. Islam has, however, always preserved the ideal of female modesty and male honour by keeping its women apart and veiling them.

Relationships between men and women in contemporary Muslim societies are governed by a dialectic in which women who were once mothers, sisters, daughters or wives are gradually becoming individualised and challenging men's status as the sole social actors in the public domain. The evolution of Muslim societies and their intensive urbanisation also mean that women have to work to ensure an adequate household income. The destruction of the concrete communities of old and the anonymity of the big city undermine the mechanisms that once protected women's modesty. Coming into contact with the middle classes of the West has given women new aspirations, and they are now making new demands. Access to higher education has changed both their mentality and their aspirations. The crisis of modernisation is leading to a new kind of patriarchalism. As the positions of men and women and their respective standings in society become more problematic, men tend to make roles within the family more rigid to compensate for the general crisis affecting the role of the individual in an increasingly anonymous world where the communitarian roles of the past no longer apply. Women's attitude towards this is often ambivalent. Because they want to intervene in the social and political field, they are part of the crisis affecting social roles but insofar as they are members of society, they too suffer when the traditional markers disappear. The new patriarchalism within the family is based upon the ideology of preserving family values, and that touches a sensitive chord. The outcome is that feminist movements that try to raise the issue in explicit and open terms are very weak. Hence the development of women's movements that try to reconcile their aspirations with a social situation characterised by the emergence of neo-patriarchal movements led by religious conservatives or neo-fundamentalists.

One of the domains to which women are denied access in Muslim societies undergoing modernisation is martyrdom. The refusal to allow them to put their lives at risk in fact denies them the right to individuation through a baptism of fire. Sacrificing one's life for a noble cause implies that others recognise one's social pre-eminence. The 'heroic individual' breaks into the social field and then becomes a true individual thanks to its secularisation. At this level, women are denied access to martyrdom because of an unbreakable social taboo rather than for political reasons. In Palestine and Chechnya, this assumption is now being challenged by some women. This tendency may be reinforced as women aspire to being men's equals. Putting their own lives at risk may guarantee them the equality they have been denied for so long.

Women's martyrdom still has no role to play in any *jihad*, and this makes them second-class citizens. Being unable to put their lives at risk, they are placed 'under the protection' of men who thus deny them the right to self-determination in the domain of the sacred and, by extension, the domain of the profane. Be it in Iran, Algeria, Egypt or Afghanistan, the refusal to allow women access to martyrdom means that they cannot dispose of their lives and deaths in the same way that men can. At this level, social dissymmetry is perpetuated, if not exacerbated. Yet many women would like to take their place in the pantheon of martyrs and thus win a collective recognition of their citizenship and equal dignity in society. In Iran, one of Hezbollah's slogans was 'The modesty of women is guaranteed by the blood of martyrs.' The refusal to grant women access to public space and keeping them under male domination are, in other words, sanctioned by the blood men spill as martyrs. Men thus acquire a legitimate status that women cannot attain because they do not have access to holy death.

## THE NEW GLOBALISED IMAGINARY

The Islamic world became part of an imaginary that was globalised thanks to the magic of oil, long before the advent of the unbridled globalisation that emerged from the ruins of the Soviet Empire. A mythical subsoil allowed its elites to acquire boundless wealth thanks to the magic of the black gold that poured billions of dollars into the coffers of patrimonial states that had no democratic legitimacy. It is no accident that the first Islamic Revolution took place in oil-rich Iran or that al-Qaeda was founded by a wealthy Saudi whose father made his money from making profitable investments when oil revenues rose in the 1970s. This vision was the first manifestation of a globalised imaginary. It was based on the belief that the spectacle of an easy opulence born of an oil miracle that implied almost no human involvement would emancipate us from the constraints of the real world. Together with more classic phenomena (the increasingly arbitrary rule of the state, the struggle against religious institutions and growing autocracy), it was this divorce from reality that lay at the origin of the Iranian Revolution. Its effects were then amplified by the technological and computer revolutions of the next decades. 'Petro-Islam' gave birth to a mentality that encouraged delusions that could coexist with those of computerised virtuality and the globalised imaginary. The mechanisms that could compensate for that loss of reality in the West did not exist.

Whilst oil stimulated some people's greed, it also accentuated a feeling of injustice on the part of those who thought it iniquitous that the wealth of a few emirates and a Saudi Arabia in the pay of America could coexist with the desolate spectacle of the poverty of the rest of the Arab and Muslim world. Saddam Hussein's invasion of Kuwait in 1990 did not provoke a wave of mass indignation in the Arab world because of the illegitimate wealth of a small population which had forgotten that the primary meaning of Islam was justice and the redistribution of wealth through Islamic taxes such as *khoms* and *zakat*. The imaginary of those who prospered thanks to oil revenues led to the disillusionment of those who, in those very same societies, were excluded from the opulence and who watched as impotent spectators while the 'happy few' became wealthy, arrogant and hostile to Islamic modesty and charity.

Oil-derived wealth has left a lasting mark on the subjects of Saudi Arabia and most countries in the Middle East, either because they had a share in the oil windfall or because they were excluded from it. Thanks to the oil imaginary, those who came to the West were no strangers to its consumerist mentality. They earned enough to live there and, in the case of the better off, had access to the benefits of modern life. But that did nothing to dispel the feeling that they were despised because they were foreigners. On the contrary. Even those who succeeded in living like the middle, or even upper classes, still felt bitter because the West hardly bothered to disguise the fact that it despised them. In the case of the diaspora's martyrs, a virtual 'cabled community' linked together by television and the internet began to gain more importance, even though its consistency was purely digital. In their view, this tragic neo-*umma* was being desecrated, violated and put to death by its own members. This worldview did not need to have any major counterweight in the real world to be credible. Traces, vestiges, a tissue of disparate facts and novel forms of identification were all that was required to make the Islamic neo-*umma* look desirable, to turn it into the basis for action and to make it a force for mobilisation. For a network like al-Qaeda, which will certainly not be the last of its kind, the imaginary and virtual neo-*umma* is just as important as its real or imaginary grievances against the West.

The role of the imaginary also finds expression in the anthropological experience of death. In the case of national martyrs, a holy death is, as we have seen, the product of a triple rupture: between life and death, between present and future, and between this world and the Paradise of the next. For the neo-*umma*'s martyrs, these three ruptures are attenuated, or even concealed, by the specificity of their mental universe. There is, so to speak, a quasi-continuity between life and death, just as there is a quasi-continuity between the virtual and the real. Similarly, the present and the future are experienced in states of weightlessness in modern cities that distort their sense of time and destroy the 'natural' categories of time and space by telescoping past and future into an artificially extended present. Everything exists in a continuous present, or even in the absence of temporality. As the real becomes virtual, it vanishes into a quasi-dream world dominated by cathode-ray tubes and electronic screens. In a world that tends to obliterate the basic difference between the real and the imaginary, the transition from life to death loses much of its terror.

The feeling that there is a break between life and death is greatly attenuated when it takes so little to move from the pole of the real to that of the unreal, from that of the concrete to that of a digitalised abstraction. The fear of dying undergoes a metamorphosis. In the case of national martyrs, a well-oiled organisation such as the Bassidj in Iran, Hamas in Palestine or the GIA in Algeria is required if they are to overcome their fear of dying by ensuring that someone stays with them during their last weeks or days on earth.

The task is, in a sense, much easier when it is a question of dying for the sacred cause of the diasporic neo-*umma*. An organisation is of course still required but it is more supple and embryonic that in the national context. The organisation is a network suited to the task, and forms of auto-suggestion and scripture mean that its members are its essential element. Just as the break between the real (life) and the virtual (death) is greatly attenuated, the transition from one to the other is much easier and does not require such an elaborate structure as other types of martyrdom. This virtual model has to be taken seriously, as diasporic believers extend it to their entire anthropological experience. The initial model is provided by electronics. In this model, anything can happen and the constraints of the real world do not apply. Players become demi-gods, provided that they understand the rules that allow them to intervene. In the interactive model, it is possible to shape the real at will and to intervene in a digitalised reality by obeying pre-established norms. This distances the players from flesh-and-blood reality, in which there are no pregiven rules to shape it or to detract from its basic unpredictability and heterogeneity. In the digital field, the real becomes a more complex virtuality that is infinitely malleable. This literally changes the meaning of the lived experience of the irreducibility of reality. Some players cross this boundary, and can therefore ignore concrete reality by identifying with the impoverished and virtual reality they see in their computer games. This can have a powerful effect on both them and others. It is not simply the specificity of electronic games or the conjuring tricks that can be performed in digitalised networks that facilitate the expansion of this quasi-virtual vision of reality. A further component comes into play and heightens its effects. I refer to everyday life in contemporary society, and life in big global cities in particular. Meanings become opaque in multicultural environments where the same act can take on a variety of heterogeneous meanings, depending on which community interprets it. When meanings lose their visibility and univocity, there is a growing sense of virtuality. The player is cut off from reality. All these phenomena give rise to a kind of anomie that might, for want of a better term, be called an-hylia: there is no more hyle or specific content. The only things that exist are the vague contours of a plurality of possible forms, each of which can be regarded as a transformation of the other. They are constantly being modified and expanded. Matter is dissolved into a multitude of forms, rather as though it could take on an infinite number of shapes. Matter or the real becomes, in other words, the virtuality of an infinite number of malleable 'morphs'. The network operates in the same way. The world turns into an avatar of 'form'. The real is nothing more than a 'signal' that has yet to be digitalised and dissolves into 'shapes' as though it were another virtuality.

The new technologies, combined with the experience of life in modern cities, operate on two fronts. They operate, on the one hand, on the front where a new digitalised world is being created, and that world generates a 'made-to-measure reality' which is experienced as an intermediary level. It has its own meaning and autonomy, exists midway between reality and a purely digital virtuality. It is at the level of virtual reality that the interactivity establishes the rudiments of a grammar with a lexicon. We move from a virtual and abstract grammar to the intermediary level of a lexicalisation that generates a sui generis reality. But this intermediary level would be no more than a game if contemporary reality did not contain elements that give consistency to this type of imaginary. The world of multinetworked big cities also tends to make reality evanescent. Ultimately, the real is nothing more than an ensemble that has yet to be explicitly coded. Road networks, distance working or modes of access to television all mean that much of our experience of daily life is now characterised by its formalism and poverty of content. Hence the disturbing convergence between the experience of interactivity in a purely digital intermediary world, and the growing impoverishment of reality in our day-to-day lives. To the extent that it is losing its substance, we are beginning to network reality.

For anyone living in the big cities, where the real is evanescent, and who is socially marginalised (but not necessarily socially excluded), it is easy to take the next step. The corollary of the 'Western arrogance' denounced by the Islamists of the diaspora is its loss of reality. Our experiences are becoming disconnected from reality and more and more influenced by the virtual, the digital and the abstract. The same applies to those who denounce this world. The aching *umma* that sprawls in front of television all day, and the neo-*umma* it believes will put an end to this humiliating suffering, both feed on the impoverishment of reality as they come into contact with a world that is increasingly abstract and out of reach. It is because it is rooted in a world where concrete forms of human experience are increasingly being replaced by complex and abstract types of formalised and digitalised relations, that the contours of the neo-*umma* are so vague. The Apocalypse it wants so much is bound up with these new forms of sociability in which the impersonal, the formal, the digital and the abstract can finally do without any reference to the real, and inspire the feeling that human relations are vacuous.

Whereas national martyrs live their tragedy in person, al-Qaeda's martyrs experience it through cables, television and digital media. It is the electronic system, defined in the broadest of senses, that provides their link with reality. Their suffering is a pathos that feeds on images and that is transmitted by proxy within a neo-*umma* where no one has given them any mandate. Their mandate is a self-proclaimed one. They award it to themselves by proxy in a fantasy world in which anyone can take the place of the victims of an act whose origins lie in global cities such as New York, Madrid, Paris or London and in ultramodern digital forms as well as in the poor areas of Algiers, the overcrowded cities of Gaza or the polluted neighbourhoods of Cairo.

# Conclusion

We have been able to identify two kinds of Islamic martyrdom in the contemporary world. The first or classic form concerns individuals who wish to build a sovereign collectivity (usually a nation) and who, when that proves impossible, embrace a sacred death either as a way of helping others to build it after their death, or to kill as many of their enemies as possible. By doing so, they make those they regard as an obstacle to the national collectivity they want so badly share their own profound despair.

There is also another sort of martyr whose aspirations are more disturbing. They wish to construct a worldwide community that is the embodiment of Islamic universalism by destroying the might of the evil forces that oppose it: the West, as personified by America and, to a certain extent, other Western societies. The second type of martyr is born of the disappearance of the old world that shaped the world order around an East–West dichotomy and of the weakening of the national imaginary that resulted from the crisis affecting allegiances and principles of identification in existing societies that resulted from globalisation. Islam is ideally suited to providing them with a pole of allegiance and to become the main, if not the only, spokesperson for this discontent. And many Muslim countries are indeed in a critical state. In some cases, independence has been confiscated by a state that has mutated into a patrimonial order, as in Algeria (a rentier state). Moreover, the conflict in the Middle East has rekindled the feeling that the Islamic world is being humiliated by Israel, which is seen as an agent of Western imperialism. A third set of causes has its origins in the emergence of new Muslim countries after the collapse of the Soviet Empire, as in Chechnya. Nation-building can scarcely be undertaken there without bloodshed, partly because of the imperialism of a new colonial power: Russia.

The multiplicity of these phenomena and the specificity of each individual case are partly concealed by the appeal to two of Islam's main themes: *jihad* and martyrdom. The appeal to these representations universalises the sufferings of the parties concerned and suggests that they all have the same motives. There is in fact a world of difference between the Palestinian who is demanding a nation, the Chechen who wants independence from Russia, the

Bosnian who demanded the withdrawal of the Serbian army, and the supporters of al-Qaeda who want to destroy Western imperialism and restore the Islamic Golden Age. The latter do not want to destroy the West so as to replace it with a tangible order, as did the revolutionary left up to the 1980s. They want to blow up a perverted and arrogant world, even though they are in no position to replace it with a universal order based on some other principle.

The temporal concomitance of the two phenomena – one national and the other transnational – means that they are interrelated. Their nature is, however, quite different. The first defines its place in a world of nations, whilst the second relates to a new world order that is coming into being. This type of martyrdom is one of its more unexpected effects. The vacuum left by nations and the collapse of the old order has resulted in the creation of a new world. These martyrs reject it, but there is no way of knowing what they want or what alternative solution they are proposing. In one sense, deaths of the second kind are both tragic and pointless. They are tragic because we are talking about the death of several thousand individuals who had no direct involvement in a war that has never been declared and that has never been clearly defined in terms of the issues involved. They are also pointless because the destruction of the entire West that these movements are demanding is impossible without the collapse of the whole world. What is mistakenly called the West is now the greater part of humanity's heritage. As it expands, it affects the imaginary and the living conditions of its enemies as well as its protagonists. Slogans such as 'The Koran is our constitution', 'Islam is a complete system' or 'Allah's Shari'a on earth' (*shari'at allah di'ardh*) may be meaningful in the context of a nation or in cases where the movements voicing them establish an Islamic theocracy. On a world scale, however, they are meaningless, unless they mean 'Apocalypse', which is precisely what the protagonists of a globalised *jihadist* Islam want.

The question that now arises is as follows: how are we to understand the death wish of these groups of men who are willing to be slain and who also aspire to slaying others?

Modern cities and especially the great 'access cities' are vast and impersonal places where the feeling of the loss of the self and the alienation caused by the general frenzy and the absence of markers lead to vertigo, even when spatially visible communities (such as Chinatowns) do exist. They are monstrous cities, if only because of the sexual licentiousness, promiscuity and 'immorality' that make them a Sodom and Gomorrah as well as a Babylon for many migrants, and for those who feel they have been left behind by an unbridled and satanic modernity. It is these cities that give rise to the feeling of a neo-*umma*, much more so than in their countries of origin, where the individual is all too often confined to a straitjacket by the state, but also by social constraints. Revolts do break out in Cairo, Tehran, the poor suburbs of Algiers (the Casbah) or the Gaza Strip (Palestine), but the outcome is a type of movement that has more to do with a Muslim nation than with the world as a whole. Even the Iranian Revolution, which attempted to export Islam to the four corners of the world, had to come to terms with the fact that it was national in character. Its real influence was confined to Lebanon, a country in crisis and without a state where it could provide Hezbollah with financial and material aid thanks to the presence of a Shi'ite community. Within a few years, the fantasy of a revolution with a worldwide vocation faded away. Defending it against the Iraqi enemy and domestic counterrevolutionaries like the People's Mujahedeen was a matter of urgency. In order to become aware of the universality of the Islamic message and to subscribe to a worldwide neo-*umma*, it is necessary to live in the very heart of the West, in its global cities where everything is present but where everything is also, in a sense, in a state of great instability, mutual rejection and cultural misunderstanding. It was in cities like New York, Paris, London, Madrid, Hamburg, Rome and Los Angeles and their suburbs that the idea of a neo-*umma* that could transcend frontiers was born in its new guise. This idea could only have germinated in the very heart of the most modern megacities of the West's heartlands, and not in the desert or in relatively unmodernised shanty towns on the periphery of Muslim countries. Those members of al-Qaeda who planned the attacks on the World Trade Center were no strangers to living in the West or to modernity. On the contrary, they were far too familiar with the Western world to believe in its intrinsic superiority. It was their feeling of humiliation by proxy that led them to begin the struggle. It was an explosive combination of involvement in modernity and what they saw as the world's refusal to recognise Islam that inspired their revolt and fed their hatred. They felt that Islam was being treated badly and that Muslims were being repressed. They also felt that the Islam that had once been at the centre of the civilised world, that had been domineering and self-confident, was now nothing more than a periphery that had been manipulated and marginalised by a truculent and immoral West intent upon offending and humiliating it so as to take away its followers' dignity and destroy the last bulwark against its illegitimate hegemony. They were also painfully aware that a small country like Israel, which has fewer than ten million inhabitants, could defy a billion Muslims, and they became their self-appointed spokesmen. The Islam that had once been one of the most feared masters of the universe was now under the domination of a West that felt not the slightest compassion for its sufferings or the afflictions of its self-proclaimed spokesmen. And yet those who reached this verdict were also, in a certain way, profoundly influenced by the West. They were not submodernised. Most of them were not ill-treated or marginalised in economic terms (in social and economic terms, many in the leadership of al-Qaeda were better integrated and much richer than many Westerners).

The Islam in whose name they oppose the West is not a different civilisation. It is the dark side of the new world civilisation, and the West is its figurehead.[1]

The martyrs and their radical Islam represent only a tiny minority within Western societies. They do, however, represent an active minority, and that is why it is so tempting to blame all Muslims for the crimes of a minority. Some claim that Islam is incapable of adapting to the modern world, to the individual, to a law-governed society and the equality it implies, and especially the equality between men and women. Equality implies the involvement of all in a pluralistic and democratic conception of politics. Half a century ago, Catholicism raised the same problems, and formulated in the same way.[2] Yet Catholicism has absorbed the essential aspects of democratic representation. There is no reason why Islam should not take the same path. If it is to do so, it requires theologians who can give a hieratic and historical interpretation of its sacred texts, and groups who espouse the customs of modern life. The first component is still in its infancy, but new intellectuals in Iran, Egypt, the Maghreb, France, England, Turkey and many other countries are trying to revitalise Islamic thought and to demonstrate that it is compatible with democratic pluralism. The second component is making good progress, and is adapting to the modern life of the Islamic diaspora. Some Muslim thinkers in Iran, Egypt and Morocco are beginning to think about democracy and Islam, and are challenging the prestige of radical Islam. The current obstacles to the democratic opening up of Muslim societies are the conflicts in the Middle East, Kashmir and Chechnya, the presence of the nepotistic or even corrupt ruling classes in their midst that are monopolising power and repressing the democratic demands of the emerging new classes. Their hold on the economic and political levers of these countries is an obstacle to the spread of democracy in this part of the world.

Martyrdom is not the infantile malady of Islam, but something that allows Muslims to recover the dignity they have been denied by Western countries whose policies are certainly biased against the Islamic world (witness their attitude towards the Palestinian and Chechen national problems). It also allows them to abdicate all responsibility for their own problems. The slim and dangerous consolation that they can take some of their enemies with them is a way of masking the fact that they are dying so as to avoid their responsibilities. So long as the major problems remain unresolved, there will always be candidates for holy death. Even if those problems are resolved, they will not necessarily disappear but their numbers will shrink to the point where they could become marginal. Societies that are at peace with themselves incite few people to embrace a sacred death. Those who do so are a tiny minority who belong to a cult of hotheads. So long as they exist in this marginal form, they can never be completely eradicated because they are products of our modern societies. These societies may well be dynamic, but they are still non-egalitarian and unfair, and the social imbalances are structural.

Hegel believed that the struggle for recognition implied a confrontation between master and slave, but not death. If the slave died, the master would be unable to exercise his hegemony and dominance over him. Modern martyrdom opens up a new space of intelligibility. The appeal to the sacred means that the struggle for recognition can now involve death to a great extent. The demography of Muslim countries allows them to mobilise part of their youth for that purpose and in order to gain an imaginary dignity in a world that denies them any real dignity. The coming century may well witness the mimetic generalisation of this form of holy death.

# Afterword to the English Edition

The globalisation of the world is becoming local or regional now, much larger and with wider implications. A new dialectic now links national, religious and ethnic problems to global problems. This is particularly true of the Palestinian, Kashmiri and Chechen national movements in the Muslim world. These movements are behind the rise of Jihadism throughout the world. The Palestinian problem, for instance, has worldwide implications in two senses. On the one hand, some Palestinians become 'human bombs' because they feel that they have been dispossessed of a territory on which they could have built their own nation.[1] But in the rest of the world – both the Muslim world and the West, where there is now a Muslim minority – it is the image of clashes between young Palestinians and Israeli tanks and missiles that brings about the profound feeling of revolt and humiliation and helps to legitimise Jihadism.[2] In some cases, it seems to be this that convinced some young French men from an immigrant background and British 'Asians' to commit themselves to the *jihad*.[3]

The conflict in Chechnya has not led to the same kind of mobilisation amongst Muslims in the West because the region is not so well known. Its people do not speak a major Islamic language. There are no major holy places in the country, whereas the Al Aqsa mosque is situated in the Palestinian territories. There is no major Chechen diaspora in the West.

Until now, terrorist groups appear to have been influenced by ethnicity, or by a transferred ethnic symbolism (in France, they are 'Arab', meaning north African; in Britain, they are Asian). Moroccan networks do, however, appear to have masterminded the attack in Madrid in 2004, and many of the terrorists involved seem to have come from the city of Tangier.

The formation of the generation that is most active in terrorist networks can be traced back to their experience in Afghanistan. Their field experience, the training they underwent in the camps and the mutual relationships established in the same camps taught them the techniques used to prepare explosives and allowed links between the various groups to be established. The various groups that went to Afghanistan, either before the departure of the Soviets in the early 1990s or after the Taliban came to power, were billeted in training camps organised on a national basis: Algerians, Moroccans, Egyptians and so on were able to get to know one another and to establish friendly links there. It was there that national or ethnic relationships were forged and reinforced. The Afghan experience was of fundamental importance in the establishment of links between the various groups of *jihadists*. Others gained experience in Iraq, where groups of foreigners established links and had direct combat experience after its occupation by American and British forces in 2003. In the West, London was the main focus for the establishment of activist groups from the rest of Europe. Many French activists of Maghrebin origin, like Zaccaria Moussaoui, served their apprenticeship in activist groups based in London. Paris also played an important role, especially for networks linked to the GIA or Moroccan groups.

The third characteristic of these groups, apart from their loosely structured and 'franchised' nature,[4] is their capacity to take the initiative at the local level, independently of other groups. This gives them the ability to carry out major operations with relatively few means.

The fourth characteristic of these groups is their extremely vague ideology. They refer to a warlike neo-*umma* and to an 'infra-ideology' that is neither coherent nor well articulated. This is a strength and not a weakness. Because this infra-ideology is so fluid and unstructured, they can both project their existential discontent on to it and find an equally flexible answer within it. The essential point is their feeling that they have been profoundly humiliated, that the West has taken away their dignity.[5] That feeling can give rise to a whole range of very specific experiences. The final main characteristic of these movements is the way they oscillate between territorialisation and deterritorialisation. Palestinian and Chechen activists know precisely what they want: a nation sanctified by Islam, now that secular nationalism has proved to be a failure. In the case of al-Qaeda, there is almost no reference to any territory: even in the early 1990s, when the struggle against America officially began, the demand for the American army to get out of the holy land of Saudi Arabia took the form of a challenge to the Saud clan's hegemony over that territory and, eventually, the struggle against all the corrupt governments in Muslims countries that support the West. This was a purely metaphorical territorialisation of Islam, but its ideology is essentially non-territorial. This means that the group can be joined by individuals who would otherwise have no reason to become involved with the nebula.

Many present determinations will change in future. Given their age, Afghan veterans will play a much less active role, at least in carrying out attacks, in the years to come. They will have to pass the baton on to a new generation. The links created between different groups in the camps in Afghanistan will become weaker as the activists involved are arrested, die or simply grow old and renounce activism. The fact that the new terrorists do not have a safe territorial base in Afghanistan (which was a safe haven under the Taliban) is a mixed blessing: on the one hand, Western governments can no longer identify them because they have been in Afghanistan, but on the other they have lost a precious base for training and socialisation.

Other camps will replace the ones that have been lost in Afghanistan. There are camps in Pakistan (despite the Pakistani army's repression of al-Qaeda), and others on the Afghan–Pakistani border. The latter are in tribal-controlled areas where the writ of neither government runs. There are also links with Iranian Baluchistan, where Sunni people speaking dialects closely related to Pashtu and Urdu have great sympathy for al-Qaeda-type ideology, not because it is anti-Western but because it is anti-Shi'ite. Being subjected to repression by the Shi'ite Iranian central government, they secretly cherish the dream of a Sunni power that finds symbolic solace in bin Laden-style activism. As the Sunnis in Iranian Baluchistan have a much higher rate of demographic growth than the Shi'ites in the same region, their numbers will increase. Tribes in Baluchistan, Warziristan (Pakistan) and the Afghan Pashtu-speakers on the borders with Pakistan and Iran are providing a new training ground for the coming generations of discontented Sunnis. Most tribes speaking Pashtu or related languages have every reason to hate the central governments that rule and repress them. Camps also exist in Chechnya, and in Muslim countries where the central government is in crisis or has lost control of its territory.

Until now, there has been no close cooperation between terrorist networks associated with al-Qaeda and other, non-Muslim groups such as ETA, dissident Irish groups, Latin American groups such as Sendero Luminoso or Shi'ite activists. Anyone wishing to work with al-Qaeda must be a Muslim, and a Sunni Muslim at that. There are no known examples of Shi'ite groups being involved with al-Qaeda.

The transformations that might affect the structure of terrorist groups close to al-Qaeda and its affiliate groups can be summarised as follows.

First, it can be assumed that the ethnic basis on which these groups have operated until now will – to some extent – be called into question. The 2004 attack in Madrid was carried out mainly by Moroccan groups, with some foreign involvement. This may not be the case in future, particularly as the absence of Afghan-trained veterans (or simply the fact that there are now fewer of them) allows the intervention of new groups that are not bound together by a common past in a specific territory or by a rigid understanding of Sunni Islam. A new ethnicity may emerge as various activists begin to cooperate more closely, and they too will become more modern as the European and American intelligence services begin to work more closely together. New forms of collaboration between Moroccans, Algerians, Pakistanis and group from the Middle East may emerge, and the groups themselves may become more ethnically mixed.

Training on the ground in Afghanistan and learning from concrete experience within integrated groups will give way to new forms of training, often involving wider use of the internet. More use will be made of modern communications networks, and that will to some extent compensate for the absence of a territorial base where members can meet and undergo intensive training. This is already the case to a certain extent.

European Islam and Europe's recognition that Islam is a domestic religion (at the moment it is usually regarded by public opinion as a foreign religion, even though many Muslim citizens have a European nationality) will in one sense marginalise activist or terrorist groups. But the fact that they are tiny minority groups will make them more cohesive and will strengthen their conviction that they must fight a Christian or godless secular order that is at war with Islam. In generations to come, there will be a 'European' Islam, but there will also be tiny minority groups that can exploit an Islam in which the old ethnic and linguistic divisions are no longer insurmountable obstacles that prevent *jihadists* from different backgrounds from communicating with one another.

The feeling of *jihad* and martyrdom feeds on the spectacle of a society that has been globalised at the level of information and communications, and in which the repression exercised by those in a hegemonic position is all the more painful for those who identify with the dominated and the repressed. Muslims in both Europe and the United States watch televised images of the despair of Palestinians facing the crushing hegemony of the Israeli army, and of Iraqis faced with the overbearing attitude of American and British soldiers and more rarely, of Russian repression of downtrodden Chechens. So long as no solution is found to these problems, one of the major symbolic causes of the alienation and frustration of Western Muslims (who may or may not be Arabs) will always be there. The Palestinian problem is no longer a territorially restricted problem concerning one particular population. It has been taken up by the Muslim minority in the West and will always be capable of mobilising the tiny minority that prefers direct actions to the legal procedures that have so far proved to have their limitations. For similar reasons, Russia and the West will draw closer, as a *jihad* in support of the Chechen cause could find positive echoes amongst a minority of Muslims in Europe.

In future, the Arab and Muslim policies of Western countries such as the United States, Britain, France and Germany, and many other countries like Italy and Spain (to cite only the most obvious examples) will no longer be a purely diplomatic problem. The Muslim minority and its views will have more significant weight and should be taken into account.

Islam is the last monotheist religion to believe in a social utopia and an eschatology that can, in the eyes of some believers, be realised here on earth. Christianity has, at least in Europe and most of the United States, given up the idea of realising its utopia in the name of religion. It is now based on male and female suffrage within democratic systems in which there is no room for faith. Judaism gave up proselytising long ago. In most Muslim countries the secular political systems bequeathed them by independence have, to a greater or lesser extent, also failed to make room for Islam. In many parts of the world, Islam has become the religion of the oppressed and the dominated. This represents a major change: Muslims were once the dominant political and military elites in the countries they ruled (India or Eastern Europe). There is every indication that the vast majority of the new citizens of Europe and the United States will accept the democratic rules by which those countries live, but a small minority – which is statistically insignificant – may go so far as to advocate *jihad* and *martyrdom*. It will have the support of outside networks, but the social and economic situation in which it finds itself will give it another reason to rise up against a society and an order that it regards as godless. In America, it is the fate of the Palestinians that is most likely to alienate part of the Muslim population; in Europe, it is the fate meted out to the excluded and practising Muslims in the name of *laïcité* (in France), racist contempt for Muslims (Islamophobia in Britain and France), or the hostility towards Muslim societies implicit in the unshakeable alliance with America (in the case of Britain) that are likely to generate new forms of alienation.

Even within Europe, alliances may be formed by extreme groups on the radicalised fringes of the Muslim population. Such groups represent only a tiny minority, but they may be able to exploit the freedom of movement and action available to them inside Europe.

Islamic extremist groups may be able to form an alliance with other radical groups (on either the far right or the far left) in Europe, should they become active and succeed in resolving their present crisis.

In the United States, new economic groupings modelled on the European common market are emerging with Canada (where there are Maghrebin networks made up essentially of Moroccans and Algerians) and Mexico. They may facilitate contacts between radicalised groups. The question is whether or not extremist groups like al-Qaeda will be able to get beyond the 'all Muslim' or 'all Sunni' phase. Whilst they are still episodic, intercontinental links between extremist Islamic groups in Europe, Asia (and especially the Middle East), Africa and America will be facilitated by new technologies. If these radical groups succeed in overcoming their ideological and religious differences, there is a strong possibility that we will find ourselves living in a more dangerous world. Self-transcendance through death may well be a way of issuing a challenge to the mighty (in, for instance, clashes between Palestinian kamikazes and the Israelis, or between Chechens and the Russian army), but it is also a way of overcoming the taboos on life and death and it may open up a new sphere of action that will prove attractive to some young men who are disoriented by their own anomie.

Women have yet to play a major role in groups like al-Qaeda. A few women activists have begun to play a role in the Palestinian and Chechen nationalist causes, but that is still a marginal phenomenon. Women are still excluded from groups like al-Qaeda. If these groups can transcend their patriarchal vision, they may be able to recruit women who will be even more devoted to the cause because they will have access to the enviable fate of the martyrs on the same basis as men. It is probable that, as the new populations adapt to life in the West, small groups of extremists will exploit this violence by involving women or even adolescent girls who would find an ideal way of asserting their newly won equality by taking the same deadly risks as men.

The case of converts merits our attention. They choose Islam because of its many attractions. It is easy to adopt the religion of Allah. The fact that there is no clergy means that everyone can interpret the law for himself. Having a 'warm' community as a point of reference gives a meaning to a collective life spent in the 'cold' and individualistic societies of the West. Islam is a very simple religion that makes a clear and decisive distinction between the Creator and his creatures, unlike the Christian trinity in which Christ is by turn the Son of God and the Son of Man. In the religion of Allah, men and women have distinct roles. This is attractive to men who feel that they have been dispossessed of their privileges in societies where men and women are, in theory, equal and in which the mental topographies of both men and women are full of grey areas. Because of all the advantages it offers, Islam finds many 'normal' recruits in the West. Many appreciate its mystical and peaceful aspects, but for a tiny minority, it is its warrior side that is attractive. Because public opinion sees it as something 'dangerous', the religion of Allah attracts groups that have rebelled against the social order. The more it is feared or despised, the more it arouses the interest of such groups.

It is, finally, possible that the increasingly lax and anomic forms of socialisation that operate in the West might encourage more families to become *jihadist*. Many of their male (and perhaps female) members may find a vocation for martyrdom because it allows them to recreate the coherence of their families and their imaginary world in the name of Islam and to fight the perverse West together.

Martyrdom and *jihad* are not just aspects of an Islamic tradition that has become mythologised and radicalised; they are also a way of appropriating and using Western modernity, and of exploiting the technological resources of a society that relies heavily upon communications. The magic of all-powerful computers and the virtual reality generated by software can bring a globalised Islam into existence,[6] and it can be an expression of the frustrations and misunderstandings that arise in increasingly complex and non-egalitarian societies in which individuals feel that they have been left at the mercy of impersonal mechanisms. Martyrdom takes on a new form, combines Islamic notions and a modern content of self-expression. It gambles with life and death because its deadly sense of the sacred has been concocted inside a purely imaginary but warlike neo-*umma*. Killing oneself and one's enemy in a generalised

Apocalypse is a way of fighting the injustice of the Crusaders from a Judaeo-Christian West who are supposedly oppressing Muslims. But the death that is inflicted in the name of a *jihadist* concept of Islam is also a way of avoiding the implications of a modernity that distributes economic opportunities and political relations on an unequal basis. *Jihadism* is a typically incoherent product of the globalisation of the last world-religion to have a social and cultural utopia that still has credibility in the eyes of some believers. It is one of the avatars of the globalisation of the world. It can be extended to other new religions or sects founded in the West.

# Notes

## INTRODUCTION

1. Nine out of ten Muslims in the world are Sunnis and belong to one of Sunnism's four official schools. Only one in ten Muslims is a Shi'ite. The Shi'ites are divided into several groups, the main ones being 'Twelvers' (who believe in the twelve imams) and the Ismailites. See Moojan Momen, *An Introduction to Shi'i Islam*, New Haven: Yale University Press, 1985; Mohammad-Ali Amir-Moezzi and Christian Jambet, *Qu'est-ce que le chiisme?* Paris: Fayard, 2004.
2. See Pierre Centlivres (ed.), *Saints, sainteté et martyre*, Neuchâtel and Paris : Editions de l'Institut d'Éthnologie and Editions de la Maison des Sciences de l'Homme, 2001.
3. See Galia Valtchinova, 'Postcommuniste et prémoderne: actualité du culte de sainte Petka dans les Balkans, une étude de cas en Bulgarie occidentale' in Centlivres, *Saints, sainteté et martyre*.
4. G. W. Bowerstock, *Martyrdom and Rome*, Cambridge: Cambridge University Press, 1995.
5. I am grateful to Marcel Swyngedauw for his bibliographical help on the topic of Christian martyrdom.
6. See Bowerstock, *Martyrdom and Rome*.
7. See Eusebius of Caesarea, *The Ecclesiastical History* (Book III), trans. Kirsopp Lake, Cambridge, MA and London: Harvard University Press and William Heinemann.
8. Eusebius, *Ecclesiastical History*.
9. Eusebius, *Ecclesiastical History*.
10. Saint Augustine, *Concerning the City of God Against the Pagans*, trans. Henry Bettenson, Harmondsworth: Penguin, 2003, p. 32.
11. See Louis E. Fennec, *Martyrdom in the Sikh Tradition*, Oxford: Oxford University Press, 2001.

## CHAPTER I

1. The Koran is cited in N.J. Daward's translation, Harmondsworth: Penguin, 2003.
2. See, *Le Saint Coran et la traduction en français de ses versets*, 1421 HA.
3. See Mark Huband, *Warriors of the Prophet: The Struggle for Islam*, Boulder, CO: Westview Press, 1999.
4. See Reuben Fierske, *Jihad: The Origins of Holy War in Islam*, Oxford: Oxford University Press, 1999.
5. The Shaafi make up one of the four Sunni schools, the others being the Hanbali, the Maliki and the Hanafi.
6. See Rudolph Peters, *Islam and Colonialism: The Doctrine of Jihad in Modern History*, The Hague: Mouton, 1979.

7. The case of the mystic Hallaj has become the paradigm in the West because of the masterly work devoted to him by Louis Massignon.

8. See Mortezâ Motahhari, achénai bâ qo'ran, djahad akhlâq e djensi ('Understanding the Koran, *jihad*, sexual morality'), Teheran: Sadrâ, nd.

9. For France, see Farhad Khosrokhavar, *L'Islam des jeunes*, Paris: Flammarion, 1997; Nancy Venel, *Musulmans et citoyens, appropriations, usages et agencements des appartenances chez de jeunes Français d'origine maghrébine*, Thesis, Université de Lille-III, 2002. Venel rightly stresses that national allegiances are no longer central to the identity of these new citizens, though this does not give rise to an antagonistic relationship with society as a whole.

10. See Yann Richard Yann, *L'Islam chiite*, Paris: Fayard, 1991.

11. For a systematic account of this modernising version, see Ali Shariati, *Entézâ, mazhabé, 'e'térâz* (lattente, a religion of protest) in Hoseyn v^ares é Adam ('Adam's heir Hosain'), Teheran: Qalam, aban 1361 (1982–83), second edition.

12. For an account of many of these interpretations, see Bakhsh Ali Qanbari, *Falsafé yé achoura az didgâh e andichmandânemosalman* (Ashura Philosophy seen by Muslim Thinkers), Teheran: Daftar barrési hâyé elsâmi, 1379 (1991–92).

13. Since the 1990s, martyrdom has become increasingly marginal in Iran and its marginalisation takes the form of a rejection of the 'kill-joy' and repressive ideology of Iranian conservatives by a new generation who, unlike their parents' generation two decades earlier, are no longer drawn to martyrdom.

14. See Bernard Lewis, *The Assassins: A Radical Sect in Islam*, London: Weidenfeld and Nicolson, 1967.

15. On schismatic and sectarian forms of Islam in the premodern age, see Henri Laoust, *Les Schismes dans l'islam*, Paris: Payot, 1965.

16. See Alexandre Popovic and Gilles Veinstein (eds), *Les Voies d'Allah*, Paris: Fayard, 1996.

17. On the other hand, we do find the 'new world' ideal in modern non-Islamic cults such as the millenarian Solar Temple or Aum.

18. See Laoust, *Les Schismes*.

19. See Patrick Michel, *Politique et religion, la grande mutation*, Paris: XXX, 1994; Olivier Roy, *L'Echec de l'islam politique*, Paris : Seuil, 1992.

20. See S.V.R. Nasr, *Mawdudi and the Making of Islamic Revivalism*, Oxford: Oxford University Press, 1996.

21. See Kepel, *The Prophet and the Pharaoh*.

22. See Olivier Carré, *l'Utopie islamique dans l'Orient arabe*, Paris: Presse de la FNSP, 1991.

23. See Olivier Carré, *l'islam laique on le retour de la grande tradition* Paris: Armand Colin, 1993.

24. See Mawdudi, *Ma'alim fil tariq*m, 1964. English translation: *Milestones*, Delhi: Markhazi Maktada Islami, 1981.

25. See Mawdudi, 'Revolutions are Never Brought About by Cowards or the Imbecilic', in Adam Parfrey (ed.), *Extreme Islam*, Los Angeles: Feral House, 2001.

26. See Saïd Amir Arjomand, *The Shadow of God and the Hidden Imam: Religion, Political Order and Social Change in Shiite Iran from the Beginning to 1890*, Chicago: Chicago University Press, 1984.

27. See Abdulazziz Abdulhussein Sachedina, *The Just Ruler in Shi'ite Islam: the Comprehensive Authority of the Jurist in Imamite Jurisprudence*, New York: Oxford University Press, 1988.

28. See Khomeini's speech on 'The Nest of Spies' (Teheran, 17 November 1979).

29. Khomeini, *Kayhan*, 7 November 1979.

30. See Roy, *L'Echec de l'islam politique*.

31. For a representative example of this tendency, see Gilles Kepel and Yann Richard, *Intellectuels et militants de l'islam contemporain*, Paris: Seuil, 1990.

32. See Malika Zeghal, *Gardiens de l'islam: Les Oulémas d'al Azhar dans l'Egypte contemporaine*, Paris: Presses de Sciences-Po, 1996.

33. Zeghad, *Gardiens de l'islam*, p. 337 and passim.

34. See Sâléhi Nadjaf Abâdi's article in *Tchechme ye nour* ('Source of Light'), Teheran: Daftar Nashr Asâr Emam, 1374 (1982–83), p. 187 and passim.

35. See Ali Shariati, 'Shahâdat' ('Martyrdom') in *Hossein, Vâres e âdam* (Husain, Adam's Heir), *Collected Works*, vol XIX, Teheran: Qalam, 1361 (1982–83), p. 187 and passim.

36. See Sheikh Abbas Qomi, *Montahi ol âmal*, vol. 1, Qom: Hadjrat, 1365 (1986–87).

37. See Eric Butel, *Le Martyre dans les mémoires de guerre iraniens, guerre Iran–Iraq, 1980–1988*, Paris: INALCO, 2000 (thesis), and Farhad Khosrokhavar, *L'Islamisme et la mort, le martyr révolutionnaire en Iran*, Paris: L'Harmattan, 1995.

38. See Shariati, *Hossein vâres e âdam* (Husain, Adam's Heir).

39. See Shariati, 'Shahâdat'.

40. Shariati, 'Shahâdat', p. 217.

41. Shariati, 'Shahâdat'.

42. Shariati, 'Shahâdat', p. 189.

43. Shariati, 'Shahâdat', p. 195.

44. Shariati, 'Shahâdat', p. 155.

45. Shariati, 'Shahâdat'.

46. Other categories of the population involved in the revolutionary movement had other demands and other aspirations, including exiled peasants, traditional categories with ties to the bazaar and the clergy, radicalised factions of the clergy, and far-left groups whose aspirations were in some ways similar to those of the modernised and destructured youth of the urban zones. See Farhad Khosrokhavar, *L'Utopie sacrifiée, sociologie de la révolution iranienne*, Paris: Presses de FNSP, 1993.

47. See Khosrokhavar, *L'Islamisme et la mort*, Paris, L'Harmalton, 1995.

48. Anderson describes nations as 'imagined communities'. Mythologised supranational communites can also exist, as in al-Qaeda. See Benedict Anderson, *Imagined Communities*, London and New York: Verso, 1991.

49. See Qutb, *Fi Zilal al-Qurán*, Cairo, 1952–56 and the summary on Ma'alam fil Tariq, 1964. See in Particular Charles Tripp, 'Sayyid Qutb: the Political

Vision', in Ali Rahnema (ed.), *Pioneers of Islamic Revivalism*, London: Zed Books, 1994.

50. See Louis Dumont, *Essai sur l'individualisme*, Paris: Seuil, 1983.

51. See Olivier Carré, *Mytique et politique: Lecture révolutionnaire du Coran par Sayyid Qutb, frèrs musulman radical*, Paris: PNSP and Cerf, 1984; S. Kotb (sic), *Social Justice in Islam*, American Council of Learned Societies, New York: Octagon Books, 1970; Charles Tripp, 'Sayyid Qutb'.

52. See Claude Lefort, *L'Invention démocratique*, Paris: Seuil 1981, *Democracy and Political Theory*, trans. David Macey, Cambridge: Polity, 1986.

53. See Amir Nipkey, *Politique et Religion en Iran contemporain*, Paris: L'Harmattan, 2001.

54. See Ali Rabnema, *An Islamic Utopia: a Political Biography of Ali Shariati*, London and New York: I.B. Tauris, 1998.

55. See Friedrich Nietzsche, *On The Genealogy of Morals*, trans. Douglas Smith, Oxford: Oxford World's Classics, 1998, Third Essay # 14; Max Scheler, *Ressentiment*, trans. William W. Holdein, New York: Free Press of Glencoe, 1961.

56. Kant demonstrates that the moral law must not make the other a means to an end. That is why, when we speak of spontaneity in Nietzschean terms, as revised and updated by Max Scheler, we are dealing with the ways affects come into being, and with the relationship with the self, others and the world rather than a rejection of reflexivity.

57. This theme is dealt with at greater length in Farhad Khosrokhavar, *L'Instance du sacré*, Paris: Cerf, 2001.

58. See Samuel Huntington, 'The Clash of Civilizations?', *Foreign Affairs*, 72, no. 3, 1993; Francis Fukuyama, *The End of History and the Last Man*, New York: Free Press, 1992.

59. The martyr Anouar Sukar from Gaza wrote to his father: 'Please forget all the mistakes I have made and our arguments. You are an educated man, and you know that martyrs act for the good of their families, in order to ensure that they will go to Paradise.' He wrote to his wife: 'Forgive the wrongs I have done you. I hope that God will give you children.' See Agnès Pavlowsky, *Hamas ou miroir des frustrations palestiniennes*, Paris: l'Harmattan, 2000.

60. See Kepel, *The Prophet and the Pharaoh*; Khosrokhavar, *l'Islamisme et la mort*.

61. '"Le Dernier soir" avant le 11 septembre', *Le Monde*, 2 octobre 2001.

## CHAPTER 2

1. The statistics are to be treated with caution. Iran's losses are estimated to have been some 500,000 dead (125,000 soldiers; the rest of the dead were Pasdaran and Basidj volunteers) and over one hundred thousand wounded. See Mehdi Amani, *Les Effets démographiques de la guerre Iran–Irak sur la population iranienne*, Paris: Institut National d'Études Démographiques, August 1992. The figures were subsequently revised downwards. Nowadays, there are estimated to have been around 300,000 casualties on the Iranian side.

2. For a detailed description see Farhad Khosrokhavar, *L'Anthropologie de la révolution iranienne*; *L'Islamisme et la mort* Paris: L'Harmatan, 1995; *l'Utopie sacrifiée*, Paris: Presses de la FNSP, See also Jean-Pierre Digard, Bernard Hourcade and Yann Richard , *L'Iran au Xxe siècle*, Paris: Fayard, 1996.

3. Other figures like Tâléghâni, Khomeini, Banisdar and Mottahari played an important role for other strata of the population, but Shariati had much greater influence over the urban youth. For a selction of text by these authors, see Mahmud Taleqani, Mortéza Mutahhari and Ali Shariati, *Jihad and Shahâdat: Struggle and Martrydom in Islam*, University of Texas, Institute for Research and Islamic Studies, 1986.

4. See Mary Hegland, 'Two images of Husain: accommodation and revolution in an Iranian village', in N.R. Keddie (ed.), *Religion and Politics in Iran*, London: Yale University Press, 1983; Paul Vieille and Farhad Khosrokhavar, *Le Discourse populaire de la révolution iranienne*, Paris: Contemporainété, 1990 (two vols).

5. Seee Ali Shariati, *Histoire et destinée: textes choisis*, Paris: Sindbad, 1982.

6. This is particularly true of the writings of Hamid Algar. See his *Religion and state in Iran, 1785–1906*, Berkeley: University of California Press, 1966; *The Islamic Revolution in Iran*, London: Open Press, Muslim Institute, 1980.

7. This did not prevent the emergence of protest movements. They were, however, usually expressions of local issues and few of them succeeded in challenging the regime. The crises occurred during interregnums or during struggles between various pretenders when the king died.

8. Except during the interregnum of Nader Shah in the eighteenth century. He was prepared to decree Shi'ism to be the fifth Sunni school. As a result, the Shi'ite Ulema left Iran for Iraq.

9. On relations between the Shi'ite 'hierocracy' and political power to the end of the nineteenth century, see Saïd Amir Arjomand, *The Shadow of God and the Hidden Imam: Religion, Political Order and Societal Change in Shi'ite Iran from the Beginning to 1890*, Chicago: The University of Chicago Press, 1984. On the Pahlavi period, see Chakroukh Akhavi, *Religion and Politics in Contemporary Iran*, Albany: SUNY Press, 1980.

10. Many middle-class groups made up of intellectuals (the Association of Iranian Writers, *kânoun'e névisandégan'e irân*), lawyers (Association of Lawyers, *kânouné vocalâ*) and autonomous associations such as the League of Human Rights (*jamiýaté hoghoughé bachar*) or the National Asociation of University Teachers (*s^azémâné mellié d^aneshgâiâne irân*) did of course play a major role in mobilising against imperial despotism. The high point of their action came in October 1977 with the Ten Nights of Poetry at the Goethe Institute in Teheran, when intellectuals and poets denounced the repression and the imperial regime. But these groups were at best a minority within the revolutionary process they had helped to launch. Their fragility and lack of support in society as a whole was revealed during the first street demonstrations against the Shah's regime. For the role of intellectuals in the early stages of the Revolution, see Nasser Pakdama, *Dah shb'e she'r, ba rési va arzyâbié yék tadjrobéh* (Ten Nights of Poetry: Analysis and Evaluation of an Experiment) Paris, 26 February 1988.

11. See Homa Katouzian, *Political Economy of Modern Iran, 1926–1979*, New York: New York University Press, 1980; Robert E. Looney, *Economic Origins of the Iranian Revolution*, New York: Pergamon Press, 1982; Mahommad H. Malek, *The Political Economy of Iran under the Shah*, London: Croom Helm, 1986; Eric Hoogland, *Land and Revolution in Iran*, Austin: University of Texas Press, 1982.

12. On this dimension of the alliance between more or less traditional strata of Iranian society, see Ahmad Ashraf, 'Bazaar-Mosque Alliance: the Social Basis of Revolts and Revolutions', *International Journal of Politics, Culture and Society* I (4), 1988.

13. On this dimension of the revolutionary movement, see Vieille and Khosrokhavar, *Le Discours populaire de la revolution iranienne*.

14. See Mehdi Bazargan, *Enghélâbé irân da do harékat* (The Iranian Revolution in Two Movements) for his analysis of how the situation was reversed shortly after the Revolution, especially when Hezbollah and Khomeini took control of the revolutionary state. See also Abolhassan Banisadr, *L'Espérance trahie*, Paris: Papyrus, 1982.

15. For all these problems see Shaul Bakhash, *The Reign of the Ayatollahs: Iran and the Islamic Revolution*, London: I.B. Tauris, 1985; Ali Rahnema and Farhad Nomani, *The Secular Miracle*, London: Zed Books, 1990; Khosrokhavar, *L'Utopie sacrifiée*; Keddie, *Religion and Politics in Iran*.

16. The full expression was *Bassidjé ârtéché bist meliouni*, meaning 'mobilisation of an army of twenty million', or in other words of almost all young men liable to be called up to defend the revolutionary government.

17. During the war with Iraq, there were two army corps: the army of the Islamic Republic of Iran and the Pasdaran army; the Bassidj was an autonomous part of the Pasdaran.

18. See Khosrokhavar, *L'Islamisme et la mort*; Vieille, 'L'Institution chiite, la religiosité populaire, le martyre et la révolution,' *Peuples méditerranéens* 16, 1981; H.G. Kipperberg, 'Jeder Tag Ashura, jeds Grab Kerbala: Zur ritualisierung des Strassenkämpf im Iran' in Kurt Greussig (ed.), *Religion und Politik im Iran*, Frankfurt am Main, 1981.

19. Far left organisations (the Moudjahdeen Khale and, to a lesser extent, the far left secular and Marxist left) were marginalised after their open break with the regime in June 1981. As for the royalists, their fate was sealed in the first months of the Revolution, when the army was purged. Their leaders had fled abroad even before the Revolution. Middle-class political organisations (Bazargan's *Nehzaté âzâdi*, *Djebhé yé melli*, the National Mossadeghst Front) were weakened, as the Shah's repression had forced them into a marginal position from which they were unable to emerge during the Revolution.

20. The Bassidj had some four hundred thousand members, as did the Pasdaran. The traditional army had almost the same number. Together, they made up the Islamic Republic's army corps in the war against Iraq.

21. See Khosrokhavar, 'Le Pur et l'impur', *Peuples méditerranéens*, 50, 1990; 'Chiisme mortifière: les nouveaux combattants de la foi', *L'Homme et la société*, 107–8, 1993; 'Le Martyre révolutionnaire en Iran,' *Social Compass* vol. 43, no. 1, March 1996.

22. They were paid between five and eight thousand toumans. In an economy with several different exchange rates, it is impossible to calculate a precise equivalent in euros. As an approximation, we can say that this corresponded to the monthly salary of the average civil servant during the war.

23. The Martyrs' Foundation was one of the financial pillars of the Bassidj and of all the organisations that financed the war. The financial resources at its disposal made it an economic colossus. It had at its disposal 50 firms, 5 in industry, 11 in stock-raising and agriculture, 14 companies constructing buildings and roads and 26 finance companies. The economic branch made 12 billion rials (just over one billion francs at the official rate of exchange) available to the Foundation. The financial branch distributed twelve billion rials' worth of medical products, dental surgery, laboratories, heating equipment, and spare parts for Mack trucks and Japanese cars. See *Ettélâât*, 20 December 1365 (1987).

24. See Bernard Hourcade, '*Vaqf* et modernité en Iran: les agro-business de l'Astân-e quods de Mashad', in Yann Richard (ed.), *Entre l'Iran et l'Occident*, Paris: Editions de la Maison des Sciences de l'Homme, 1989.

25. In one working class family, the son joined the Committee whilst the daughter, who was two or three years older, joined the Moudjahideen. Many similar examples could be observed during the Revolution.

26. See Vieille, *Féodalité et Etat en Iran*, Paris: Anthropos, 1975.

27. This calls into question the thesis that, for the young people who took part in it, the revolutionary movement was traditionalist or neo-traditionalist. See in particular Saïd Amir Arjomand, *The Turban for the Crown, the Islamic Revolution in Iran*, New York: PBUN, 1988. According to Arjomand, the Islamic Revolution was a neo-traditionalist movement: it was led by radicalised traditional actors (the clergy and groups associated with it, the bazaar and other traditional urban couches) who were reacting against the Pahlavis' modernization because it was a threat to their way of life.

28. See Farhad Khosrokhavar, 'Le Quasi-individu: de la néo-communauté à la nécro-communauté', in François Dubet and Michel Wieviorka (eds.), *Penser le sujet: autour d'Alain Touraine*, Paris: Fayard, 1995 (Colloque de Cérisy).

29. For a case-study of a small town and of the transformation of its Committee into a state repressive apparatus, see Farhad Khosrokhavar, 'Le Comité dans la révolution iranienne: le cas d'une ville moyenne, Hamadan,' *Peuples méditerranéens* 9, 1979.

30. See Ian Brown, *Khomeini's Forgotten Sons: the Story of Iran's Boy Soldiers*, London: Grey Seal Books, 1990; Werner Schmucher, 'Iranische Märtyrtestamente', *Die Welt des Islams* 27, no. 4, 1987; Farhad Khosrokhavar, 'Bassidhe, auxiliaries juveniles de la révolution iranienne', *Culture & Conflicts*, 18, 1995.

31. These included cheap apartments, and trips to Syria and Libya where they were paid in dollars that were worth several times more than on the market. It should be noted that the price of dollars was kept artificially high during the war, but only carefully selected officials had access to them. As a result they quickly became rich. Others had to buy dollars on

the open market. At the end of the war, the dollar was worth 20 times more than it had been before the Revolution.

32. See Hourcade, '*Vacf* et modernité en Iran'.

33. See the section on morbid neo-mysticism below.

34. Bassidji testaments are full of these considerations. They were published throughout the war, with the active support of the press and the many publications of the Bassidj and its affiliated associations, but the depths of despair they express are real and could be observed in the field. See Khosrokhavar, *L'Islamisme et la mort*, Eric Butel, *Le Martyre révolutionnaire: strategies et discours néo-communitaires de la jeunesse populaire iranienned*, DEA INACLO-EHESS, 1995; Alain Chaouli, *Un Groupe minoritaire d'adolescents révolutionnaries iraniens*, memoire, EHESS, 1996.

35. Hence the many tales of martyrs' lives and the many stories written by them in which a visionary old man appears to them at the front. He could be either the Imam of Time or his representative Khomeini. For examples, see Khosrokhavar, *L'Islamisme et la mort* and Butel, *Le Martyre révolutionnaire*.

36. Imam Husain, the third Shi'ite Imam, is the Paragon or Prince of Martyrs. See Mahmoud Ayoub, *Redemptive Suffering in Islam*, The Hague: Mouton, 1978; Jean Calmard, 'Le Patronage des ta'ziéh: Eléments pour une étude globale', in Peter J. Chelkowski (ed.), *Ta'zieh, Ritual and Drama in Iran*, New York: New York University Press, 1979; George Thaiss, 'Religious symbolism and social change: the drama of Husain', in Nikki R. Keddie (ed.), *Scholars, Saints and Sufis*, Los Angeles: University of California Press, 1972.

37. For a comparative analysis of the failure of Islamic movements, see Olivier Roy, *L'Echec de l'islam politique*, Paris: Seuil, 1992.

38. See Fatima Mernissi, *Le Harem politique: Le Prophète et les femmes*, Paris: XXX, 1987.

39. The many cases reported in the media include that of a family that originally came from Arâk, but which had been living in the suburbs of Teheran for a generation. Of its five sons, two died martyrs' deaths and three were seriously wounded at the front. One broke his shoulder and the other broke his spinal chord, which left him paralysed for the rest of his life. The third had both legs amputated. The father volunteered for the front in 1987. The newspapers are full of similar stories. See, for example, *Résalat*, 28 January 1987, pp. 1, 2 for an account of how four sons from the same family died as martyrs (one was reported missing).

40. Martyropathic families can be compared with cults which, like the group at Waco (1992) or the Solar Temple in Switzerland (1994), attempt to commit collective suicide. Such cults are likely to become more common as modernity's destructuring effects increase.

41. There are no reliable statistics on the number of martyrs from different regions, provinces and cities. Any analysis therefore has to be based upon individual observations and qualitative data.

42. See the section on Khomeini in Khosrokhavar, *l'Utopie sacrifiée*.

43. See Ali Farâtsi, 'Kizéche hâyé sé sale gozachté irân, marhaléy'e boloughé mobârézâté mardomin' ('Movements in Iran over the last three years:

popular struggles reach the stage of maturity'), *Navidé Moghâvémat* (Paris) 7, Spring 1996.

44. See Mohsen Mottaghi, 'Rowshanfekrane eslâh talab e didni bologhe mob^arzâtê mardomi' ('Reformist religious intellectuals and civil society') *Iran Naméh*, vol. XIX, no. 4, Autumn 1380 (Autumn 2001), Bethesda, and the rest of this special issue on reforms in Iran, edited by Farhad Khosrokhavar.

45. See Farhad Khosrokhavar and Olivier Roy, *L'Iran: comment sortir d'une révolution religieuse?*, Paris: Seuil, 1999.

46. See Pénélope Larzillière, 'Construction national et construction de soi: l'évolution de la contestation politique des jeunes Palestiniens de la première à la deuxième Intifada', *Egypte-Monde Arabe*, Cairo: CEDEJ, Autumn 2002.

47. See Agnès Pavlowsky, *Les Femmes palestiniennes entre soumission et emancipation* (ongoing thesis, EHESS, Paris).

48. See Läetitia Bucaille, *Gaza: la violence de la paix*, Paris: Presses des Sciences-Po, 1998.

49. For a theoretical justification of these fourfold dimensions see Farhad Khosrokhavar, *L'Instance du sacré*, Paris: Presses des Science-Po, 1998.

50. See Zéev Schiff and Ehud Ya'ari, *Intifada*, Paris: Stock, 1991.

51. See Läetitia Bucaille, *Générations Intifada*, Paris: Hachette, 2002.

52. Examples include a 46 year old kamikaze called Daoud Ali, who owned land near one of the settlements but was unable to work it. See 'Un Kamikaze très ordinaire', *Le Monde*, 18 Janary 2002.

53. This section draws on discussions with Agnès Pavlowsky and Pénélope Larzillière.

54. Each Palestinian has roughly seven litres per day, whereas even Jewish settlers have the right to 350 litres (they are Jews and not simply Israelis, as Israeli Arabs and Druzes do not have the right to live in the settlements).

55. See Jean-François Legrain, 'Palestine: les Banoustans d'Allah', *Cahiers de Cermoc Palestine* 17, 1997; Alain Dieckhoff, *La Nation dans tous ses états*, Paris: Flammarion, 1996.

56. In martyrs' testaments, these grievances are pathetically expressed in what is supposed to be religious language, but their content is determined by the concrete situation and living conditions of Palestinians. See the testaments at www.palestine-info.org. Edna Yaghi's 'You Have Made Me Your Human Bomb' provides a good summary of these grievances, which are not in themselves religious.

57. The expression 'apartheid' is used by figures like the writer Grossman and Judge Michael Ben Yäir. See the latter's, 'Non à l'apartheid, pour sauver le sionisme', *Le Monde*, 10–11 February 2002. Personalities like the pacifist Yuri Avneri, reserve general Dov Tamari and even Knesset leader Avrham Burg have reached the same conclusion. According to Burg, 'The occupation is a source of corruption; to be more specific, it has corrupted us. Discrimination is becoming our norm, and insensitivity a way of being.' Without a withdrawal from the Occupied Territories, according to Ehud Barak, 'It will be Bosnia or South Africa here.' See 'La montée d'un camp moral humaniste (en Israël)', *Le Monde*, 10–11 February 2002.

58. See Lambert Dolphin, 'There's a War on, Folks – the Coming Tribulation', in Adam Parfrey (ed.), *Extreme Islam*, Los Angeles: Feral House, 2001; 'Holy War Zero' in the same volume for the output of a website run by apocalyptic Christian supporters of Zionism.

59. The supporters of Greater Israel, who include the members of the National Unity Party and even some members of Likud want a massive transfer of the Palestinian population away from the Occupied Territories. For the comments of Benyamin Elon, who speaks of 'transferring the Palestinians', see *Le Monde*, 10–11 February 2002. The Gush Emunim group has tried to blow up the Al Aqsa mosque. It plans to bring Greater Israel into existence by physically eliminating Palestinians. See Yosef Hermoni, 'Gush Emunim's View of Zionism' in *Parfrey, Extreme Islam*.

60. See René Girard, *La Violence et le Sacré*, Paris: Grasset, 1972.

61. According to Israeli security sources, there were 13 'living bombs' in 1993, seven in 1994, 8 in 1996, four in 1997, and then two in 1998, none in 1999, four in 2000, 36 in 2001 and 28 in 2002. The moment of respite in the cycle of violence came in 1999, when no suicide bombings were reported. See *Time*, 15 April 2002.

62. See Agnès Pavlowsky, *Hamas ou le miroir des frustrations palestiniennes*, Paris: L'Harmalton, 2000.

63. In September 1995, there was a clash between a section of Force 17 and the civilian police. See Graham Usher, 'What kind of nation? The rise of Hamas in the Occupied Territories', *Race and Class* 37 (2), October–December 1995. Other clashes occurred in Gaza City in June 1996.

64. See Khaled Hroub, *Hamas: Political Thought and Practice*, Washington, DC: Institute for Palestinian Studies, 2000.

65. See Emile Habibi, *Les Aventures de Saïd le 'peptimist'*, Paris: Gallimard, 1997.

66. This may, however, involve large numbers of people. Some 40,000 young Palestinians are reported to have left the Occupied Territories since the beginning of the second Intifada.

67. See Avishai Margalit, *The Decent Society*, tr. Naomi Goldblum, Cambridge, MA and London: Harvard University Press, 1996. Margalit outlines a decent society in which institutions respect individuals. He uses the example of Palestine to argue that the ideal of decency is more important than that of justice.

68. See *Time*, 15 April 2002.

69. See Bucaille, *Générations Infifada*.

70. See *Council on Foreign Relations, Terrorism: Questions & Answers* http://cfrterrorism.org/home. This report describes 90 per cent of Hamas's activities as cultural and social, according to the Israeli specialist Reuven Paz: www.terrorismansweres.co/groups/hams3.html

71. See Pavlowsky, *Hamas*.

72. See Stéphanie Nolen, 'Portrait of a suicide bomber', *Palestine Report* (Jerusalem, 15 March 1996).

73. See Pavlowsky, *Hamas*.

74. See *Time*, 15 April 2002, citing Israeli security sources.

75. In an opinion poll carried out in the Gaza Strip, 78 per cent of the population supported the suicide bombers, and only 60 per cent were in favour of continued peace negotiations. See *Time*, 15 April 2002.

76. Nasra Hassan, 'An arsenal of believers: talking to the "human bombs"', *The New Yorker*, 19 September 2001.

77. See *Terrorism: Questions 7 Answers*.

78. See Paris, 'Un Kamikaze très ordinaire'.

79. See Pavlowsky, *Hamas* , p. 184.

80. See Bernard Lempert, *Critique de la pensée sacrificielle*, Paris: Seuil, 2000.

81. See Dr Eyad Serraj, 'Understanding Palestinian terror', www.middleeast. org. Dr Serraj is a member of the Human Rights Commission. In 1996, he was jailed three times by the Palestine National Authority.

82. For an account of morbid religiosity in a situation where distress has been internalised, see Khosrokhavar, *L'Utopie sacrifiée*, *L'Islamisme et la mort*, and *L'Anthropologie de la révolution iranienne*.

83. In Iran, the expression 'living martyr' applies to those who aspired to die a holy death in military operations in the war with Iraq but who did not die, despite suffering serious wounds or mutilations.

84. See Hassan, 'An arsenal of believers'.

85. Human bombs always persuade Israeli society to vote for the right, or even the far right, as they did in the latest legislative elections when Sharon was elected in preference to the Labour candidate Ehud Barak. When, on the other hand, Israeli governments wish to postpone peace talks with American emissaries, they liquidate a Hamas or Islamic Jihad leader, knowing full well that the response will not be slow in coming, that there will be a living bomb and deaths, and that the subsequent collective emotions will justify the decision to postpone the talks sine die.

86. Texts by the Christian and Jewish Zionists who want to build the Third Temple of Solomon on the ruins of Jerusalem's Al-Aqsa mosque can be consulted at www.templemountfaithful.org.

87. This is particularly true of Ahmad Thomson, whose *Dajjal the Antichrist* combines neo-Nazi ideas with an apocalyptic vision. See the section on the 'absent community'.

88. His *The Day of Wrath: Is the Intifada of Rfajab only the Beginning?* can be consulted at www.azzam.com

89. See Issa Mahhlouf, *Beyrouth ou la fascination de la mort*, Paris: Editions de la Passion, 1988; Georges Corm, *Le Proche-Orient éclaté*, Paris: La Découverte, 1983.

90. Maklouf, *Begrouth*.

91. See Patrick Meney, *Même les tueurs ont une mère*, Paris: La Table Ronde, 1986.

92. This was an inversion of the master-and-slave dialectic described by Hegel in *The Phenomenology of Mind*. According to Hegel, killing the slave would put an end to the master's hegemony. That is why he must avoid killing him at all costs. The master is a master only because the slave is there, which means that the slave is indispensable to the continued feeling of mastery and slavery. One configuration escapes Hegel's notice: the death of the other gives a feeling of omnipotence that can be heightened

by the very spectacle of the slave's death. It is a manifestation of an omnipotence that makes the master almost God-like, and the repetition of the act becomes an essential ingredient of his very mastership. This means that his mastery can only be perpetuated if there is a supply of slaves that can be renewed at will. The master can then kill the slave in order to experience his own superiority.

93. See Saoudi Fathia, *L'Oubli rebelle*, Beirut, 1982, Paris: L'Harmattan, 1986; Issa Makhlouf, *Begrouth*.

## CHAPTER 3

1. See Moussa Khedimellach, *De l'Obscurité à la lumière. Da'wa, subjectivation et resocialistion: le cas des jeunes hommes engagés dans la Tablighi Jama'a en Lorraine*, Diplôme d'études approfondies, EHESS, Paris, September 1999.

2. See John R. Hall, Philip D. Schuyler and Sylvaine Trinh, *Apocalypse Observed*, London and New York: Routledge, 2000.

3. Some of the prisoners were on remand and had not yet been tried. Others had been jailed for their involvement in terrorist activities relating to Algeria. Their cases were being reinvestigated because of their al-Qaeda involvement. For obvious reasons, they cannot be named.

4. See Zygmunt Bauman, *Life in Fragments*, Oxford: Blackwell, 1995. Alain Ehrenberg, *La Fatique d'être soi*, Paris: Odile Jacob, 1998 also offers a fine account of this. The author rightly stresses the importance of depression, but fails to see the manic dimension that is also characteristic of the modern individual's mood swings.

5. See Alain Touraine and Farhad Khosrokhavar, *La Recherche de soi*, Paris: Fayard, 2000.

6. The allusion is to the al-Alaq ('clots of blood') *surah*, which begins: 'Recite in the name of your Lord who created – created man from clots of blood …' (The French translation cited has 'Lis': 'Read').

7. See Saskia Sassen, 'Whose City Is It? Globalization and the Formation of New Claims,' *Public Culture* 19, 1996; *Cities in a World Economy*, Thousand Oaks: Pine Forge/Sage, 1994.

8. See Dale Eickelman and James Piscatori, *Muslim Travellers*, Berkeley: University of California Press, 1990; Susanne Hoeber, Rudolph and James Piscatori, *Transnational Religion and Fading States*, Boulder: Westview Press, 1997. See also the contributions by Valérie Amiraux, Michel Peraldi and Rémi Leveau, *Cultures & Conflicts* 33–34, Spring–Summer 1999 (special issue on 'Les Anonymes de la mondialisation', ed. Jocelyne Cesari).

9. This is the case with the London-based Hizb ul-Tahrir, which hopes to rebuild the caliphate on a world scale.

10. The Tamils began to use human bomb tactics in 1987, and eventually killed India's Prime Minister Rajiv Ghandi in 1991, and the President of Sri Lanka in 1993. It should be noted that almost one third of the suicide bombers were women, who often passed themselves off as pregnant.

11. The expression 'terrorism' is used in a neutral sense, even though it is impossible to avoid its negative connotations.

12. François Heisbourg, *Hyperterrorisme: la nouvelle guerre*, Paris: Odile Jacob, 2001.

13. See Yossef Bodansky, *Bin Laden: the Man who Declared War on America*, Rocklin: Forum, 2000; Florent Blanc, *Ben Laden et l'Amérique*, Paris: Fayard, 2001.

14. See Brett McCrea, 'US Counter-Terrorist Policy: A Proposed Strategy for a Non-Traditional Threat', *Low Intensity Conflict and Law Enforcement*, Winter 1994.

15. See Michel Wieviorka, *Sociétés et terrorisme*, Paris: Fayard, 1988. Wieviorka rightly stresses that there is a dissociation between terrorist actors and the cause they claim to embody (they claim, for example, to be representatives of the working class, but are nothing of the kind).

16. See Khaled Ahmed, 'Le Harkat, l'islamisme pur et dur', *Courrier international* 604, 3 May – 2 June 2002. This is an abridged version of an article first published in *The Friday Times* (Lahore).

17. See Manuel Castells, *Le Pouvoir de l'identité, l'ère de l'information*, Paris: Fayard, 1997.

18. See Heisbourg, *Hyperterrorism*; Blanc, *Bin Laden*.

19. See Roland Jacquard, *Au Nom d'Oussama bin Laden*, Paris: Editions Jean Picollec, 2000.

20. See Bodansky, *Bin Laden*; Roland Jacquard, *Au Nom*; for an overall account, see Gilles Kepel, *Jihad: The Trail of Political Islam*, trans. Anthony F. Roberts, London: I.B. Tauris, 2003.

21. See Jacquard, *Au Nom*.

22. Gérard Chaliand, 'Ce n'est pas une guerre, c'est le stade ultime du terrorisme classique', *Le Monde*, 18 September 2001.

23. *Islam and the Death of Democracy* is the title of one of Ian Dallas's books. It can be consulted on his website. Extracts can be found in Adam Parfrey (ed.), *Extreme Islam*, Ferad House, 2002.

24. See Ahmad Thomson, *Dajjal the Antichrist*, Novus Ordo Secolorum, 1997.

25. Shi'ites take the view that the institution of the caliphate was illegitimate because it was not Ali, the prophet's son-in-law and cousin, but Abu Bakr who was appointed Caliph when the Prophet died. Ali only became Caliph after Omar and Osman. Later Caliphs and their representatives, such as the Ottoman Sultans, often repressed the Shi'ites, who regarded them as usurpers. Even though radical Shi'ites preach the unity of Islam and call for its long-term political unification, their point of reference is not the Caliphate, but the reign of the Prophet in Medina and the reign of Ali, the fourth Caliph (the other three are not recognised as legitimate).

26. See Suah taji Farouki, *A Fundamentalist Quest: Hizb al Tahrir and the Search for the Islamic Caliphate*, London: Grey Seal, 1996.

27. See Werner Schiffauer, *Die Gottesmänner, Turkische Islamisten in Deutschland*, Frankfurt am Main: Suhrkamp Taschenbuch.

28. On the origins of the Taliban movement in Afghanistan, see Michael Griffin, *Reaping the Whirlwind: The Taliban Movement in Afghanistan*, London: Pluto Press, 2001.

29. See Michael Elliott, 'Al Qaeda Now,' *Time*, 3 June 2002.

30. See Marc Sageman, *Understanding Terror Networks*, Philadelphia: University of Pennsylvania Press, 2004. Sageman divides al-Qaeda's membership into four categories: leaders, those who come from South-East Asia, Arabs from the Middle East, and those from North Africa. For a review of this remarkable book and other new conceptions of terrorism, see Olivier Roy, *Le Terrorisme entre stratégie, métaphysique, psychiatries et mise en scène*, Paris: Revue Critique, 2004.

31. See Peter L. Bergen, *Bin Laden: Running a 'Holy War Inc.'*, London: Weidenfeld & Nicolson, 2001; Kepel, *Jihad*; Jacquard, *Au Nom*.

32. See Blanc, *Bin Laden*.

33. See Kepel, *Jihad*.

34. See Jacquard, *Au Nom*.

35. See Michael Elliott, 'Al-Qaeda now', *Time*, 3 June 2002.

36. The Jewish almoner in one of the prisons I visited told me that some Maghrebin inmates began to call him a 'dirty Jew' in March 2002. That was when television coverage of the behaviour the Israeli army in the Occupied Territories was at its most intense. Television is the inmates' sole source of news.

37. See Anthony Giddens, *Modernity and Self-Identity*, Cambridge: Polity, 1991.

38. See Djalal Al-Ahmad, *L'Occidentalité*, Paris: L'Harmattan, 1988.

39. See Johanes J.-G. Jansen, *The Neglected Duty: the Creed of Sadat's Assassins and Islamic Resurgence in the Middle East*, New York: Macmillan, 1986.

40. Interviews with Islamists in prisons in the Paris region, March–April 2002.

41. See Philippe Bataille, *Le Racisme au travail*, Paris: La Découverte, 1997.

42. See 'Moi, Khaled Kelkal', *Le Monde*, 7 October 1995 (interview with Dietmar Loch, 13 October 1992).

43. Olivier Roy describes this as 'neo-fundamentalism'. See his 'Le Post-islamisme', *Revue des mondes musulmans et de la Méditerranée*, 85–86, Aix-en-Provence: Edisud, 1999.

44. See Denis Duclos, *Société-monde: le temps des ruptures*, Paris: La Découverte and Syros, 2002.

45. The anti-terrorist legislation of 2001 and 2002 has led to a partial change of attitude in this respect.

46. For a comparative account of suburban identities in France and Germany, see Nikola Tieze, *Islamische Identitäten, Frome Muslimischer Religiosität jünger Männer in Deutschland und Frankeich*, Hamburg: Hamburger Edition, 2001.

47. See, for example, Paul Kelso, 'Terror Recruits Warning: Young Muslims "Fall Prey to Extremists"', *Observer*, 27 December 2001.

48. See Steven Morris, 'Volunteers, Shock for Neighbours at Briton's Fate', *Guardian*, 27 October 2001.

49. In prisons close to towns where there are problems in the *banlieues* (Lyon, Marseille, Metz or Lille) up to 72 per cent of inmates are either directly (born in the Maghreb) or indirectly (Maghrebin parents) of North-African origin.

50. For a sometimes idyllic account of American Muslims, see M.A. Muqtedar Khan, *American Muslims: Bridging Faith and Freedom*, Beltsville, MD: Amana Publications, 2002.

51. See Leonard Karen Isaksen, *Muslims in the United States: The State of Research*, New York Russell Sage Foundation, 2003.

52. In a prison near Paris, television news broadcasts showing the Israeli army repressing Palestinians periodically trigger waves of anti-Semitism and hatred of America. When interviewed, some young prisoners make no secret of their wish to join the Palestinians to take revenge on Israel, or to join al-Qaeda to take their revenge on the West because it had humiliated Palestinians. When the issue of Chechnya was raised, they expressed sympathy, but not to the same degree. Chechens are not Arabs. Some Muslims know little about them. Chechnya is not home to any of Islam's holy places, such as the Al-Aqsa mosque in Jerusalem. Above all, Chechnya receives much less media attention. See Farhad Khosrokhavar, *L'Islam dans les prisons*, Paris: Editions Balland, 2004.

53. See Ziauddin Sardar, 'Mobilising Islam against Terror', *Observer*, 16 February 2003; Fareena Alam, 'How War Brought Hope to British Muslims' *Observer*, 23 March 2003.

54. See, for example, Fareena Alm, 'My Battle is in the Living Room', *Observer*, 30 March 2003.

55. 'British Muslims Killed in Air Raid', *Manchester Evening News*, 29 October 2001.

56. See the websites of Forum Against Islamophobia and Racism (FAIR) and the Islamic Human Rights Commission.

57. See Hugh Muir, 'Mosques Launch Protests over "Terror" Arrests,' *Guardian*, 13 December 2003.

58. See Daniel Klaidman, Mark Hosenball, Michael Isikiff and Evan Thomas, 'Al-Qaeda in America: the Enemy Within', *Newsweek*, 19 June 2003; Elaine Shannon and Michael Weisskopf, 'Khaled Sheikh Mohammed Names Names', *Time* 24 March 2003.

59. For an account that puts too much emphasis on the attacks, see Steven Emerson, *American Djihad: The Terrorists Living Among Us*, New York: The Free Press, 2002.

60. On the Black Muslim phenomena, see Edward E. Curtis, *Islam in Black America: Identity, Liberation and Difference in African-American Islamic Thought*, Albany: State University of New York Press, 2002.

61. See Dietmar Loch's interview with Kelkal, *Le Monde*.

62. See Gabriel A. Almond, R. Scott Appleby and Emmanuel Sivan, *Strong Religion: the Rise of Fundamentalism around the World*, Chicago and London: University of Chicago Press, 2003.

63. After September 11, and given the general suspicion that hangs over some Muslims in the United States, together with the Bush administration's pro-Sharon policies, it is possible that a small segment of the American Muslim population will become radicalised by the same *ressentiment* that is experienced by their counterparts in Europe (a feeling of deep humiliation, of being rejected by society, the absence of any future prospects, an irreversible stigmatisation).

64. See Anne Pelous, 'Les Tribulations d'une famille islamiste,' *Le Monde*, 23 February 2004.

65. Pelous, 'Les Tribulations'.

66. See *Le Monde*, 17 March 2004.

67. For a detailed description of so-called 'martyropathic' *jihadi* families, see Khosrokhavar, *L'Islamisme et la mort*.

68. My interpretation of *jihadist* and martyrological phenomena is completely different to that of commentators such as Daniel Pipes, who thinks that terrorists come from groups that have not been modernised. *Jihadists* are, rather, characterised by a mental and subjective modernisation, together with a feeling of rejection and humiliation, which can be defined in either class or cultural terms or in terms of their relationship with everyday life. Most of them have studied modern subjects, have lived in the West for a long time and display absolutely no signs of non-modernity or of involvement in any culture other than a world-civilisation that they regard as profoundly unjust and prejudiced against them. See Daniel Pipes, *Militant Islam Reaches America*, New York: W.W. Norton, 2002.

69. See Danièle Hervieu-Léger, *La Pèlerin et le converti*, Paris: Flammarion, 1999.

70. See 'Killing Infidels in Chechnya: a foreign Mujahid's Diary', in Parfrey, *Extreme Islam*.

71. See Dominique de Courcelle, 'Un Lieu pour la raison des "Lumières": la conversion à l'Islam d'Adam Neuser au XVIe siècle', in Mercedes Garcia-Arenal (ed.), *Conversions islamiques*, Paris: Maisonneuve & Larose, 2001.

72. See Khosrokhavar, *L'Islam des jeunes*, Paris: Flammarion, 1997; Nikola Tietze and Farhad Khosrokhavar, 'Violences, médias et intégration', in Michel Wieviorka (ed.), *Violence en France*, Paris: Seuil, 1991.

73. See François Dubet and Danilo Martucelli, *Dans quelle société vivons-nous?*, Paris: Seuil, 1998.

74. Despite his verbosity and his deliberate waywardness, Baudrillard is the best commentator on this state of affairs, in which the individual oscillates between televised unreality and a reality in which there are no rough patches. See his *Simulacra and Simulation*, trans. Sheila Faria Glaser, Ann Arbor: University of Michigan Press, 1994.

75. See Frank Kermode, *The Sense of an Ending*, Oxford: Oxford University Press, 1967.

76. See Baudrillard, *Simulacra*. Baudrillard fails to see that, as the simulacra multiply, the unreality-effects they induce can, as continuity is inverted into rupture, turn into a truly deadly reality.

77. See Farhad Khosrokhavar and Chahla Chafiq, *Sous le voile islamique*, Paris: Editions du Félin, 1995.

## CONCLUSION

1. It can be seen as one of the faces of a modernity that is, by definition, multiple. It is, however, difficult to say if it is a form of modernisation, or the dark face of certain types of modernity. See the contributions by

S.N. Eisenstadt and Bilufer Göle, 'Multiple Modernities', *Daedelus*, vol. 129 no. 1, Winter 2000.

2.  See Jose Casanova, 'Civil Society and Religion: Retrospective Reflections of Catholicism and Prospective Reflections of Islam', *Social Research* vol. 68 no. 4, Winter 2001.

### AFTERWORD

1.  See Joyce M. Davis, *Martyrs: Innocence, Vengeance and Despair in the Middle East*, New York: Palgrave Macmillan, 2003; Penelope Larzillière, *Etre jeune en Palestine*, Paris: Ballard, 2004.
2.  The problem can be seen in the context of a global clash of fundamentalisms. The history of the Muslim world's conflictual relationship with the West has long been punctuated by *jihads* and crusades. See Tariq Ali, *The Clash of Fundamentalisms: Crusades, Djihads and Modernity*, London and New York: Verso, 2002.
3.  Both Al-Muhajiroun and Hizb al-Tahrir exploit these feelings of revolt and indignation, and translate them into broadly anti-Semitic terms.
4.  Olivier Roy uses the expression 'franchised' several times in documents that were not intended for publication.
5.  For a purely instrumentalist interpretation that takes no account of the *jihadis*, subjectivity see, for example, John R. Martin (ed.), *Defeating Terrorism: Strategic Issue Analyses*, Carlisle, PA: Strategic Studies Institute, US Army War College, 2002.
6.  See Olivier Roy, *L'Islam mondialisé*, Paris: Seuil, 2002.

# Index